Lecture Notes in Computer Science

Edited by G. Goos, J. Hartmanis and J. van Leeuwen

Springer
Berlin
Heidelberg
New York
Barcelona
Hong Kong
London
Milan
Paris
Singapore
Tokyo

Brian Lings   Keith Jeffery (Eds.)

Advances in Databases

17th British National Conference on Databases, BNCOD 17
Exeter, UK, July 3-5, 2000
Proceedings

 Springer

Series Editors

Gerhard Goos, Karlsruhe University, Germany
Juris Hartmanis, Cornell University, NY, USA
Jan van Leeuwen, Utrecht University, The Netherlands

Volume Editors

Brian Lings
University of Exeter, Department of Computer Science
Prince of Wales Road, Exeter EX4 4PT, UK
E-mail: brian@dcs.exeter.ac.uk

Keith Jeffery
CLRC Rutherford Appleton Laboratory
Department for Computation and Information
Chilton-Didcot, OX11 0QX Oxon, UK
E-mail: kgj@rl.ac.uk

Cataloging-in-Publication Data applied for

Die Deutsche Bibliothek - CIP-Einheitsaufnahme

Advances in databases : proceedings / 17th British National Conference
on Databases, BNCOD 17, Exeter, UK, July 3 - 5, 2000. Brian Lings ;
Keith Jeffrey (ed.). - Berlin ; Heidelberg ; New York ; Barcelona ;
Hong Kong ; London ; Milan ; Paris ; Singapore ; Tokyo : Springer, 2000
(Lecture notes in computer science ; Vol. 1832)
  ISBN 3-540-67743-7

CR Subject Classification (1998): H.2, H.3, H.4

ISSN 0302-9743
ISBN 3-540-67743-7 Springer-Verlag Berlin Heidelberg New York

Springer-Verlag is a company in the BertelsmannSpringer publishing group.
© Springer-Verlag Berlin Heidelberg 2000
Printed in Germany

Typesetting: Camera-ready by author
Printed on acid-free paper   SPIN: 10721967   06/3142   5 4 3 2 1 0

Foreword

After a decade of major technical and theoretical advancements in the area, the scope for exploitation of database technology has never been greater. Neither has the challenge.

This volume contains the proceedings of the 17th British National Conference on Databases (BNCOD 2000), held at the University of Exeter in July 2000. In selecting the quality papers presented here, the programme committee was particularly interested in the demands being made on the technology by emerging application areas, including web applications, *push* technology, multimedia data, and data warehousing. The concern remains the same: satisfaction of user requirements on quality and performance. However, with increasing demand for timely access to heterogeneous data distributed on an unregulated Internet, new challenges are presented.

Our three invited speakers develop the theme for the conference, considering new dimensions concerning user requirements in accessing distributed, heterogeneous information sources.

In the first paper presented here, Gio Wiederhold reflects on the tension between requirements for, on the one hand, precision and relevance and on the other completeness and recall in relating data from heterogeneous resources. In resolving this tension in favour of the former, he maintains that this will fundamentally affect future research directions.

Sharma Chakravarthy adds another dimension to the requirement on information, namely timeliness. He shares a vision of just-in-time information delivered by a *push* technology based on reactive capabilities. He maintains that this requires a paradigm shift to a user-centric view of information.

Peter Buneman's paper raises the new and increasingly important issue of data provenance - something which impacts on precision, relevance, and timeliness. He notes that existing database tools are severely lacking when it comes to considering provenance, requiring great circumspection – in particular when using digital library sources.

The contributed papers are presented under four groupings, the first of which concerns performance and optimisation. Lawder and King report on work within the TriStarp group at Birkbeck on a new approach to multi-dimensional indexing. They present an excellent review of the area, and detail algorithms and performance results for the approach. Manegold *et al.* present a heuristic for optimising multiple queries typical in data mining, and consider the practical performance of their query optimiser for sequential and parallel environments. Finally, Waas and Pellenkoft address the important problem of optimisation of join order for medium to large queries. Their technique uses non-uniform sampling of query plans, using bottom-up pruning.

The second grouping addresses user requirements on large systems. Engström *et al.* characterise a quality framework for data warehouse maintenance, justifying their thesis that a user-centric view of quality issues is currently largely missing and proposing a framework to rectify this. Paton *et al.* address the issue of systematic comparison of the functionality and performance of spatial database systems. Little has so far been published on such comparisons, so this is a welcome addition to the literature. Their benchmark allows conclusions to be drawn on the relative efficiency of spatial storage managers. Finally in this group, Gray *et al.* propose a means of offering views over collections of objects at different levels of aggregation. Their *collection views* protect the user from having to anticipate queries and adapt method code themselves. They show the applicability of their ideas in the context of Bioinformatic databases.

The third grouping addresses the increasingly important area of global transactions, both within the context of distributed databases and the web. Türker *et al.* present a systematic model for describing termination issues in multiple-site databases. They propose a protocol to address the problem that atomic commitment of global transactions is not sufficient to deal correctly with termination of global transactions. Multiple database transactions on the web pose other problems, which are excellently reviewed by Younas *et al.* Their paper contributes a number of insights into the state of the art, and is a very timely contribution. Timeliness is very much the concern of Cheng and Loizou, whose paper proposes a framework for associating documents and resources from a company with its targeted customers within the context of *push* technology for e-commerce. At the heart of the system is an object-oriented organisational model; its application in a prototype to support a commercial insurance firm is discussed.

Our final grouping addresses the ever increasing interest in interoperability via the web, with specific reference to XML. Behrens addresses one of the most important web issues, namely DTD integration. The paper introduces problems with a simple grammar-based model approach, and proposes a solution – so-called *s-xschemes*. Kemp *et al.* consider the very topical issues of CORBA for implementing client-server database architectures and XML for information interchange. With the use of examples from a biological database, the implications of different design choices, from coarse grain to fine grain, are detailed. Finally, Wood describes a procedure for optimising queries in XQL subject to functional constraints derived from an XML DTD.

1   Acknowledgements

We are deeply indebted to the members of the programme committee for their helpful cooperation throughout the reviewing process. All deadlines were once again met. Many thanks to Suzanne Embury, who enthusiastically fielded numerous enquiries using her experience from BNCOD16 and organised the PhD Summer School associated with the conference. Thanks also to Alex Gray, who has for many years been the guiding force behind BNCOD, and whose calm steering has been very much appreciated.

April 2000   Brian Lings and Keith Jeffery

Conference Committees

Programme Committee

Keith Jeffery (Chair)	CLRC Rutherford Appleton Laboratory
Peter Barclay	Napier University
David Bell	University of Ulster
David Bowers	University of Surrey
Richard Connor	University of Strathclyde
Richard Cooper	University of Glasgow
Suzanne Embury	Cardiff University
Alvaro Fernandes	University of Manchester
Mary Garvey	University of Wolverhampton
Carol Goble	University of Manchester
Alex Gray	Cardiff University
Mike Jackson	University of Wolverhampton
Graham Kemp	University of Aberdeen
Jessie Kennedy	Napier University
Brian Lings	University of Exeter
Nigel Martin	Birkbeck College, University of London
Ron Morrison	University of St Andrews
Norman Paton	University of Manchester
Alex Poulovassilis	Birkbeck College, University of London
Brian Read	CLRC Rutherford Appleton Laboratory
Mike Worboys	Keele University
Howard Williams	Heriot-Watt University

Organising Committee

Brian Lings (Chair)	University of Exeter
David Bowers	University of Surrey
Wendy Milne	University of Exeter
Suzanne Embury (PhD Summer School)	Cardiff University
Tracy Darroch (Administration)	University of Exeter
Ross Purves (Webmaster)	University of Exeter

Steering Committee

Alex Gray (Chair)	Cardiff University
Nick Fiddian	Cardiff University
Carole Goble	University of Manchester
Peter Gray	University of Aberdeen
Roger Johnson	Birkbeck College
Jessie Kennedy	Napier University
Mike Worboys	Keele University

Table of Contents

Invited Paper

Interoperability Using XML

Precision in Processing Data from Heterogeneous Resources

Gio Wiederhold

Computer Science Department, Stanford University, Stanford CA 94305-9040
gio@cs.stanford.edu.

"The certitude that any book exists on the shelves of the library first led to elation, but soon the realization that it was unlikely to be found converted the feelings to a great depression", Luis Borges: *The Infinite Library*, 1964.

Abstract. Much information is becoming available on the world-wide-web, on Intranets, and on publicly accessible databases. The benefits of integrating related data from distinct sources are great, since it allows the discovery or validation of relationships among events and trends in many areas of science and commerce. But most sources are established autonomously, and hence are heterogeneous in form and content. Resolution of heterogeneity of form has been an exciting research topic for many years now. We can access information from diverse computers, alternate data representations, varied operating systems, multiple database models, and deal with a variety of transmission protocols. But progress in these areas is raising a new problem: semantic heterogeneity. Semantic heterogeneity comes about because the meaning of words depends on context, and autonomous sources are developed and maintained within their own contexts. Types of semantic heterogeneity include spelling variations, use of synonyms, and the use of identically spelled words to refer to different objects. The effect of semantic heterogeneity is not only failure to find desired material, but also lack of precision in selection, aggregation, comparison, etc., when trying to integrate information. While browsing we may complain of 'information overload'. But when trying to automate these processes, an essential aspect of business-oriented operations, the imprecision due to semantic heterogeneity can be become fatal. Manual resolutions to the problem do work today, but it forces businesses to limit the scope of their partnering. In expanding supply chains and globalized commerce we have to deal in many more contexts, but cannot afford manual, case-by-case resolution. In business we become efficient by rapidly carrying out processes on regular schedules. XML is touted as the new universal medium for electronic commerce, but the meaning of the tags identifying data fields remains context dependent. Attempting a global resolution of the semantic mismatch is futile. The number of participants is immense, growing, and dynamic. Terminology changes, and must be able to change as our knowledge grows. Using precise, finely differentiated terms and abbreviations is important for efficiency within a domain, but frustrating to outsiders. In this paper we indicate research directions to resolve inconsistencies incrementally, so that we may be able to interoperate effectively in the presence of inter-domain inconsistencies. This work is an early stage, and will provide research opportunities for a range of disciplines, including databases, artificial intelligence, and formal linguistics. We also sketch an information systems

B. Lings and K. Jeffery (Eds.): BNCOD 17, LNCS 1832, pp. 1-18, 2000.

architecture which is suitable for such services and their infrastructure. Research issues in managing complexity of multiple services arise here as well. The conclusion of this paper can be summarized as stating that today, and even more in the future, precision and relevance will be more valuable than completeness and recall. Solutions are best composed from many small-scale efforts rather than by overbearing attempts at standardization. This observation will, in turn, affect research directions in information sciences.

1 Introduction

A study by Inktomi and NEC Research Institute showed that the Internet at the end of 1999 provided access to at least one billion unique indexable web pages [Inktomi:00]. Finding relevant information in such a massive collection is hard. Indexing here means that text from words that the pages contain can be extracted to direct its search engine. Inktomi performs automated searches as a service for Yahoo and its customers, while Yahoo itself uses human specialists to categorize a small, but high-value portion of the web. This cooperation between automation and expert inputs provides a direction for improving Internet-based information systems.

1.1 Getting Information Rather Than Data

We define information, following tradition, to be data that transmit something not known to the receiver, and that will cause the state of the world of the receiver to be altered [ShannonW:48]. The need for assistance in selecting actual information from the world-wide-web was recognized early in the web's existence [BowmanEa:94]. A succession of search engines have provided rapid advances, and yet the users remain dissatisfied with the results [Hearst:97]. Complaints about `information overload' abound. Most searches retrieve an excess of references, and getting a relevant result, as needed to solve some problem requires much subsequent effort in actual analysis of the content. And yet, in all that volume, there is no guarantee that the result is correct and complete.

Searches through specific databases can be complete and precise, since the contents of a database, say the list of students at a university, and their searchable attributes, as maintained by the registrar, is expected to be complete. Not obtaining, say, all the Physics students from a request, is seen as an error in precision, and receiving the names of any non-Physics student is an error of relevance.

When using the web for more complex queries than simple fact retrieval, we access multiple sources [ChangGP:96]. For purchasing or investment planning, comparison of alternatives is essential. The benefits of integrating related data from diverse sources may be even greater, since it allows the discovery or validation of relationships among events and trends in many areas of science and commerce.

1.2 Business Needs

In this paper we consider professional needs, especially those that arise in business situations, other aspects are addressed in an earlier report [Wiederhold:99]. Business requirements include the need to get tasks done expeditiously. The need for repetitive human processing of obtained information should be minimal. These means that the information obtained should be highly reliable and relevant.

In manufacturing, for instance, the traditional needs are obtaining information about inventory and personnel, the best processes, equipment, and material to produce merchandise, and the markets that will use those goods. In distribution industries, the information needed encompasses the producers, the destinations, and the capabilities of internal and external transportation services. In these and other situations data from local and remote sources must be reliably integrated so they can be used for recurring business decisions.

The needs and issues that a business enterprise deals with include the same needs that an individual customer encounters, but place a higher value on precision. In business-to-business interaction automation is desired, so that repetitive tasks don't have to be manually repeated and controlled [JelassiL:96]. Stock has to be reordered daily, fashion trends analyzed weekly, and displays changed monthly. However, here is where the rapid and uncontrolled growth of Internet capabilities shows the greatest lacunae, since changes occur continuously at the sites one may wish to access.

Modeling the business customers' requirements effectively requires more than tracking recent web requests. First of all a customer in a given role has to be disassociated from all the other activities that an individual may participate in. We distinguish here customers, performing a specific role, and individuals, who will play several different roles at differing times. In a given role, complex tasks can be modeled using a hierarchical decomposition, with a structure that supports the divide-and-conquer paradigm that is basic to all problem-solving tasks [W97:M].

2. Problems in Integration of Information

The major problem facing all types of users is the ubiquity and diversity of information. Finding the right information takes time, effort, and often luck. Just as the daily newspaper presents an overload of choices for the consumer in its advertising section, the world-wide web contains more alternatives than can be investigated in depth. When leafing through advertisements the selection is based on the organization of the presentation, the prominence of the advertisement, the advertised price, the convenience of getting to the advertised merchandise in one's neighborhood, the reputation of quality, personal or created by marketing, of the vendor, and unusual attractive features. The dominating factor differs based on the merchandise, commodity goods being more distinguished by price, and piece goods more by quality attributes. Similar factors apply to online purchasing of merchandise and services. Lacking the convenience of leafing through the newspaper, greater dependence for selection is based on selection tools.

2.1 Getting Complete Information

Getting all of the possibly relevant, the complete information, is a question of breadth. In bibliographic settings completeness of coverage is termed `recall'. The indexes used for automated searching depend on words, but the usage of words throughout the web is inconsistent. If relevant goods or services are described with unexpected terms their information will not be recalled. Conversely, when words have multiple interpretations, depending on context, excess information will be produced, resulting in loss of precision, or relevance.

To improve completeness a number of methods have been employed to widen the search beyond direct matches. Most depend on thesauri, which expand the search term with similar terms, terms used for its subsidiary concepts, and perhaps even terms that are generalizations of the search term. A well-known example is the Unified Medical Language System (UMLS), which aggregates terms from several medical subdomains, as patient's problem lists, diagnostics, pathology, and bibliographic categorizations to increase recall when perusing the medical literature [HumphreysL:93]. However, any broadening is likely to lead to loss of precision, since irrelevant citations will now be collected and reported as well. Figure 1 sketches the relationship among these parameters. The curvature of the precision and recall metrics indicate the effectiveness of the methods used.

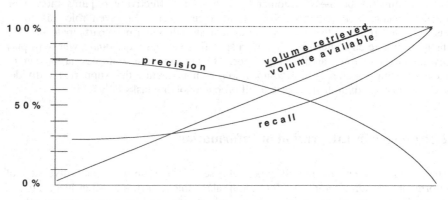

Fig. 1. Typical relationships between data volume retrieved, recall, and precision.

Unfortunately, poor relevance causes a loss of actual recall. If the increase of citations or other data is significant, the required effort which has to process and analyze good and bad citations is likely to be so great that human researchers will give up, and ignore potentially useful information. We all have had this experience when web-browsing. In the world of statistics the amount of irrelevant information retrieved is termed `false positives'. Even a small fraction of false positives can be devastating, since to distinguish true and false positives requires follow-up. The cost of follow-up is always relatively high when compared to search, since it involves human jusdgement. Minimal follow-up means retrieving more complete information, checking the contents, and deciding on actual relevance. For instance, if we deal with

100 000's of instances, a 1% false positive rate means following up on 1000 false leads, easily overwhelming our capabilities.

2.2 Consistency Is Local

Precision in on-line commerce requires a consistent structure and a consistent terminology, so that one term always refers to the same set of objects. For example when we talk about equipment for a `sports-car' both partners in a business transaction want to refer to exactly the same set of vehicles. But no law or regulation can be imposed on all suppliers in the world that define what a sports-car is. Consistency is a local phenomenon. There might be a professional society, say a sports-car club, which will define the term for its membership, and not allow in its annual show a convertible without a roll bar to be entered. A manufacturer may sell the same type of car as a sports car after installing a stiffer suspension and a nice paint job. Within a closeknit group the terms used are well understood because they refer to real objects in our neighborhood or are abstractions built from other known terms [RoyH:97].

Terms, and their relationships, as abstraction, subsets, refinements, etc. are hence specific to their contexts. We denote the set of terms and their relationships, following current usage in Artificial Intelligence, as an *ontology* [WG:97]. Many ontologies have existed for a long time without having used the name. Schemas, as used in databases, are simple, locally consistent ontologies. Foreign keys relating table headings in database schemas imply structural relationships [Chen:76]. Included in ontologies are the values that variables can assume; of particular significance are codes for enumerated values used in data-processing [McEwen:74]. For instance, names of states, counties, suppliers, etc., are routinely encoded to enhance consistency. When such terms are used in a database the values in a schema column are constrained, providing another level of a structural relationship.

There are thousands of local, corporate, or organizational ontologies, often maintained by domain specialists. Today many ontologies are being created within DTD definitions for the eXtended Markup Language (XML) [Connolly:97]. Large ontologies have been collected with the objective to assist in common-sense reasoning (CyC) [LenatG:90]. However, large ontologies, collected from diverse sources or constructed by multiple individuals over a long time, will contain substantial inconsistencies. In these efforts the objective is again to increase breadth or recall, rather than precision or relevance.

Many ontologies have textual definitions for their entries, just as found in printed glossaries. These definitions will help human readers, but cannot guarantee precise semantic matching of entries outside of their contexts, because the terms used in the definitions also come from their own source domains.

Experimental communication languages that specify the ontology to be used, as KQML [LabrouF:94] and OML [Kent:99], provide a means to clarify message contexts, but have not yet been used in practical situations.

2.3 Inconsistency

Inconsistency of among distinct sources is due to their autonomy, which allows and even encourages heterogeneity. Inconsistency among heterogeneous sources has many facets, by technical progress has removed has overcome most mechanical issues. We can access data independent of location, computer hardware, operating systems, programming language, and even data representations. Not well handled today is the inconsistency of semantics among sources. The problem with matching terms from diverse sources is not just that of synonyms – two words for the same object, say *lorry* and *truck* -- or one word for completely different objects, as *miter* in carpentry and in religion. Many inconsistencies are much more complex, and include overlapping classes, subsets, partial supersets, and the like.

Languages exist in working contexts, and local efficiency determines the granularity and scope of word usage. Few terms refer to instances of real-world object instances, say Exeter cathedral, most terms refer to abstract groupings, and here different interpretations abound. The term 'vehicle' is different for architects, when designing garage space, from that of traffic regulators, dealing with right-of-way rules at intersections. The term *vehicle* is used differently in the transportation code than in the building code, although over 90% of the instances are the same. A vendor site oriented towards carpenters will use very specific terms, say *sinkers* and *brads*, to denote certain types of nails, but those terms will not be familiar to the general population. A site oriented to homeowners will just use the general category of *nails*, and may then describe the diameter, length, type of head, and material.

Avoiding inconsistency by enforcing consistency seems attractive, but fails for several reasons. First of all, we see that each source develops is language in its own context, and uses terms and classifications that are natural and efficient to its creators and owners. The homeowner cannot afford to learn the thousands of specialized terms needed to maintain one's house, and the carpenter cannot afford wasting time by circumscribing each nail, screw, and tool with precise attributes.

Attempting to maintain consistency just among interacting domains is not a viable approach because of scale and dynamics. Carpenters interact with hardware, lumber, and tool suppliers as well as homeowners, and the same suppliers interact with businesses, who in turn interact with shippers, and airlines, etc. In the end global consistency would be required. However, global consistency would take a very long time to achieve, and during that time new terms and relationships will make earlier ontological agreements obsolete.

2.4 Recognizing Inconsistency

When dealing with disjoint groups the meaning of terms can differ arbitrarily. To be safe we should make the default assumption that no terms will match unless specific arrangements have been made. Most insidious are cases when terms in closely related contexts differ slightly. Then the differences may not be easily observed, and only when computations give erroneous results will the misunderstandings be discovered. An example of such a semantic difference is the use of the term *employee*, which in payroll system includes all persons being paid, and in a personnel system includes all people available to do work. In a realistic and large organizations there are nearly always some people that do not fall into both categories: staff taking early retirement, employees on loan to outside projects, specialists on consulting contracts, etc. Hence, the differences found are rational, since the departments had to satisfy different objectives: check generation and tracking of work and space assignments

Intranets, operating within one enterprise, should have a fairly consistent ontology. However, as the *employee* example showed, it's best to check all assumptions. Aberrations can easily be demonstrated in by computing the differences of the membership from their respective databases. If ignored, computations based on their match will be wrong. Within a specific business domain the contexts must be clear and the ontology unambiguous. Once the rules are known, integration can be made precise and unambiguous [ElMasriW:79]. When access to information becomes world-wide, and contexts become unclear, imprecision results, making business transactions unreliable. In large multi-national corporations and companies that have grown through mergers, differences are bound to exist. These can be dealt with if the problems are formally recognized, but often they are isolated, and solved over and over in an ad-hoc fashion.

2.4 Improving Recall

To achieve a high recall all possibly relevant sources should be accessed. On the Interner that number is open-ended. A number of *worm* programs scan the web continuously, scanning pages as input to their indexing schemes. Terms for deemed useful for subsequent retrieval and links to further pages are collected. The effort to index all publicly available information is immense. Comprehensive indexing is limited due to the size of the web itself, the rate of change of updates to the information on the web, and the variety of media used for representing information [PonceleonSAPD:98]. To keep abreast of changes sites that appear to change frequently will be visited by the worms more often, so that the average information is as little out of date as feasible [Lynch:97]. However for sites that change very rapidly, as news broadcasts, creating indexes is nearly futile. Some services cache retrieved pages, so that the data, even though obsolete, remains available.

Automatic indexing systems focus on the ASCII text presented on web pages, primarily in HTML format. Documents stored in proprietary formats, as Microsoft Word, Powerpoint, Wordperfect, Postscript, and Portable Document Format (PDF) [Adobe:99] are ignored today. Valuable information is often presented in tabular form, where relationships are represented by relative position. Such representations are hard to parse by search engines, although specialized tools have been developed for that purpose in the past.

Also generally inaccessible for search are images, including icons and corporate logos, diagrams and images [Stix:97]. Some of these images contain crucial embedded text; if deemed important, such text can be extracted [WangWL:98]. Several specialized vendors and museums provide large image libraries on-line, and for them the quality of retrieval depends wholly on ancillary descriptive information [DeYoung:00]. Iterative refinement then can employ feature search on content parameters as color or texture [Amico:98], but purely content-based methods are typically inadequate for initial selection form large libraries. There are also valuable terms for selection in speech, both standalone and as part of video representations [PonceleonSAPD:98]. The practice of video-clip indexing, supported by broadcasters, is relatively mature [MPEG:00]. Its problems have been addressed by brute force, using heavyweight indexing engines and smart indexing engines combining speech, voice prints, and closed captioning for the hard-of-hearing, when available.

Web sites that derive their information from databases will only provide access to selected metadata, and not to their actual contents. How well those meta-data represent its actual contents depends on the effort and competence of the database owners. Some prefer not to be visited by worms at all, preferring that customers find them directly, while some seek maximum exposure. HTML pages can contain a header forbidding access to worms. On the other hand some web sites try to fool the search engines, by including excessive and even false meta-information, hoping to generate more visits to their web-sites.

The consumer of information will typically find it too costly to produce indexes for their own use only. Schemes requiring cooperation of the sources have been proposed [GravanoGT:94]. Since producing an ontology is a valued-added service, it is best handled by independent companies, who can distinguish themselves by comprehensiveness versus specialization, currency, convenience of use, and cost. Those companies can also use tools that break through access barriers in order to better serve their population. For scientific objectives there is a role here for professional societies [ACM:99], since these communities are not likely to be well served by commercial interests.

3. Articulation

Inconsistent use of terms makes simplistic sharing of information based on term matching from multiple sources incomplete and imprecise. The problems due to inconsistency are more of a hindrance to business than to individuals, who deal more often with single queries and instances. In business similar tasks as purchasing and shipping occur regularly, and should be automated. Luckily, interoperation of source domains in businesses is limited and constrained to specific applications. In our approach to dealing with semantic heterogeneity we focus on the intersection of domains that related by common application use. We define an *articulation* to manage that intersection.

A domain is defined as having a consistent internal ontology. If there is an explicit ontology, and that ontology has been enforced, the task of defining the domain is simplified. In practice we often start with database schemas. An entity-relationship model used for design can provide important relationships among the tables. Constraints on table values, often documented as lists or look-up tables can augment the domain ontology further.

3.1 Defining an Articulation

For integration of information we will have two or more domains with their ontologies. Traditional database integration mandated that complete schemas be considered, but a business application needs only to consider terms used for matching specific data. For instance, in purchasing, only the objects to be purchased need to be matched, together with those attributes that play a role in selecting objects for purchase, as *size*, various specifications, and *price*. Personnel and manufacturing data can be ignored. Defining the articulation can still involve much work, and typically involves human expertise, but once the matching rules are established the actual purchase transactions can be automated. The concept is illustrated in Figure 2.

Rules for articulation can be as simple as equating obvious terms: $shoe_s$ in the shoe store equals $shoe_f$ in the shoe factory, define tabular matches as $color_s$:= $colorfunction(color_f)$, or can have conditionals, say, $size_s$ if $location_f$ = 'Europe' :=$size_f$, else := $sizefunction(size_f)$. We see that the definition of a top-level articulation often requires subsidiary definition, for instance *Europe* will probably require a table of countries using metric shoe sizes. A general definition of *Europe* from a global geographic ontology is likely to be wrong in the shoe-purchasing articulation. Mismatches are rife when dealing with geographic information, although localities are a prime criterion for articulation [MarkMM:99]. For instance, maps prepared for property assessment will use different identifiers and boundaries than the terms used in giving driving directions. When the directions prove inadequate, say because of a road closure, an appropriate map is needed to allow matching points to be found.

3.2 Maintaining Articulations

An articulation creates a new, limited ontology, sufficient only for making the required linkages to the source ontologies for a particular application. Many such ontologies will be needed as the number of applications requiring access to multiple sources increases. The limited scope and independence of application-specific articulated ontologies simplifies their individual maintenance. Having a formal articulation permits computer systems to automate work performed today by many humans, performing a variety of brokering services. The benefit will be a significant increase in the speed of setting up multi-domain, business-to-business transactions.

When humans perform articulation, either on the phone or in direct interaction on the Internet, the problems of semantic mismatch are less obvious. After automation the role of the humans becomes creation and maintenance of the articulation rules. Logical organizations to be responsible for broader articulation ontologies would be societies serving brokering industries, as say the National Drug Distributors Association (NDDA) in the USA.

Most of those individuals or organizations will not be sophisticated users of computing, so that tools will have to be developed for the collection and maintenance of articulation rules [JanninkSVW:98]. The articulations in turn will be embedded as mediating nodes in our information systems, as discussed in Section 4.

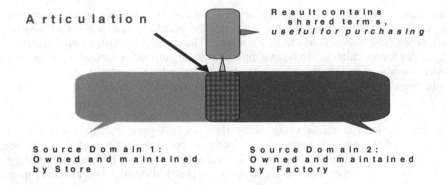

Fig. 2. Typical relationships between data volume retrieved, recall, and precision.

3.3 Multiple Articulations

Multiple articulations among identical domains are likely to be needed as well. Medical findings of interest to a pathologist will be confusing to patients, and advice for patients about a disease should be redundant to the medical specialist. Some partitioning for distinct application roles within single sources exists now; for instance, Medline has multiple access points [Cimino:96]. It is unclear if the sources are the best judges of their own relevance, or of such assessments are best left to outside experts. When there multiple sources there is certainly a role for mediating modules to interpret meta-information associated with source sites and use that information to filter or rank the data obtained from those sites [Langer:98]. Doing so requires understanding the background and typical intent of the customer and the application. Note that the same individual can have multiple customer roles, as a private person or as a professional; we revisit that issue in Section 4.5.

3.4 Combining Articulations

There will be many applications that cannot live within a single articulated ontology. For example logistics, which must deal with shipping merchandise via a variety of carriers: truck, rail, ship, and air, requires interoperation among diverse domains, as well as among multiple companies located in different countries. To resolve these issues we have proposed an ontology algebra, which uses rules to resolve differences in the intersection of base ontologies [MitraWK:00]. Having an algebra promises to provide a basis for scalability and optimization. A capability for arbitrary composition removes pressure to create large source ontologies or even large articulations, keeping maintenance local. Large compositions may have multiple evaluation paths, and optimizers can make choices that are efficient, since the sizes of intermediate results, and their access costs may vary greatly.

3.5 An Example: Dealing with Bioinformatics Computations

Precision becomes crucial when the data quantities become large. For instance, in bioinformatics applucations deal with the 3 billion base pairs of the human genome, and shorter, but still massive strands from other species. To exploit this data for diagnostics and therapeutics we must match abnormalities to about 10 000 protein-coding regions and their disease-causing variations. Genetic variations affect every single one of our 6 billion world population. At the same time, researchers in chemical genomics are generating systematically an increasing fraction of the few million small organic molecules. These molecules are candidates for pharmaceuticals that can switch protein generation or protein effectiveness on and off, affecting the several hundred metabolic pathways that control our six billion lives, and many more lives in future generations. The linkages are sketched in Figure 3.

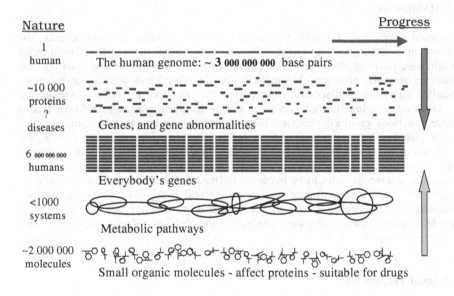

Fig. 3. Quantities of some potential data objects in bioinformatics

When navigating through this huge space for opportunities to develop drugs that can help specific subsets of mankind, we are faced with the dilemma of recall versus precision. Missing some potential effects due to poor recall is a loss of an unknown magnitude, but the cost associated with a false positive lead has a high cost that can be estimated, since the follow-up analyses are very resource intensive. Precision will be critical -- whenever we deal with 100 000's of instances, even a 1% false positive rate means following up on 1000 false leads, easily overwhelming our research capabilities.

4. Architecture

System designer make a distinction in distributed architectures between clients and severs, although the architecture of the web allows clients to be servers and vice versa without any constraints. There are active debates about the benefits of thin clients versus thin servers. The relative amount of fat in a node is due to the amount of services it provides, but we have argued above that we prefer to have small, domain specific sources, and then intermediate services, also of modest size, that can be composed to serve a wide variety of equally modest application clients. The outcome of that view is that we prefer information processing architectures to have three conceptual layers, where the middle layer is independent of the sources, but can exploit them, and serve as many clients as feasible, given application needs for domain simplicity, consistency and precision.

4.1 Middleware

So-called middleware provides the needed network linkages between clients and servers in a heterogeneous world. However, much of the existing commercial middleware provides little capabilities for information integration and even less for resolving semantic problems. Is simplicity, on the other hand, means that it can be installed without domain-specific expertise and be maintained by technical specialists.

However viewing the linkages as a strictly technical means to achieve binary interconnections ignores the added value provided now by human intermediaries. For travel planning we had travel agents, for logistics we had shipping agents, for publications filtering was performed by editors and librarians, and for supply-chains we relied on distributors. The cost and delays associated with human intermediaries causes these intermediaries to be bypassed in Internet-based technologies, since their operations are incommensurate with milli-second world-wide communications. Disintermediation causes a loss of services that increased precision when these people, selected, filtered, digested, integrated, and abstracted data for specific topics of interest [Resnick:97].

4.2 Agent Technology

At the same time, there is an increased interest in agent technology, software which provides added value services for a client, as in locating resources and retrieving information [HuhnsS:97]. Agent software is intended to overcome the loss or the delays associated with human agents in moving to Internet-based commerce. Those agents must count on consistent meta data in order to carry out their tasks, but most agent literature does not define where the maintenance responsibilities lie. Often shared ontologies are assumed, that will bind sources, agents, and clients together [ChavezM:96]. Agents may count on middleware to resolve problems due to technical heterogeneity.

4.3 Mediators

Middleware, as well as agent technology deserves a well defined architectural niche. These services should be not attached to sources, since they may integrate multiple sources, nor to clients, since the required knowledge acquisition and and its maintenance only becomes economical when shared among multiple clients. Mediators are then services inside the web, while clients and sources will occupy the periphery and can remain of modest size [W:92].

To remain thin mediators should also be specialized. We discussed the need for partitioning of the tasks of semantic mismatch resolution in Section 2.2. That task however, while challenging, is just one of the tasks that needs to be performed at an intermediate level. Tasks performed by middleware, namely resolving technical heterogeneity and efficiently transporting data from servers to clients find a home in a mediated architecture. Tasks foreseen for agents, as locating, and validating sources find a home base in the mediating modules as well, even if their computational tasks extend over the network. Integration, improved by semantic mismatch resolution, is central to mediation. Reporting results to thin clients may involve summarization and abstraction to increase the value per data-unit transmitted. Such services become crucial for mobile clients, and we see already examples of such technologies attached to several servers [HadjiefthymiadesM:99].

The composition of synergistic functions grows a mediator into a substantial service. Such a service is best envisaged as a module within the networks that link customers and resources, as sketched in Figure 4. There is today a small number of companies building such mediators [W:98]. However, the technology is not yet suitable to be shrink-wrapped and requires substantial adaptation to individual settings.

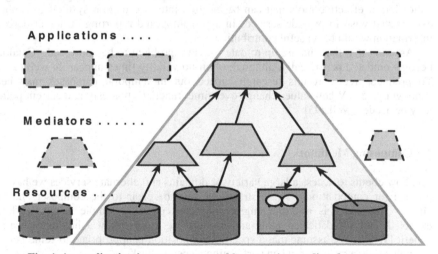

Fig. 4. An application instance composed by accessing mediated resources.

4.4 Other Services that Enhance Precision

We focused on semantic term mismatch in addressing solutions to enhance precision, but many other aspects of information processing are candidates. For instance, many businesses and consumers are interested in quality [NaumannLF:99]. Whereas today we routinely can compare prices of goods offered for sale on the web, obtaining quality metrics is much more difficult. Purchasing a cheap product that fails prematurely can be much more costly than the original price differential. Quality can be conveyed by corporate reputation, by guarantees given, by consumer reports, or by explicit metrics.

If guarantees are given, trust is still required that the guarantee will be honored. There are organizations now that give a Seal-of-Good-Housekeeping to other companies. These companies have to be trusted as well, and the same issues of trust recurr at one level higher. Payment and delivery guarantees may require escrow services [KetchpelGP:97]. If failed objects have to be returned shipping costs become a factor. Guarantees in the service arena are harder to specify, say, for the design or repair of software. Services cannot be returned, and the person providing the service may not be able to carry the burden of non-payment. Again intermediaries may be needed to support a reasonable business model. Little software and systems support exists to help new service businesses.

Quality metrics can also be gathered by surveying customers. Some web services, as Epinions have started to serve clients by encouraging reporting of purchase experiences. While such information always lags, and is easily biased, it represents actual outcome evaluations rather than promises. Bias occurs because of self-selection of customers and unbalanced response rates. Stable customers are reached more easily. Unhappy customers are more likely to respond. Again, having a collection of effective tools that can be inserted into information systems to support experts that wish to provide services in aggregating and reporting customer-derived information would be a useful contribution.

Assuring that the data are up-to-date is also a problem to be addressed. Catalogs become outdated periodically, although often no validity times appear on web pages. To produce precise results research carried out in temporal databases may help [Snodgrass:95]. When values change over time, functions that estimate current points may be needed [WJL:93].

4.4 Composing Mediators

To allow clients to access a large variety of domains and alternate services we have to provide for composition. These structures must be clear to the composer and the client. Simplicity is a prime engineering concept: only simple things work as expected, and sophisticated tools and models are more likely a hindrance than a benefit [W:97]. We assume that a specific composition is appropriate to some person or application, a *customer*, when performing a specific task.

As indicated in Figure 4 we expect that customer needs can be served by hierarchical models, although the underlying world of information resources is much more complex [WG:97]. Searching through a hierarchy has a logarithmic cost, and a factor that depends on the breadth of the tree at each level. When humans search the list at one level, their perception can deal with 7 ± 2 items at one time. That means a well-structured tree of 10 000 items can be searched fully with 6 actions. That cost is acceptable to most customers. We have seen that resources gathered from the web can be effectively presented as hierarchies of semi-structured data items [ChawatheEa:94]. A hierarchy also presents an effective model for task decomposition in workflow models.

4.5 Use of Multiple Compositions

Individuals may switch tasks and move among application domains. In our terms, that means that they may use multiple customer models at distinct times.   The composition that represents one customer model may be abandoned, temporarily or permanently.   Such switching must be recognized, and prior task models during a session must be retained to be re-enabled if the individual returns to a past customer model. How to recognize that a context switch is occurring and how to provide appropriate services cleanly is a difficult research question.

Customer models that are used by an individual within one session will typically be related. We find now again an intersection, where items belong to two models. There will be an *articulation point* between them. At an articulation point there will be some semantic match, even if the actual terms and representation do not match. Moving, for instance, from the domain of vacation travel planning for a *trip segment* to the airline domain the term *flight* is equivalent. Here the connection is easy, and either domain model could help in the match. But care is still needed, since a *flight segment* is at a lower level of granularity than the trip segment. Precision in matching of such task models becomes essential in repetitive business transactions, where one cannot afford to spend human efforts to correct semantic mismatches every time.

5. Conclusion

Information is created at the confluence of knowledge and data [CollettHS:91]. Data is obtained from observations, and its values should be objectively verifiable. Knowledge is gained through processing of observations, gained by experience, teaching, and the more formal processes we will focus on. Knowledge is compact, it applies to many data instances. Much important knowledge to deal with real-world complexities s is now held by human experts who function as intermediaries. To use the knowledge in automation it must be formalized into programs and rules.

Creating knowledge from data is not a one-way path. The processes that convert data to knowledge themselves require knowledge. We need knowledge to select and filter appropriate data from an ever-increasing flow of observations, and assess their correctness. We need knowledge to classify instances and aggregate their parameters. We need knowledge to integrate the plethora of diverse sources. We need knowledge to select analyses and understand the meaning of the results. Knowledge is needed to understand and abstract the results into effective knowledge and information.

Information presented to customers must have a value that is greater than the human cost of obtaining and digesting it. More is hence not better nor efficient. We will need to focus increasingly on assuring that the information our systems provide is highly relevant to the customer in their roles.   Precision is an important aspect of information, and will be increasingly important. There are many components to precision. We have focused on improving precision due to rule-based matching of terms from semantic distinct domains. Other areas where precision should be is in metadata describing objects such as their quality, and in the processing models we need to manage complex transactions.

Moving to the desired state, world-wide efficient interoperation of information and business transactions, requires much research [LockemanEa:97]. Many short term solutions are being implemented in industry today. Analyzing industrial solutions has two benefits for researchers: it shows where needs exist and, invariably. also shows where ad-hoc solutions will fail in terms of scalability, generalizability, and maintainability. We have learned that solutions that are formally grounded will provide growth, and reliable infrastructures for the future.

In the base report [Wiederhold:99] we analyzed the status and changes expected over a wide range of topics related to information technology. In this paper we focused on semantic modeling issues requiring research. Novel software will require more powerful hardware, but we are confident that hardware-oriented research and development is healthy, and will be able to supply the needed infrastructure [Hamilton:99]. To be effective issues of technology transfer must be considered as well.

Acknowledgement

The material for this paper came in part from a study prepared for JETRO [Wiederhold:99], and in turn was based on many published resources as well as on discussions with wonderful people that I have encountered in my work and studies. Research on articulation is supported by the AFOSR New World Vistas Program. A large number of students and colleagues have contributed and demonstrated concepts and validations.

References

[ACM:99] Neal Coulter, et al: ACM Computing Classification System
    http://www.acm.org/class
[Adobe:99] Adobe Corporation: PDF and Printing;
    http://www.adobe.com/prodindex/postscript/pdf.html
[Amico:98] Art museum image consortium (AMICO) http://www.amico.net/docs/vra
[BowmanEa:94] C. Mic Bowman, Peter B. Danzig, Darren R. Hardy, Udi Manber and Michael F. Schwartz: The HARVEST Information Discovery and Access System"; *Proceedings of the Second International World Wide Web Conference*, Chicago, Illinois, October 1994, pp 763--771.
[ChangGP:96] Chen-Chuan K. Chang, Hector Garcia-Molina, Andreas Paepcke : Boolean Query Mapping Across Heterogeneous Information Sources ; *IEEE Transactions on Knowledge and Data Engineering*; Vol.8 no., pp.515-521, Aug., 1996.

[ChavezM:96] Anthony Chavez and Pattie Maes: „Kasbah: An Agent Marketplace for Buying and Selling Goods'; *First International Conference on the Practical Application of Intelligent Agents and Multi-Agent Technology*, London, UK, April 1996.

[ChawatheEa:94] S. Chawathe , H. Garcia-Molina , J. Hammer , K. Ireland , Y. Papakonstantinou , J. Ullman , J.Widom: The TSIMMIS Project: Integration of Heterogeneous Information Sources; *IPSJ Conference*, Tokyo Japan, 1994.

[Chen:76] Peter P.S. Chen: The Entity-Relationship Model --- Toward a Unified View of Data; *ACM Transactions on Database Systems*, March 1976.

[Cimino:96] J.J. Cimino: „Review paper: coding systems in health care"; *Methods of Information in Medicine*, Schattauer Verlag, Stuttgart Germany, Vol.35 Nos.4-5, Dec.1996, pp.273-284.

[ColletHS:91] C. Collet, M. Huhns, and W-M. Shen: ``Resource Integration Using a Large Knowledge Base in CARNOT"; *IEEE Computer*, Vol.24 No.12, Dec.1991.

[Connolly:97] Dan Connolly (ed.): *XML: Principles, Tools, and Techniques*; O'Reilly, 1997.

[ElMasriW:79] R. ElMasri and G. Wiederhold: Data Model Integration Using the Stuctural Model; *ACM SIGMOD Conf. On the Management of Data*, May 1979, pp.191-202.

[GravanoGT:94] L. Gravano , H. Garcia-Molina ,and A. Tomasic: „Precision and Recall of GlOSS Estimators for Database Discovery"; *Parallel and Distributed Information Systems*, 1994.

[HadjiefthymiadesM:99]   Stathes Hadjiefthymiades and Lazaros Merakos: „A Survey of Web Architectures for Wireless Communication Environments"; *Computer Networks and ISDN Systems*,   Vol.28,   May   1996,   p.1139, http://www.imag.fr/Multimedia/www5cd/www139/overview.htm.

[Hamilton:99] Scott Hamilton: Taking Moore's Law into the Next Century; *IEEE Computer*, Jan. 99, pp. 43-48.

[Hearst:97] Marty Hearst: "Interfaces for Searching the Web"; in [SA:97].

[HuhnsS:97] Michael Huhns and J.Singh: *Readings in Agents*; Morgan Kaufmann, October, 1997, pp.185-196.

[HumphreysL:93] Betsy Humphreys and Don Lindberg: „The UMLS project : Making the conceptual connection between users and the information they need"; *Bulletin of the Medical Library Association*, 1993, see also http://www.lexical.com

[Inktomi:00] Inktomi and NEC: Size of the Web; http://www.inktomi.com/webmap/, 17Jan2000).

[JanninkSVW:98] Jan Jannink, Pichai Srinivasan, Danladi Verheijen, and Gio Wiederhold: "Encapsulation and Composition of Ontologies"; *Proc. AAAI Workshop on Information Integration*, AAAI Summer Conference, Madison WI, July 1998.

[JelassiL:96] Th. Jelassi, H.-S. Lai: CitiusNet: The Emergence of a Global Electronic Market, INSEAD, The European Institue of Business Administration, Fontainebleau, France; http://www.simnet.org/public/programs/capital/96paper/paper3/3.html;   Society   for Information Management, 1996.

[Kent:99] Robert   E.   Kent: Ontology   Markup   Language; http://wave.eecs.wsu.edu/CKRMI/OML.html, Feb.1999

[KetchpelGP:97] Steven P. Ketchpel, Hector Garcia-Molina, Andreas Paepcke : Shopping Models: A Flexible Architecture for Information Commerce; Digital Libraries '97, ACM 1997.

[LabrouF:94] Y. Labrou and Tim Finin: A Semantics Approach for KQML, a general Purpose Language for Software Agents; *Proc. CIKM 94*, ACM, 1994.

[Langer:98] Thomas Langer: „MeBro - A Framework for Metadata-Based Information Mediation"; *First International Workshop on Practical Information Mediation and Brokering, and the Commerce of Information on the Internet*, Tokyo Japan, September 1998, http://context.mit.edu/imediat98/paper2/

[LenatG:90] D. Lenat and R.V. Guha: Building Large Knowledge-Based Systems; Addison-Wesley (Reading MA), 372 pages.

[LockemanEa:97] Peter Lockeman et al.: „The Network as a Global Database: Challenges of Interoperability, Proactivity, Interactiveness, Legacy"; *Proc. 23 VLDB*, Athens Greece, Morgan Kaufman, Aug. 1997.

[Lynch:97] Clifford Lynch: „Searching the Internet"; in [SA:97].

[MarkMM:99] David Mark et al.: "Geographic Information Science: Critical Issues in an Emerging Cross-Disciplinary Research Domain"; NCGIA, Feb. 1999, http://www.geog.buffalo.edu/ncgia/workshopreport.html.

[McEwen:74] H.E. McEwen (ed): *Management of Data Elements in Information Processing*; NTIS, US. Dept.of Commerce pub.74-10700, 1974.

[MitraWK:00] Prasenjit Mitra, Gio Wiederhold, and Martin Kersten: „A Graph-oriented Model for Articulation of Ontology Interdependencies"; in Zaniolo, Locckeman, chll and Grust: *Advances in Database Technology -- EDBT 2000*, Springer Verlag LNCS Vol. 1777, March 2000, pp. 86-100.

[MPEG:00] Motion Picture Group: Proposed standard for Video Metadata, MPEG7; www.cselt.it/mpeg, 2000.

[PonceleonSAPD:98] D. Ponceleon, S. Srinivashan, A. Amir, D. Petkovic, D. Diklic: „Key to Effective Video Retrieval: Effective Cataloguing and Browsing"; *Proc.of ACM Multimedia '98 Conference*, September 1998.

[Resnick:97] Paul Resnick "Filtering Information on the Internet"; in [SA:97].

[RoyH:97] N.F. Roy and C.D. Hafner: „The State of the Art in Ontology Design"; *AI Magazine*, 1997, Vol.18 No.3, pp.53--74.

[SA:97] Scientific American Editors: *The Internet: Fulfilling the Promise*; Scientific American March 1997.

[ShannonW:48] C.E. Shannon and W.Weaver: *The Mathematical Theory of Computation*;1948, reprinted by The Un.Illinois Press, 1962.

[Snodgrass:95] Richard T. Snodgrass (editor): *The TSQL2 Temporal Query Language*; Kluwer Academic Publishers, 1995.

[Stix:97] Gary Stix: „Finding Pictures"; in [SA:97].

[WangWL:98] James Z. Wang,, Gio Wiederhold, and Jia Li: „Wavelet-based Progressive Transmission and Security Filtering for Medical Image Distribution"; in Stephen Wong (ed.): *Medical Image Databases*; Kluwer publishers, 1998, pp.303-324.

[W:92] Gio Wiederhold, Gio: "Mediators in the Architecture of Future Information Systems"; *IEEE Computer*, March 1992, pages 38-49.

[WJL:93] Gio Wiederhold, Sushil Jajodia, and Witold Litwin: Integrating Temporal Data in a Heterogenous Environment; in Tansel, Clifford, Gadia, Jajodia, Segiv, Snodgrass: *Temporal Databases Theory, Design and Implementation;* Benjamin Cummins Publishing, 1993, pp. 563-579.

[W:97] Gio Wiederhold: "Customer Models for Effective Presentation of Information"; Position Paper, Flanagan, Huang, Jones, Kerf (eds): *Human-Centered Systems: Information, Interactivity, and Intelligence*, National Science Foundation, July 1997, pp.218-221.

[WG:97] Gio Wiederhold and Michael Genesereth: "The Conceptual Basis for Mediation Services"; *IEEE Expert, Intelligent Systems and their Applications*, Vol.12 No.5, Sep-Oct.1997.

[W:98] Gio Wiederhold: "Weaving Data into Information"; *Database Programming and Design*; Freeman pubs, Sept. 1998.

[W:99] Gio Wiederhold: Trends in Information Technology; report to JETRO.MITI, currently available as http://www-db.stanford.edu/pub/gio/1999/miti.htm.

Just-in-Time Information: To *Push* or Not to *Push*

Sharma Chakravarthy

The University of Texas at Arlington, USA
sharma@cse.uta.edu

Abstract. Today, there is a greater need for *just-in-time* information than ever before. Information systems have evolved from distributed and homogeneous to network-centric and heterogeneous. The number of users dependent on these information sources for personal, business, and mission critical needs has increased by orders of magnitude. Yet the way in which users have been accessing information has not undergone the paradigm shift needed for making the „just-in-time" information happen. In this talk we differentiate between data-centric and user-centric approach to information access and management. We argue that the success of web-based information usage is grounded in user-centric view of the information where the user is the one to whom information should flow rather than the user approaching the information (as in the data-centric case). In order for this to happen, we propose that the push technology should be incorporated into all aspects of information management. Push technology is based on the reactive (or trigger) capability and has a well-grounded formalism for adapting it to network-centric architectures. We overview the state-of-the-art in reactive capability and elaborate on its potential for just-in-tine information management.

B. Lings and K. Jeffery (Eds.): BNCOD 17, LNCS 1832, p. 19, 2000.
© Springer-Verlag Berlin Heidelberg 2000

Using Space-Filling Curves for Multi-dimensional Indexing

J.K. Lawder and P.J.H. King

School of Computer Science and Information Systems,
Birkbeck College, University of London,
Malet Street, London WC1E 7HX, United Kingdom
{jkl, pjhk}@dcs.bbk.ac.uk

Abstract. This paper presents and discusses a radically different approach to multi-dimensional indexing based on the concept of the space-filling curve. It reports the novel algorithms which had to be developed to create the first actual implementation of a system based on this approach, on some comparative performance tests, and on its actual use within the TriStarp Group at Birkbeck to provide a Triple Store repository. An important result that goes beyond this requirement, however, is that the performance improvement over the Grid File is greater the higher the dimension.

1 Introduction

Underlying any dbms is some form of repository management system or data store. The classic and dominant model for such repositories is that of some form of logical record or data aggregate type with a collection of instances conforming to that type usually termed a file. Such file systems are, of course, also used directly in many applications. The data model of a dbms may be radically different from this underlying repository model, the mapping between the two being a function of the dbms. With the well known relational systems, however, the mapping from the simple tabular data model to a collection of such repository files is generally straightforward.

The indexing of files can be either one-dimensional or multi-dimensional and we briefly review the two approaches in sections 2 and 3 of this paper. We then present our work on multi-dimensional indexing using the Hilbert Curve which was suggested by Faloutsos [4] although the idea was not fully developed. We are not aware of any actual implementation based on this approach prior to our own, but there has been some useful theoretical work supported by simulation on the clustering properties of the curve [5], [11], [13] and [10]. These studies generally agree on the superior clustering properties of the Hilbert Curve.

Section 4 introduces the concept of a space-filling curve using the Hilbert Curve as illustration. Sections 5 to 8 then discuss our own work on the Hilbert Curve in some detail, followed by Sect. 9, which discusses other types of curve, and Sect. 10 which summarizes our conclusions and further planned research.

B. Lings and K. Jeffery (Eds.): BNCOD 17, LNCS 1832, pp. 20–35, 2000.

2   One-Dimensional File Structures

With one-dimensional file structures, the record type specifies the fields or attributes which a record may contain. In one of these fields, usually termed the primary key, a value is required in all records and all values must be distinct.

A characteristic of one-dimensional systems is that the primary key values are used to determine the placement of records in physical storage organized as a collection of pages, a page containing a number of records. The page is located using some form of physical address, or value from which such an address can be determined, known as a *page-key*. Given a primary key value, there is an algorithmic process of some kind, a B-tree index, hashing, etc which yields a page-key thus determining the page on which the corresponding record is to be placed in the case of a store operation or is to be found, if it exists, in the case of a retrieval operation. We assume in this paper that the reader is familiar with such one-dimensional file structures and with aspects such as page splitting, page merging, etc. The B-tree in particular is now well developed and has come to be the dominant technology for one-dimensional file systems.

Whilst one-dimensional indexing provides for efficient retrieval on the primary key, retrieval by the specification of other attribute values, if not to be by exhaustive search, requires the maintenance of supplementary or secondary indexes. For these the values are not required to be unique and, given a particular value, the index simply provides the primary keys for those records having this value which are then retrieved in the usual way. Although some gain can be had by operating on primary key lists prior to actual retrieval such as intersecting lists from different secondary indexes, organizing the placement of records to optimize retrieval other than for the primary key is not possible.

3   Multi-dimensional Indexing

Multi-dimensional indexing is based on the notion that more than one field or attribute of a record type should be specified as constituting the *primary key set* for records of that type and that all keys in the key set should play an equal role in determining the physical placement of a record in store and hence in optimization issues. Whilst every member of the key set must be defined for a record, uniqueness is required only for the set as a whole and not of its individual components. To fix ideas consider the indexing of objects at points in three-dimensional space; objects can lie on the same plane or line and thus can have any one or any two key values in common, but no two objects can occupy the same point and thus all three co-ordinates cannot be the same.

With multi-dimensional indexing we have the important facility of the retrieval of sets of records on partially specified keys. Thus with a three component key set we may wish for example, to retrieve all those records for two specified values of the key set but with any value for the other one; or with just one component specified and any values for the other two; or with intervals in all three dimensions, all the records whose key set values lie within the defined cuboid. Unlike the one-dimensional file structures therefore, with multi-dimensional structures the algorithms for retrieval are considerably more complex than those which determine the placement of a given record in physical storage and their development is a matter of research.

A landmark paper in work on multi-dimensional indexing is that of Nievergelt et al [14] in which the potential values of key sets are regarded as points in an n-dimensional cartesian product space. This product space we term the *key-space* and the points which correspond to actual records we term *datum-points*. The key-space is divided into cuboids with each cuboid being in one-one correspondence with a page of data in physical store, the records on that page being those that correspond to the datum-points in the cuboid. When a page which becomes full is split the cuboid is split correspondingly and similarly with recombination of under-used pages. This paper left open a number of questions relating to the structuring of the index to the key-space and the choice of dimensions for splitting. These were addressed by Derakhshan [3] whose work resulted in the repository system used by the TriStarp Group for the past decade in both its three and four dimensional versions. An evaluation and critique of this implementation is to be found in Lawder [12].

An important development along the same lines as the Grid File is the Bang File of Freeston [6]. In this approach the key-space cuboids are not disjoint but nested and whilst there are data pages in one-one correspondence with the cuboids, for only the innermost cuboids do they contain the records for all datum-points within it, in general containing only the records for the datum-points within it less those in the contained cuboids. This approach avoids the recombination deadlock problems which can occur with the Grid File and a method of indexing has also been developed. However no retrieval method for partial match or interval queries has yet been published and nor is such a method readily apparent.

A review of multi-dimensional indexing methods, including Guttman's R-Tree [8], is given by Gaede and Günther [7].

4   Hilbert's Space-Filling Curve

Space filling curves became a topic of interest to leading pure mathematicians in the late 19th century, the first paper being that of Peano in 1890 [16]. A more readable paper, however, is that of David Hilbert in 1891 [9] who gave the first geometrical interpretation. We briefly summarise his argument, using the same diagrams he used.

Without loss of generality we consider a mapping between the points of a square and a finite line using the definition of a point on the line as the limit of an infinite sequence of nested intervals whose length tends to zero and of a point in two dimensions as being the limit of an infinite sequence of nested squares whose area tends to zero. Figure 1 reproduces the figures in Hilbert's paper, except that we number the points from 0 rather than from 1. Figure 1(a) shows the initial square and line each divided into four, the numbers showing corre-

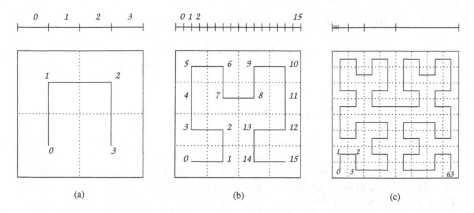

Fig. 1. Approximations of the Hilbert curve in 2 dimensions

spondences between sub-squares and line intervals established so that adjacent line intervals always correspond to adjacent sub-squares; the line connecting the centres of the sub-squares emphasizes their ordering. Figure 1(b) shows the next step in which each square and its corresponding line interval have been further subdivided with re-orientations of the sub-square sequences for the first and last sub-squares of Fig. 1(a) to ensure that the adjacency property is everywhere preserved. Figure 1(c) indicates the third step in the sequence.

If this process is continued to infinity then for any arbitrary point in the square there is a unique infinite sequence of nested squares for which this point is its limit. The corresponding infinite sequence of nested intervals on the line also defines a unique point. This argument also goes the other way and thus a one-one mapping is established between all points of the line and all points of the square. The points on the line are plainly ordered and this ordering thus gives the points of the square an ordering now known as the Hilbert Curve. Since this curve passes through every point in the square once and once only it is said to be space filling. The curve is everywhere contiunuous and nowhere differentiable. Intuitively one can see that the continuity results from the persistence of the adjacency property at every step and the non-differentiability from the sharp changes of direction at each step. For more on the mathematics and on other curves see Sagan [17].

But these mathematicians were concerned with limits at infinity whereas computer scientists are more concerned with the finite albeit large. We therefore say the curve in Fig. 1(a) is the First Order Hilbert Curve and is in a finite two dimensional space comprising only four points. It clearly "fills" this space. Likewise Fig. 1(b) shows the Second Order Hilbert Curve which fills a finite two-dimensional space of 16 points, and so on.

To specify the coordinates of the points in the space of Fig. 1(a) we need only a single bit but for the ordinal positions on the line two bits. The ordinal mapping established by the First Order Hilbert Curve is thus:

$$\langle 0, 0 \rangle \to 00, \langle 0, 1 \rangle \to 01, \langle 1, 1 \rangle \to 10 \text{ and } \langle 1, 0 \rangle \to 11.$$

For the points in the space of the Second Order Curve we require two bits for the coordinates and four bits for the ordinal numbering and the mapping established by this curve begins:

$$\langle 00, 00 \rangle \to 0000, \langle 01, 00 \rangle \to 0001, \langle 01, 01 \rangle \to 0010, \langle 00, 01 \rangle \to 0011, \ldots$$

In practice we are interested in somewhat higher order curves. With 32 bit coordinates we would need the 32nd Order Hilbert Curve and would have 64 bit ordinal numbers. We therefore need some algorithmic procedures for the mapping which, given coordinates, produces the ordinal number and vice versa. These are discussed in Sect. 7.

Thus far we have discussed only two dimensions since in this paper we aim only to illustrate concepts. However the Hilbert Curve extends readily to any number of dimensions. In three the First Order Curve passes through the eight sub-cubes into which the initial cube is divided and the mapping is to a line divided into eight intervals, the adjacency property now being that consecutive sub-cubes have a common surface. For four dimensions the First Order Curve orders 16 cuboids with consecutive cuboids having a common three dimensional hypersurface. And so on! For more information on how the algorithms scale up and the general formulae see the thesis of Lawder [12], the working software of which can be parameterised to up to 16 dimensions and which could be modified to go beyond.

5   Indexing Using Space-Filling Curves

To construct an index to a multi-dimensional file we use a finite Hilbert Curve of appropriate order to give a linear ordering to the datum-points in the key-space. These datum-points are then partitioned by dividing the curve into consecutive sections. Each section is then put into correspondence with a page of storage which contains the actual records. The sequence number or *derived-key* of the first datum-point on a curve section is used as the corresponding page-key which gives the pages a logical ordering. The page-keys are then indexed using a conventional B-Tree or some variant which gives the physical page addresses.

An important point to note in our approach is that it indexes partitions of data rather than partitions of the key-space. This contrasts with most alternative approaches, including the Grid and Bang Files. Our approach enables us to avoid problems arising from partitions overlapping within the index, which are common in other approaches, including those based on the R-Tree and the Bang File.

6   A Tree Representation of the Hilbert Curve

As a result of the recursive way in which a space-filling curve is constructed, the correspondence between the points on a finite space-filling curve and their sequence numbers can be expressed as a tree structure, its height corresponding to the order of the curve. Not only does this provide an insight into how mappings are performed but, more importantly, a tree-like conceptual view greatly aids the development of algorithms which are used to facilitate the execution of queries. We use the 2-dimensional Hilbert Curve in describing the construction of the tree but the process is applicable to other curves and to higher dimensions. In what follows, we use the term *n-point* for the concatenation of the coordinates of a point on the first order curve; note that on a first order curve coordinates are single bit values.

We begin by placing a first order curve at the root of the tree. If we express the coordinates of points lying on a first order curve as n-points then the correspondence between one-dimensional sub-interval sequence numbers and co-ordinates given in Sect. 4 above results in a root node comprising the set of ordered pairs: $\langle 00, 00 \rangle$, $\langle 01, 01 \rangle$, $\langle 10, 11 \rangle$ and $\langle 11, 10 \rangle$. In this notation, the first value of each pair is the sequence number and the second value is the n-point representation of a point lying at the centre of a sub-square.

In the transformation to a second order curve each of these ordered pairs becomes the parent of a node similar to the root and so the height of the tree increases to 2. The middle two child nodes express a first order mapping which is the same as that of their parent and the other two express mappings which are different. An example of a tree whose height is 3 is given in Fig. 2. Tree level 1 corresponds to Fig. 1(a), level 2 corresponds to Fig. 1(b) and level 3 corresponds to Fig. 1(c).

The process of growing the tree can then be continued for each node at the lowest current level as the order of the curve increments. We note that the fanout of the tree equals the number of points on a first order curve.

The set of ordered pairs in all of the leaves corresponds to the finite set of points through which the curve passes while non-leaf nodes correspond to sub-squares which contain a sub-set of points at the leaf level.

7   Mapping between n and One Dimensions

An algorithm by which the derived-key, D, of a point, P, is calculated is readily illustrated with the aid of the tree representation of the Hilbert curve and entails a traversal from root to leaf. This is given in Algorithm 1, where the most significant bit of a value is designated 'position 1'. The inverse mapping, from a derived-key to the coordinates of a point, is carried out in a similar manner.

It is not a practical option, however, to base the mapping implementation on storing the tree representation of a curve explicitly and traversing it from root to leaf since the number of nodes would be excessive. Furthermore, the size of a node increases exponentially with the number of dimensions. There is, however, a finite number of distinct node types, ie orientations of the first order curve, and this number is independent of the height of a tree. This is apparent from Fig. 2. Thus it is possible to represent the tree as a state diagram in which each node type corresponds to a state. Once the height of the tree exceeds a relatively

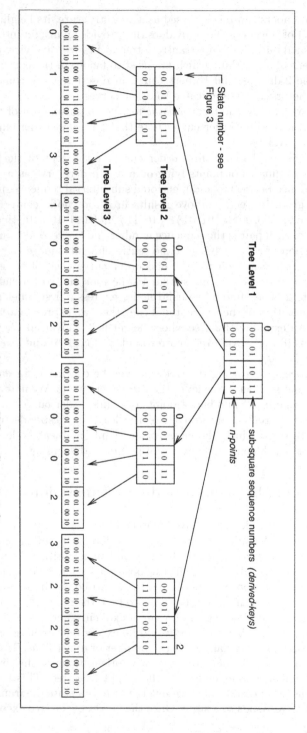

Fig. 2. The tree representation of the third order Hilbert Curve in 2 dimensions

---

Algorithm 1 Finding the *derived-key* of a Point by Traversing the Tree Representation of the Hilbert Curve

---

1: *current_level* ⇐ 1
2: *current_node* ⇐ *root*
3: D ⇐ the empty bit-string
4: **repeat**
5:    p ⇐ one bit in position *current_level* taken from each coordinate in P, concatenated into an *n-point*
6:    d ⇐ the n-bit *derived-key* taken from *current_node* corresponding to p
7:    append d to D
8:    **if** *current_level* < *leaf level* **then**
9:       *current_node* ⇐ node pointed to by the ordered pair ⟨ p, d ⟩ within *current_node*
10:    **end if**
11:    *current_level* ⇐ *current_level* +1
12: **until** *current_level* > *leaf level*

---

low threshold, there are more nodes than states. A state diagram thus enables us to express the tree in a compacted form, since the states are not replicated in the diagram. The state diagram for 2 dimensions is given in Fig. 3.

The use of state diagrams for Hilbert Curve mappings was suggested in a technical report by Faloutsos [4] which refers to a method for generating state diagrams proposed by Bially [1]. Bially's technique is not specifically oriented towards the Hilbert Curve and comprises an incomplete set of rules requiring a manual process of trial-and-error in the generation of state diagrams.

Lawder [12] adapts Bially's technique to enable the automatic construction of state diagrams for the Hilbert Curve. State diagrams are useful in up to 10 dimensions for the Hilbert Curve, beyond which memory requirements become prohibitive. In higher dimensional space, the calculation method of mapping from one to n dimensions given by Butz [2] is used. Some improvements to Butz' method are given by Lawder, together with details of the inverse mapping.

8 Query Execution

8.1 Overall Approach

We noted earlier that a page represents a section of curve, ie a contiguous set of points, and will contain the records for datum-points which lie on that section. A query region, which is a hyper-rectangle, will always overlap one or more sections of the curve with intervening lengths joining them lying outside of the region. In other words, the curve may enter, leave and re-enter the query region a number of times.

Our querying algorithm therefore identifies every page whose curve section overlaps one or more of the curve sections of the query region. These pages are identified in ascending page-key order and any page whose curve section lies wholly outside the query region is, in effect, 'stepped over'. An example

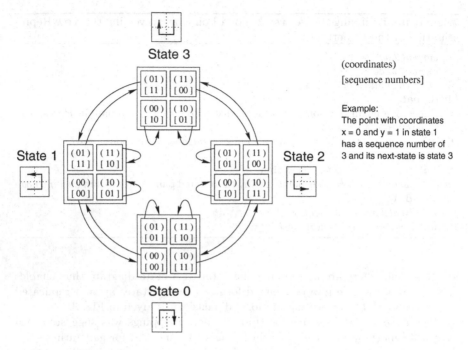

Fig. 3. A state diagram for the Hilbert curve in 2 dimensions

illustrating the concept is given in Fig. 4. To effect the stepping-over, a function is required which, given as input a derived-key value, i, will calculate and output the <u>lowest</u> derived-key which is equal to or greater than i and which corresponds to a point lying in the query region. We call this function *calculate_next_match* and the output value the *next-match*.

Once a page, intersecting with the query region, has been identified, retrieved and searched, the page-key of the next page is used as input to the *calculate_next_match* function. We then retrieve for searching the page which will contain the point mapping to the output of the function, if it is a datum-point. We identify the first page to be searched after calculating the lowest derived-key of any point in the query region by supplying the value of zero as input to the *calculate_next_match* function.

A description of the *calculate_next_match* function in more detail is given in the next section.

8.2   Algorithm for Calculating the *next-match* on a Hilbert Curve

We refer to the input to the *calculate_next_match* function as the *current-page-key* and refer to the sub-spaces resulting from a first order division of a space as *quadrants* regardless of the number of dimensions. Recall that a first order curve passing through a space connects the centre-points of these quadrants, which

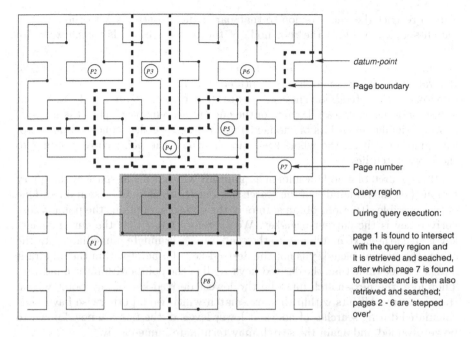

Fig. 4. Example range query on points mapped to the Hilbert curve

total 2^n in number. Also recall that the sequence number of a quadrant is also a derived-key and that the derived-key of a quadrant is an n-bit value.

Our search for a next-match, if one exists, is equivalent to finding the appropriate path in a descent, from root to leaf, of the tree representation of the partitioning of space induced by the Hilbert Curve. This descent is an iterative process. During each iteration, a node is searched to attempt to find within it a quadrant intersecting with the query region and mapping to the lowest derived-key equal to or greater than that of the quadrant holding the point corresponding to the current-page-key. The child node pointed to by this quadrant may then be searched in the next iteration but, as described below, sometimes the search for a next-match can be simplified and accelerated, sometimes back-tracking is required and sometimes the search fails thus signifying completion of the query execution.

The searching of a node is not straightforward when using the Hilbert curve since quadrants can be ordered differently in different nodes. The manner in which this problem is resolved is detailed by Lawder [12].

We recall that nodes correspond to sub-spaces and we call a node which is being searched during any particular iteration of the algorithm the *current-search-space*. As the tree is descended, at the end of each iteration, the current-search-space is restricted to one of its quadrants and thus is reduced in size by a factor of 2^n since a node contains this many quadrants. It is convenient also to restrict the query region to that part which intersects with the current-search-space. Note that the root node of the tree corresponds to the whole of the key-space.

On successful completion of each iteration of the search process, n bits of the value of the next-match are identified and provisionally appended to any previously calculated bits. These n bits are the sequence number of the quadrant found following a successful search of the current-search-space. Thus the highest, or most significant, n bits of the next-match designate the sequence number of the quadrant within the whole key-space in which the point corresponding to the next-match lies.

If the search of a node results in a quadrant which is a sub-space of the query region then the remainder of the search for a next-match may be simplified. One of two possible situations obtains. In one, the quadrant contains the point whose derived-key is the current-page-key. We therefore know that the current-page-key is itself the next-match and so the search may terminate immediately. In the other, the current-page-key is not the derived-key of a point within the quadrant and is a lower value than the derived-keys of all of the points within the quadrant. Therefore, the next-match must be the lowest derived-key of any point within the quadrant. All bits within the next-match which would otherwise have been calculated during searches of nodes at lower levels of the tree are now known to be zero-valued and again the search may terminate immediately.

Alternatively, the search of a node may result in a quadrant which intersects with but is not a sub-space of the query region. Again, one of two possible situations obtains. In one, the quadrant contains the point corresponding to the current-page-key and so the quadrant sequence number is appended to the next-match, as described above, and the search continues in the next lower level of the tree. In the other, the quadrant does not contain the point corresponding to the current-page-key and so the remainder of the search can be simplified since a next-match is guaranteed to exist. It will be the lowest derived-key of any point lying within the intersection of the quadrant and the query region. Thus the value of the current-page-key is of no further interest and there will be no possibility of a requirement to back-track, as described below.

Sometimes the search of a node fails to find any quadrant both intersecting with the query region and also having a derived-key equal to or greater than that of the quadrant containing the point corresponding to the current-page-key. Determining the next-match then requires back-tracking to a higher level in the tree where a node was previously found to contain at least one quadrant intersecting with the query region and containing points mapping to higher derived-keys than the current-page-key. If no such node, to which back-tracking may take place, was found previously then no next-match can exist and the search terminates. The lack of a next-match also signifies that the query process itself is complete.

Sub-sets of quadrants to which back-tracking can return may be found at more than one level of the tree as it is descended. In order for a next-match to be minimally higher than the current-page-key, back-tracking, if required, entails ascending the tree by the least possible number of levels, ie to the 'most recently' identified such sub-set of quadrants. For each level of ascension of the tree, n low order bits of the next-match are removed and must be recalculated once descent resumes.

If back-tracking is possible and takes place, then a similar situation arises as described above where the search results in a quadrant not containing the point corresponding to the current-page-key. Additionally, the quadrant may be a sub-space of the query region, also as described above.

The algorithm implemented as the *calculate_next_match* function is given in Algorithm 2 and for simplicity assumes a tree representation of the Hilbert Curve.

Algorithm 2 Algorithm to calculate the Hilbert *next-match*

1: *current_level* $\Leftarrow$ 1
2: *current-search-space* $\Leftarrow$ *root*
3: **repeat**
4:     $X \Leftarrow$ the *derived-key* of the quadrant in the *current-search-space* containing the *current-page-key*
5:     $Y \Leftarrow$ the lowest *derived-key* of any quadrant in the *current-search-space* intersecting with the *current-query-region*, such that $Y \geq X$
        {this entails a binary search of the *current-search-space*, the recording of sub-spaces to which back-tracking may be required and may aslo entail backtracking (if possible)}
6:     *current-search-space* $\Leftarrow$ the quadrant whose *derived-key* = Y
7:     *current-query-region* $\Leftarrow$ the intersection of the *current-query-region* and the *current-search-space*
8:     append Y to the *next-match*
9:     **if** $X = Y$ **then**
10:        **if** *current-query-region* = *current-search-space* **then**
11:           return the *current-page-key* as the *next-match*
12:        **end if**
13:    **else**
14:        **if** *current-query-region* = *current-search-space* **then**
15:           all remaining unresolve bits of *next-match* $\Leftarrow$ 0
16:           return the *next-match*
17:        **else**
18:           calculate the *next-match* as the lowest *derived-key* of any point in the *current-query-region*
19:           return the *next-match*
20:        **end if**
21:    **end if**
22:    *current_level* $\Leftarrow$ *current_level* +1
23: **until** *current_level* > *leaf level*

---

9   Other Space-Filling Curves

The approach described in this paper can be used for finite space-filling curves other than the finite Hilbert Curve by the substitution of appropriate mapping functions and some minor modifications to the *calculate_next_match* function.

Most notable is the Z-order curve, which has been applied, for indexing regions (eg the Bang File) and for spatial data (eg Orenstein's PROBE Project [15]). A Z-order derived-key is 'assembled' very simply by cyclically taking a bit from each coordinate of a point and appending it to those taken previously. This is sometimes referred to as 'bit interleaving'. Thus the 2 dimensional point P with coordinates

$$\langle\, x_1 x_2 x_3 \ldots x_k,\ y_1 y_2 y_3 \ldots y_k \,\rangle$$

maps to a derived-key of

$$x_1 y_1 x_2 y_2 x_3 y_3 \ldots x_k y_k,$$

where each x_i is a bit in a coodinate in dimension x, and similarly each y_i. The curve is illustrated in Fig. 5.

First Order   **Second Order**   **Third Order**

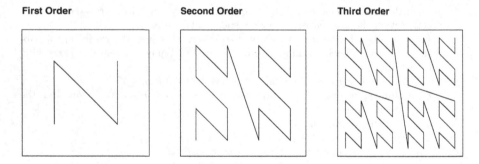

Fig. 5. Approximations of the Z-order curve in 2 dimensions

The direct relationship between individual bits in coordinates and Z-order derived-keys enables us to adopt a different algorithm for the *calculate_next_match* function which is more computationally efficient. This relies on manipulating bit values rather than conceptually descending a tree.

Where the page-key is not the next-match it must be incremented which entails changing a zero-valued bit to 1. In order to increment the page-key minimally, the algorithm first finds the lowest possible highest bit which must change and lower bits are then reduced in value, where possible. The method is given in outline in Algorithm 3, in which a *page-key-point* is the point corresponding to a page-key.

Other curves, but of less interest than the Z-order Curve, include the Gray-code, Scan and Snake Curves and are discussed by Lawder [12].

Algorithm 3 Algorithm to calculate the Z-order *next-match*

1: *next-match* $\Leftarrow$ *page-key*
2: check each coordinate in the *page-key-point* to find the highest bit in the *next-match* which must change:

    (a) from 1 to 0 because a *page-key-point* coordinate > the corresponding coordinate in the range upper bound
       or
    (b) from 0 to 1 because a *page-key-point* coordinate < the corresponding coordinate in the range lower bound

3: where the highest bit to change arises from condition (a) in some coordinate:

    find the lowest but higher bit in the *next-match* determined by some other coordinate which can be changed from 0 to 1, such that if all lower bits are set to 0, the coordinate value remains *leq* the corresponding coordinate in the range upper bound

4: set to 1 the bit identified in the *next-match* as being the highest zero-valued bit which must be incremented
5: set all lower bits in the *next-match* to 0
6: for each coordinate of the point corresponding to the *next-match*, if any is < the corresponding coordinate of the range lower bound, then increment the corresponding bits in the *next-match* to the values in the range lower bound

---

10   Conclusions and Future Work

The work reported in this paper has taken the idea of using space-filling curves for multi-dimensional indexing and the Hilbert Curve in particular and resolved the outstanding problems required to make such an approach practically usable; in particular the key problem of discovering a general algorithm for the all important query process. This has led to a working system which provides for the multi-dimensional indexing of records in up to 16 dimensions and which could readily be extended to higher dimensions if required.

This software has now been used practically for three dimensions as a Triple Store repository within the TriStarp Group and we have carried out preliminary experiments using randomly generated data to compare the system with the Group's existing multi-dimensional indexing sytstem based on the Grid File. These tests have indicated that the space-filling curve approach is more to be preferred the higher the dimensionality required. Comparisons with Guttman's R-Tree using 2-dimensional randomly generated spatial data showed a 75% saving in time taken to populate a data store and over 90% saving in time taken to execute range queries. Further details of performance tests undertaken can be found in Lawder's thesis [12]. We have also modified our software to give versions which use other space-filling curves and made some comparisons with the Hilbert Curve software. Our provisional conclusion is that none is better than the Hilbert Curve but more work is needed on this aspect.

Considerable scope remains for carrying out further experimentation and a number of potentially significant improvements need investigating. One interesting possibility is not to regard the pages as covering the whole curve. This could be effected by indexing each page using the minimum and maximum derived-keys for the datum-points which it contains. The maximum derived-key of one page and the minimum derived-key of the next then specify a section of curve which contains no datum-points. This should reduce the number of pages which have to be searched for a query and in some cases require no pages at all to be searched.

Thus far our attention has been principally focussed on point data as datum-points of records. We are aware, however, that multi-dimensional indexing using space-filling curves has potential application to spatial data which is another area meriting further work. We would be pleased to make our software available for bona fide experimental use to anyone with a multi-dimensional indexing requirement.

References

1. Theodore Bially. Space-Filling Curves: Their Generation and Their Application to Bandwidth Reduction. *IEEE Transactions on Information Theory*, IT-15(6):658–664, Nov 1969.
2. Arthur R. Butz. Alternative Algorithm for Hilbert's Space-Filling Curve. *IEEE Transactions on Computers*, 20:424–426, April 1971.
3. Mir Derakhshan. A Development of the Grid File for the Storage of Binary Relations. PhD thesis, Birkbeck College, University of London, 1989.
4. Christos Faloutsos and Shari Roseman. Fractals for Secondary Key Retrieval. Technical Report UMIACS-TR-89-47, University of Maryland, 1989. http://www.cs.cmu.edu/ christos/cpub.html.
5. Christos Faloutsos and Yi Rong. DOT: A Spatial Access Method Using Fractals. In: *Proceedings of the Seventh International Conference on Data Engineering, April 8-12, 1991, Kobe, Japan*, pages 152-159. IEEE Computer Society.
6. M. Freeston. The BANG File: A New Kind of Grid File. In: Umeshwar Dayal and Irving L. Traiger (eds): *Proceedings of the Association for Computing Machinery Special Interest Group on Management of Data Annual Conference*, May 27-29, 1987, San Francisco, California, pages 260-269. ACM Press.
7. Volker Gaede and Oliver Günther. Multidimensional Access Methods. ACM Computing Surveys, 30(2):170–231, June 1998.
8. Antonin Guttman. R-Trees: A Dynamic Index Structure for Spatial Seaching. In: *SIGMOD '84: Proceedings of the Annual Meeting, volume 14(2) of SIGMOD Record*, pages 47–57. ACM, 1984.
9. David Hilbert. Ueber stetige Abbildung einer Linie auf ein Flachenstuck. *Mathematische Annalen*. 38:459–460, 1891.
10. H.V. Jagadish. Analysis of the Hilbert curve for representing two-dimensional space. *Information Processing Letters*, 62(1):17–22, April 1997.
11. Akhil Kumar. A Study of Spatial Clustering Techniques. In: Dimitris Karagiannis (ed): *Proceedings of the 5th International Conference on Database and Expert Systems Applications (DEXA '94)*, volume 856 of Lecture Notes in Computer Science, pages 57–71. Springer-Verlag, Sept 1994.

12. Jonathan Lawder. The Application of Space-Filling Curves to the Storage and Retrieval of Multi-dimensional Data (Submitted for PhD). Technical Report JL/1/99, Birkbeck College, University of London, 1999.
13. Bongki Moon and H.V. Jagadish and Christos Faloutsos and Joel H. Saltz. Analysis of the Clustering Properties of the Hilbert Space-Filling Curve. Technical Report CS-TR-3611 / UMIACS-TR-96-20, University of Maryland, 1996.
14. Jürg Nievergelt and Hans Hinterberger and Kenneth C. Sevcik. The Grid File: An Adaptable, Symmetric Multikey File Structure. *ACM Transactions on Database Systems (TODS)*, 9(1):38–71, 1984.
15. Jack A. Orenstein and F.A. Manola. PROBE: Spatial Data Modeling and Query Processing in an Image Database Application. *IEEE Transactions on Software Engineering*, 14(5):611–629, 1988.
16. Giuseppe Peano. Sur une courbe, qui remplit toute une aire plane (On a curve which completely fills a planar region). *Mathematische Annalen*, 36:157–160, 1890.
17. Hans Sagan. Space-Filling Curves. Springer-Verlag, 1994.

A Multi-Query Optimizer for Monet[*]

Stefan Manegold, Arjan Pellenkoft, and Martin Kersten

CWI, P.O. Box 94079, 1090 GB Amsterdam, The Netherlands
{Stefan.Manegold,Arjan.Pellenkoft,Martin.Kersten}@cwi.nl

Abstract Database systems allow for concurrent use of several applications (and query interfaces). Each application generates an "optimal" plan—a sequence of low-level database operators—for accessing the database. The queries posed by users through the same application can be optimized together using traditional multi-query optimization techniques. However, the commonalities among queries of different applications are not exploited.

In this paper we present an efficient inter-application multi-query optimizer that re-uses previously computed (intermediate) results and eliminates redundant work. Experimental results on a single CPU system and a parallel system show that the inter-application multi-query optimizer improves the query evaluation performance significantly.

1 Introduction

Much effort has been spent on designing and implementing algorithms for database query optimization. Almost all current query optimizers are targeted at finding the best (or at least a good) execution plan for a single query at a time [SAC+79, IK90, GLPK94, VM96]. This is a reasonable approach for ad-hoc querying and traditional applications firing isolated, but rather complex queries at a time.

Modern database applications, such as data mining, however, strongly interact with the DBMS by sending a stream of query batches. This stream typically reflects a kind of navigation through the solution space of the data mining algorithms. Its batches consist of rather simple queries to be solved. Depending on the results of one step—consisting of a single query, or of a set of queries—an interactive user or an automated mining algorithm decides how to proceed. Typically, only a few parameters are changed in order to have a closer, i.e., more detailed look at a certain part of the database. Hence, it is very likely that subsequent data mining steps are similar and can easily benefit from re-using previously created intermediate results. This property can be used by applications to optimize access to a database at the cost of replicating parts of the query optimizer code within each application.

Further, data mining systems are typically multi-user systems, i.e., several users operate on the same database via the same or different mining applications.

---

[*] This work has been supported by the HPCN-CONQUER project.

Although the users act independently, formulating different queries, it is not unusual that the database system has to execute identical basic (but expensive) operations several times to satisfy the different requests. Unfortunately, this property cannot be exploited by a single product/application, as it is outside its scope of control.

Obviously, there are two sources of optimization that can be exploited if multiple queries are considered: re-use of previously calculated (and cached) intermediate results and elimination of redundant work. This calls for a new type of *inter-application* multi-query optimizer that is able to detect and exploit such optimization opportunities in a stream of individually optimized queries that originate from various applications.

The issue itself, *multi-query optimization* (MQO), has received limited attention in the database research community. As query optimization was shown to be NP-complete [IK84, SM97] it is not surprising that the problem of MQO is also NP-complete [SG90]. MQO can therefor only be achieved using heuristics [Jar85] or probabilistic techniques.

Early works [Fin82, Sel88] show that ad hoc queries can benefit from using materialized results generated by earlier queries, even if only equivalent expressions are considered. The savings can be considerable when compared to single query processing. Shim et al. [SSN94] propose improved heuristics to search for the global optimum in the state space that models all alternatives for evaluating a batch of queries. Chakravarthy and Minker [CM86] use a multi-query graph for representing multiple SPJ queries. Again, heuristics are used to identify common subexpressions and transform the graph into an evaluation strategy without applying a search algorithm. Chen and Dunham [CD98] improve these heuristics by, o.a., considering partial overlapping selection predicates.

All previous work on MQO considered a single application which allows for a unified query abstraction level to perform common subexpression elimination. However, a multi-query optimizer at the inter-application level, as we study in this paper, cannot take advantage of these techniques.

In [RC88, AR92], frameworks for analyzing the MQO problem are proposed. One of the issues addressed is that each type of (multi) query optimization should be done at the appropriate level of abstraction — e.g., one level for determining the appropriate join order and one to determine the join implementation. Furthermore, they point out that a multi-query optimizer should at least perform as well as a single query optimizer. Illustrative for this approach is the paper [KDB94], where the MQO is done at the algorithm-level to exploit the re-use of (temporary) hash tables.

In this paper we introduce a novel architecture to bring inter-application query-optimizer back into the mainstream of research. The prime innovation is to organize the query optimization problem into three tiers: *Strategic optimization, Tactical optimization* and *Operational optimization*. At each tier, different sources of optimization are exploited. The strategic tier uses the application (-model) knowledge, such as foreign-key dependencies, semantic integrity constraints, and user-application focus to derive a query execution plan.

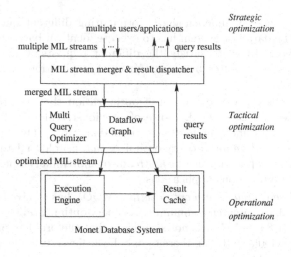

Figure 1. System Architecture

The tactical optimizer is geared at balancing the resources amongst competing queries. This involves both recognition of commonalities amongst (inter- and intra-application) requests and methods to exploit potential parallelism and replication at the database back-ends.

The operational optimizer decides at run time which is the most suitable algorithm for performing low-level database operation, e.g., it chooses between a hash join or a nested loops join. Also the re-use of dynamically created hash tables is done at this level.

In this paper, we present a multi-query optimizer for the middle tier (tactical optimization) that is focused on but not limited to query workloads generated by a specific, commercial data mining application. The optimizer keeps a history of calculated intermediate results to re-use them in subsequent queries and it detects common subexpressions of multiple queries to avoid redundant work.

Section 2 provides a short overview of the system and our focal data mining product. Section 3 illustrates by an extensive example the opportunities for inter- and intra-application in a data mining context. Section 4 reports on the results obtained using the DD Benchmark, a metric for judging the capabilities of a DBMS for interactive data mining. We conclude with a short outlook on the extensions planned for the tactical optimizer.

2   System Architecture

Our system architecture in depicted in Figure 1. The Monet database engine [BK95] is used as back-end server for multiple applications. The applications use the Monet Interpreter Language (MIL) [BK99], an algebraic query language,

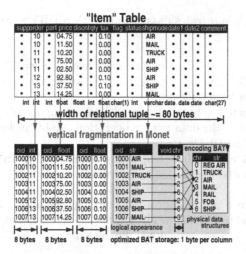

Figure 2. Vertically Decomposed Storage in BATs

to communicate with the back-end engine. Each application first optimizes its query individually on a logical level, e.g., algebraic operators are re-ordered to minimize the data volume to be handled. Then, the application translates each query into a sequence of MIL statements.

Our multi-query optimizer is placed between the applications and Monet. It takes the unified stream of MIL statements from the applications as input and produces an optimized stream of MIL statements to be sent to Monet for execution. We will describe the multi-query optimizer in detail in Section 3.

2.1 Monet

Monet is a main-memory database kernel developed at CWI. It is targeted at achieving high performance on query-intensive workloads, such as created by OLAP or data mining applications. Monet uses the Decomposed Storage Model (DSM) [CK85], storing each column of a relational table in a separate binary table, called a Binary Association Table (BAT). A BAT is represented in memory as an array of fixed-size two-field records [OID,value], or Binary UNits (BUN). The OIDs in the left column are unique per original relational tuple, i.e., they link all BUNs that make up a original relational tuple (cf. Figure 2). The major advantage of the DSM is that it minimizes I/O and memory access costs for column-wise data access which occurs frequently in OLAP and data mining workloads [BRK98, BMK99].

2.2 Data Surveyor

Most existing data mining tools employ specialized data structures and algorithms to manipulate mass data outside the DBMS. Data Surveyor of Data

Distilleries, however, integrates data mining with a DBMS using a 3-tier architecture:

GUIs taking the form of Java applets. Apart from a powerful expert data mining interface, Data Surveyor provides pre-cooked user interfaces tailored to special end-user requirements.

Data Mining Kernel containing tens of data-mining specific algorithms. This component directs the data mining operations and translates a data mining task into multiple DBMS queries.

DBMS back-end can be all SQL-speaking commercial (parallel) DBMSs. Further, Monet can be used as high-performance back-end.

To facilitate the translation of a data mining task into DBMS queries, the Data Mining Kernel uses a unique algorithmic framework that decomposes data mining algorithms in three orthogonal dimensions:

- a *modeling language* for expressing hypotheses,
- a *quality function* for testing the quality of a hypotheses, and
- a *search strategy* for looking for interesting hypotheses.

2.3 DD Benchmark

The Drill Down Benchmark (short: DD Benchmark) is designed to measure DBMS performance on a typical data mining query load. The benchmark is formulated as a typical data mining task, which in turn is translated into DBMS queries. The mining task mimics a customer loyalty application, a common and prototypical data mining problem. In this task, a company wants to find profiles for (un)reliable groups of customers.

The DD Benchmark uses decision rules as the modeling language to describe such customers, where the rules are simple conjunctions of selections on the attributes of the mining table. The quality of such rules is expressed as a confidence interval and a beam-search algorithm is used to find interesting hypotheses.

The mining table contains 1 million customer records, consisting of 100 attributes. Six attributes play a role in the mining task. A detailed description of the DD Benchmark is available in [BRK98].

3   Multi-Query Optimizer

In this Section, we present an overview of the multi-query optimization facilities embodied by our prototype optimizer.

3.1   Concept

Our optimizer mainly focuses on the following optimization potentials:

elimination of common (sub-)expressions Especially in a data mining scenario, it is very likely that several queries to the same database will shared at least some subexpressions. Evaluating identical subexpressions several times (once per query) is of course redundant work. Hence, our optimizer identifies such common subexpressions, schedules each subexpression only once for evaluation and ensures that all queries can use the respective intermediate result without any additional costs once it has been generated.

re-use of cached intermediate results Common subexpression may not only occur among queries that are optimized at the same time. Rather, a query might also require an intermediate result that has already once been calculated for an earlier query. Hence, we keep intermediate results materialized in main memory for later re-use.

parallelization Monet and MIL offer the possibility of parallel query execution. On a shared-memory multi-processor machine, for instance, a multi-threaded Monet engine can evaluate multiple independent MIL statements concurrently. Our optimizer takes care of that by identifying independent statements and scheduling them for concurrent execution.

3.2 Example

As a simple example, consider a relation "customer" with four attributes ("gender", "age", "marital", "reliable") and the following four SQL queries taken from the DD Benchmark. Besides selections, the queries contain groupings and aggregations, the most frequent tasks in data mining.

> **Q1:** SELECT age, reliable, count(*)
> FROM customer
> WHERE gender = 'f'
> GROUP BY age, reliable;
>
> **Q2:** SELECT marital, reliable, count(*)
> FROM customer
> WHERE gender = 'f'
> GROUP BY marital, reliable;
>
> **Q3:** SELECT age, reliable, count(*)
> FROM customer
> WHERE gender = 'm'
> GROUP BY age, reliable;
>
> **Q4:** SELECT marital, reliable, count(*)
> FROM customer
> WHERE gender = 'm'
> GROUP BY marital, reliable;

In Monet, the relation is stored in five BATs: "C_gender", "C_age", "C_marital", and "C_reliable". The SQL queries translate to the following four MIL programs. The "Vij" are variables that store the materialized intermediate results.

P1: V11 := CTgroup(C_age);
      V12 := select(C_gender,'f');
      V13 := semijoin(C_reliable,V12);
      V14 := CTgroup(V11,V13);
      V15 := histogram(V14);
      print(C_age,C_reliable,V15);

P2: V21 := CTgroup(C_marital);
      V22 := select(C_gender,'f');
      V23 := semijoin(C_reliable,V22);
      V24 := CTgroup(V21,V23);
      V25 := histogram(V24);
      print(C_marital,C_reliable,V25);

P3: V31 := CTgroup(C_age);
      V32 := select(C_gender,'m');
      V33 := semijoin(C_reliable,V32);
      V34 := CTgroup(V31,V33);
      V35 := histogram(V34);
      print(C_age,C_reliable,V35);

P4: V41 := CTgroup(C_marital);
      V42 := select(C_gender,'m');
      V43 := semijoin(C_reliable,V42);
      V44 := CTgroup(V41,V43);
      V45 := histogram(V44);
      print(C_marital,C_reliable,V45);

In MIL, groupings are materialized in a *cross-table* BAT that holds in the head column identifiers of all objects of interest, and in the tail a unique group identifier. The "CTgroup" operators construct such cross-tables. The unary "CTgroup" is executed on an [OID,value] BAT. It returns an [OID,OID] BAT with the same head column as the input and a group-id in the tail column for each BUN. Each group-id is chosen from the collection of OIDs from the head of its group members. The binary "CTgroup" refines a cross-table by subdividing the groups according to an additional [OID,value] BAT.

The "histogram" operation creates a histogram of the tail values of a BAT. It returns a BAT with each distinct tail value of the input in its head column and the number of occurances of that value in its tail column. Applied on a cross-table, the histogram calculates the group sizes.

The "print" operation finally performs a multi-BAT equi-join on the head columns, printing a multi-column table consisting of the respective tail columns. In our example, "print" creates the required query result, a table that consists of the grouping attributes and the group sizes.

The operations "CTgroup(C_age)", "CTgroup(C_marital)", "select(C_gender,'f')", and "select(C_gender,'m')" occur twice creating pairwise identical results V11≡V31, V21≡V41, V12≡V22, and V32≡V42. Hence, "semijoin(C_reliable,V12)" and "semijoin(C_reliable,V22)" are identical as well as "semijoin(C_reliable,V32)" and "semijoin(C_reliable,V42)". The multi-query optimizer has to detect these commonalities and avoid redundant work.

3.3   Implementation

The optimizer takes a stream of MIL statements as input. This stream is the merged output of several applications (or multiple mining threads) and contains a set of queries, each optimized in isolation. The optimizer stores the queries in a dependency graph. Each distinct MIL statement makes up a node of the graph. The nodes are connected by directed edges representing the data dependencies between the nodes (i.e., the MIL statements). Hence, the dependency graph forms a directed acyclic graph (DAG).

Elimination of Common Subexpressions At database startup time, the dependency graph consists of a set of non-connected nodes. Each of these nodes represents a persistent BAT stored in the database. When receiving input, the optimizer adds a new node for each distinct MIL statement. The node then represents the intermediate result created by that very MIL statement. Additionally, the optimizer adds edges to the dependency graph, representing the dependency of an intermediate results on the parameters (i.e., persistent BATs and previous intermediate results) of the respective MIL statement. To eliminate common subexpressions, the optimizer identifies identical MIL statements by their signature (i.e., operator name and parameters) and maps them to the same node in the dependency graph. Hence, each distinct intermediate result occurs only once in the dependency graph.

Figure 3 shows the dependency graph for our simple example. The equivalent operations are identified and mapped to a single node.

Parallelization When the execution engine becomes idle, the optimizer scans the dependency graph for independent statements to be executed next. Independent statements are nodes that depend only on persistent BATs or on intermediate results already calculated. In other words, independent statements are ready to be evaluated immediately. For each independent node, the optimizer checks whether there is a linear path starting at the independent node, whose nodes successively become independent as soon as their very predecessor in the path is executed. If such a path exists, all nodes of that path (including the original independent node) are gathered into a single task. Otherwise, the task consists only of the original node. All statements within a task are evaluated sequentially according to their dependencies. Gathering linear paths into sequential tasks ensures that intermediate results are used as soon as possible and preferably by the same thread/CPU that created them. Parallelism is exploited by sending several/all independent tasks to the execution engine to be evaluated concurrently, each by a separate thread.

The grey-shadings in Figure 3 depict sequential tasks and parallel blocks. The optimized MIL program is given in Figure 4. Operations within a sequential task

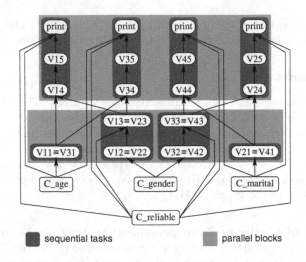

Figure 3. Sample Dependency Graph

("{...}") are are executed one after another. All operations or tasks within a parallel block ("{|...|}") are executed concurrently.

Re-use of Cached Intermediate Results The execution engine keeps all intermediate results materialized in main memory. Hence, they are instantly available for later re-use.[1]

By annotating the nodes in the dependency graph appropriately, the optimizer keeps track of which intermediate results are already available and which statements still need to be executed. Thus, the optimizer can easily detect, when a new statement requests an intermediate result that has already been calculated earlier.

4   Experiments

To analyze the benefits of multi-query optimization in a data mining scenario, we run experiments using the DD Benchmark [BRK98]. The DD Benchmark creates a typical Data Mining workload. It consists of 5 batches of queries, 133 queries altogether. All queries perform selections, groupings, and aggregations on a subset of the attributes of a single relational table. The query batches mimic the behavior of a beam-search algorithm to generate decision trees.

To run the DD Benchmark against the Monet database, we use the MIL programs as generated by Data Distilleries' mining tool Data Surveyor. In this form, the whole DD Benchmark consists of some 1200 MIL statements altogether.

---

[1] Currently, we implicitly assume an unlimited memory capacity. Cache management facilities are to be added in the near future (cf. Section 5).

```
{|
    {
        V11 := CTgroup(C_age);
    }{
        V12 := select(C_gender,'f');
        V13 := semijoin(C_reliable,V12);
    }{
        V32 := select(C_gender,'m');
        V33 := semijoin(C_reliable,V32);
    }{
        V21 := CTgroup(C_marital);
    }
|}{|
    {
        V14 := CTgroup(V11,V13);
        V15 := histogram(V14);
        print(C_age,C_reliable,V15);
    }{
        V34 := CTgroup(V11,V33);
        V35 := histogram(V34);
        print(C_age,C_reliable,V35);
    }{
        V24 := CTgroup(V21,V13);
        V25 := histogram(V24);
        print(C_marital,C_reliable,V25);
    }{
        V44 := CTgroup(V21,V33);
        V45 := histogram(V44);
        print(C_marital,C_reliable,V45);
    }
|}
```

Figure 4. Optimized MIL Program

Table 1 compares the performance of executing the non-optimized and the optimized MIL program running a single-threaded Monet server on an Intel PentiumII 400 MHz based PC with 512 MB main memory.

The results show, that our optimizer is able to detect overlap among the queries and eliminate common subexpressions (i.e., redundant work) efficiently. The total optimization overhead is approximately 400 milliseconds, i.e., negligible. The improvements increase with each additional batch of queries, as the execution can then benefit from re-using previously calculated intermediate results. In batch 4, the number of instructions that is actually executed is reduced by factor 5.1, the elapsed time it even reduced by factor 17.3. The overall improvement for the whole benchmark is factor 3.7.

Table 1. Experimental Results: sequential Monet Server on PC

batch	non-optimized		optimized		improvement (factor)	
	# stat's	time [ms]	# stat's	time [ms]	# stat's	time
0	14	1,940	14	1,940	1.0	1.0
1	18	4,864	12	3,339	1.5	1.5
2	345	43,350	135	17,444	2.6	2.5
3	444	38,621	114	7,059	3.9	5.5
4	447	27,802	87	1,608	5.1	17.3
0-4	1,268	116,578	362	31,898	3.5	3.7

Table 2. Experimental Results: sequential Monet Server on Origin2000

batch	non-optimized		optimized		improvement (factor)	
	# stat's	time [ms]	# stat's	time [ms]	# stat's	time
0	14	1,664	14	1,664	1.0	1.0
1	18	3,926	12	2,615	1.5	1.5
2	345	39,811	135	15,574	2.6	2.6
3	444	36,429	114	6,382	3.9	5.7
4	447	26,889	87	1,422	5.1	18.9
0-4	1,268	108,720	362	27,795	3.5	3.9

We ran the same experiments on an SGI Origin2000 with 24 MIPS R12000 CPUs (300 MHz) and 48 GB of main memory. Table 2 shows the results using a single-threaded Monet server. The improvements are similar to those on the PC.

Table 3 depicts the results using a multi-threaded Monet server, i.e., using parallel execution. In the non-optimized version, each query forms a sequential task. All queries within one batch are independent and can be evaluated concurrently. With increasing degree of parallelism, the improvement of the optimized version over the non-optimized version slightly decreases. The reason being that most improvement is gained from the fact that several statements can re-use an intermediate result that is created only once. The Origin2000 is a ccNUMA machine with distributed shared memory. Thus, memory access costs differ significantly between local and remote memory access. With higher parallelism, it becomes more likely, that a thread re-uses a result that has been created by another thread, and is hence stored on another (remote) CPU board. But even with 9 threads, the improvement is still factor 2.5.

Finally, Figures 5 and 6 show the speedup curves for the non-optimized and the optimized version, respectively. Both figures show 6 speedup curves, 5 of them representing the individual performance of each batch and the last one representing the overall performance.

In both cases, batch 0 and batch 1 show rather limited speedup. This is due to the fact that the two batches contain only 7, respectively 6, queries. The other batches consist of more that 30 queries each, i.e., there is sufficient

Table 3. Experimental Results: parallel Monet Server on Origin2000

threads	non-optimized time [ms]	optimized time [ms]	improvement (factor)
1	108,720	27,795	3.9
2	54,944	15,598	3.5
3	39,089	12,221	3.2
4	30,288	9,451	3.2
5	25,874	8,893	2.9
6	21,934	7,549	2.9
7	19,793	7,670	2.6
8	18,587	7,072	2.6
9	18,808	7,436	2.5

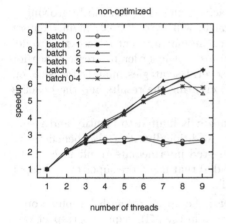

Figure 5. Speedup: non-optimized   **Figure 6.** Speedup: optimized

potential for parallelism. Doing redundant work on local data in parallel, the non-optimized version achieves near-linear speedup for the remaining batches and for the overall performance. The optimized version, however, avoids redundant work. Hence, several threads might re-use the same intermediate result, causing remote memory access (see above). Although there is sufficient potential for parallelism, the extra costs for remote memory access limit the achievable speedup on a ccNUMA machine.

5   Conclusion and future research

In this paper, we showed that data mining applications provide some inter-query optimization potentials that traditional query optimizers cannot exploit. We proposed and implemented an application-independent inter-application multi-query optimizer. The optimizer avoids redundant work by eliminating common subexpressions and re-using cached intermediate results. Performance experiments with the Drill Down Benchmark showed, that the optimizer yields significant improvements of up to factor 4, while causing hardly any optimization overhead.

The architecture provides an outlook on the novel three-tier optimization scheme under development for the Monet DBMS. The underlying hypothesis is that by breaking the optimizer into distinct tiers, we can both simplify the optimization process at each level and further benefit from the inter- and intra-application dependencies. This approach has already been shown beneficial at the operational level in [BK95, BK99] and at the tactical level in this paper.

The research agenda for the tactical optimizer includes the following near-term extensions:

cache management Main memory capacity—although constantly growing—is not unlimited. Hence, the result cache will exceed (real) main memory capacity, eventually. To prevent this, cache management is necessary to decide when and which (old) results to discard in order to create space for new results. We plan to investigate several strategies, mainly focusing on taking into account the costs for (re-) creating the results and the benefits of keeping certain results.

re-using supersets Currently, the optimizer is limited to identify and re-use equivalent intermediate results, only. Additionally, it is also beneficial to re-use the smallest superset of a requested intermediate result in case the equivalent result is not available, provided that using the superset is cheaper that using the original persistent BAT.

pattern rewriting Finally, we will extend the optimizer with 'peephole optimization rules' to detect certain patterns in the MIL sequence, respectively in the dependency graph, in order to replace them with less expensive ones. This approach releases the applications from taking care of any tactical optimization. Instead, applications only need to generate straightforward MIL code. The tactical optimizer then takes care of optimizing the code before actually executing it. In particular, when the Monet engine is extended by a new operator that implements a sequence of operators more efficiently, it will enable arbitrary applications to use the new implementation, without changing the applications; the application even doesn't have to know about the existence of the new operator.

In general, many of the decisions that have to be taken by these extensions at run time cannot be formulated as static rules or heuristics. Hence, we will provide the optimizer with the required cost information to support its decisions.

Acknowledgements. We would like to thank Florian Waas for his contributions to a prototype of the multi-query optimizer.

References

[AR92]   J. R. Alsabbagh and V. V. Raghavan. A Framework for Multiple-Query Optimization. In *Proc. Research Issues on Data Eng.: Transaction and Query Processing*, Tempe, AZ, USA, February 1992.

[BK95]   P. Boncz and M. Kersten. Monet: An Impressionist Sketch of an Advanced Database System. In *Proc. Basque International Workshop on Information Technology*, San Sebastian, Spain, July 1995.

[BK99]   P. Boncz and M. Kersten. MIL Primitives For Querying a Fragmented World. *The VLDB Journal*, 8(2), October 1999.

[BMK99]   P. Boncz, S. Manegold, and M. Kersten. Database Architecture Optimized for the New Bottleneck: Memory Access. In *Proc. of the Int'l. Conf. on Very Large Data Bases*, pages 54–65, Edinburgh, Scotland, UK, September 1999.

[BRK98]   P. Boncz, T. Rühl, and F. Kwakkel. The Drill Down Benchmark. In *Proc. of the Int'l. Conf. on Very Large Data Bases*, pages 628–632, New York, NY, USA, June 1998.

[CD98]   F.-C. F. Chen and M. H. Dunham. Common Subexpression Processing in Multiple Query Processing. *IEEE Trans. on Knowledge and Data Eng.*, 10(3):493–499, May/June 1998.

[CK85]   G. P. Copeland and S. Khoshafian. A Decomposition Storage Model. In *Proc. of the ACM SIGMOD Int'l. Conf. on Management of Data*, pages 268–279, Austin, TX, USA, May 1985.

[CM86]   U. S. Chakravarthy and J. Minker. Multiple Query Processing in Deductive Databases using Query Graphs. In *Proc. of the Int'l. Conf. on Very Large Data Bases*, pages 384–390, Kyoto, Japan, August 1986.

[Fin82]   S. J. Finkelstein. Common Expression Analysis in Database Applications. In *Proc. of the ACM SIGMOD Int'l. Conf. on Management of Data*, pages 235–245, Orlando, FL, USA, June 1982.

[GLPK94]   C. A. Galindo-Legaria, A. Pellenkoft, and M. Kersten. Fast, Randomized Join-Order Selection – Why Use Transformations? In *Proc. of the Int'l. Conf. on Very Large Data Bases*, pages 85–95, Santiago, Chile, September 1994.

[IK84]   T. Ibaraki and T. Kameda. Optimal Nesting for Computation N-Relational Joins. *ACM Trans. on Database Systems*, 9(3), September 1984.

[IK90]   Y. E. Ioannidis and Y. C. Kang. Randomized Algorithms for Optimizing Large Join Queries. In *Proc. of the ACM SIGMOD Int'l. Conf. on Management of Data*, pages 312–321, Atlantic City, NJ, USA, May 1990.

[Jar85]   M. Jarke. Common Subexpression Isolation in Multiple Query Optimization. In W. Kim, D. S. Reiner, and D. S. Batory, editors, *Query Processing in Database Systems*, pages 191–205. Springer-Verlag, 1985.

[KDB94]   M. H. Kang, H. G. Dietz, and B. Bhargava. Multiple-query optimization at algorithm-level. *Data and Knowledge Engineering*, 14(1), November 1994.

[RC88]   A. Rosenthal and S. Chakravarthy. Anatomy of a Modular Multiple Query Optimizer. *Proc. of the Int'l. Conf. on Very Large Data Bases*, pages 230–239, 1988.

[SAC+79]   P. G. Selinger, M. M. Astrahan, D. D. Chamberlin, R. A. Lorie, and T. G. Price. Access Path Selection in a Relational Database Management System. In *Proc. of the ACM SIGMOD Int'l. Conf. on Management of Data*, pages 23–34, Boston, MA, USA, May 1979.

[Sel88]   T. K. Sellis. Multiple-Query Optimization. *ACM Trans. on Database Systems*, 13(1), March 1988.
[SG90]   T. Sellis and S. Ghosh. On the Multiple-Query Optimization Problem. *IEEE Trans. on Knowledge and Data Eng.*, 2(2):262–266, Jun 1990.
[SM97]   W. Scheufele and G. Moerkotte. On the Complexity of Generating Optimal Plans with Cross Products. In *Proc. of the ACM SIGACT-SIGMOD-SIGART Symposium on Principles of Database Systems*, pages 238–248, Tucson, AZ, USA, May 1997.
[SSN94]   K. Shim, T. Sellis, and D. Nau. Improvements on a Heuristic Algorithm for Multiple-Query Optimization. *Data and Knowledge Engineering*, 12(2):197–222, March 1994.
[VM96]   B. Vance and D. Maier. Rapid Bushy Join-order Optimization with Cartesian Products. In *Proc. of the ACM SIGMOD Int'l. Conf. on Management of Data*, pages 35–46, Montreal, Canada, June 1996.

Join Order Selection (Good Enough Is Easy)

Florian Waas* and Arjan Pellenkoft

CWI, P.O.Box 94079, 1090 GB Amsterdam, The Netherlands
{Florian.Waas,Arjan.Pellenkoft}@cwi.nl

Abstract. Uniform sampling of join orders is known to be a competitive alternative to transformation-based optimization techniques. However, uniformity of the sampling process is difficult to establish and only for a restricted class of join queries techniques are known.

In this paper, we investigate non-uniform sampling devising a simple yet powerful algorithm that is generally applicable. The key element of the algorithm is a mapping of randomly generated sequences of join predicates to query plans. We take advantage of the bottom-up constructing of query plans by simultaneously computing the costs and discarding partial plans as soon as they exceed the best costs found so far, which implements a highly effective cost-bound pruning component.

Sampling does not produce *the* optimal plan but a near-optimal solution which is fully sufficient as the cost function grows more and more inaccurate with increasing query size. In return, our algorithm establishes a well-balanced trade-off between result quality and time invested in the optimization process.

1 Introduction

Join-ordering is one of the most persistent problems in query optimization. Over the last decade, special attention has been devoted to probabilistic techniques that proofed superior to heuristics [SMK97]. Galindo-Legaria *et al.* made out a good case for using uniform random sampling of plans rather than transformation-based algorithms like Simulated Annealing [GLPK94]. They showed that sampling matches randomized algorithms in quality but outruns them in terms of convergence, i.e. finds high quality solutions earlier. The nucleus of this work is the one-to-one mapping between plans and ordinal numbers. Generating random numbers and un-ranking the associated query plan then establishes a mechanism to sample plans with uniform probability. However, the algorithm devised is a complex construction and the deployment is limited to acyclic graphs only [GLPK95]. This limitation—though popular with previous work—is a distinct restriction. Queries as for instance in the standard data warehouse benchmark suite of TPC-H/R contains indeed cyclic queries [Tra98]. But this algorithm does show the way how to exploit the characteristic features of the search space successfully.

---

* Current address: Universitá di Bologna, 40136 Bologna, Italy

B. Lings and K. Jeffery (Eds.): BNCOD 17, LNCS 1832, pp. 51–67, 2000.
© Springer-Verlag Berlin Heidelberg 2000

In this paper, we investigate how to overcome this restriction without loss of performance. And more general, we address the question whether uniformity of the sampling is a necessary prerequisite.

QUICKPICK, the algorithm we develop in this paper, performs biased sampling by selecting edges from the join graph and adding the respective joins to the query plan. To cut down on the running time we add a cost-bound pruning strategy: We simultaneously compute the costs while building up the plan and partial plans that exceed the costs of the currently best plan are discarded as early as possible. The algorithm is distinguished by its high result quality and short running times. Additionally, QUICKPICK is of low complexity both in time complexity and implementation, and is applicable to any query graph overcoming the restriction for uniform sampling.

To analyze the algorithm and explain its superior performance, we scrutinize cost distributions, i.e. the frequencies of cost values in the entire search space. Reviewing previous work and complementing it with own experiments, we abstract cost distributions making them accessible to formal reasoning. This way we can derive accurate approximations of the quality of the results of sampling. Our investigations indicate that uniform sampling provides upper bounds for our new algorithm.

Road-Map. In Section 2, we briefly outline the model for the problem and discuss cost distributions and quality measures. In Section 3, we introduce the sampling algorithm and give a quantitative assessment of it in Section 4. We review related work in Section 5. Section 6 contains our conclusions and outlook to further research.

2   Preliminaries

Since the join-ordering problem has been discussed in detail in previous work we give only a short outline of the basic setting here. More detailed descriptions can be found e.g. in [SAC+79,SG88,IK91,SM97,SMK97].

A join query is given by a *join* or *query graph* whose nodes correspond to the base tables used in the query. Its edges are annotated with the predicates of the query, and denote which tables are to be joined. A *query plan* is a binary tree where each inner node corresponds to a predicate of the query; the leaves correspond to the base relations. Each such query plan is of certain *costs*, computed according to a *cost function* or *model*. Both components together make up the join ordering problem of finding the query plan with the least costs.

Since cost models have to reflect the query engine which will execute the plan, cost models differ in general from one system to another, yet there are properties all cost models have in common as we will point out later.

2.1   Cost Distributions

The term *cost distribution* refers to the frequencies of all possible cost values occurring in the entire search space. They reflect the ratio of high to low quality solutions. Cost distributions are closely interconnected with the object function. As a consequence, cost distributions are characteristic for a given combinatorial optimization problem, i.e. all instances of a problem display cost distributions with similar properties. The degree of variation is problem specific but limited in its extent; apart from pathological cases. For example, the Symmetric Traveling Salesman Problem is characterized by normal distributions with heavy tails [Waa99]. The cost distributions in query optimization differ substantially from that due to the different nature of the cost function. They display a strong asymmetry with a distinct concentration of cost values close to the optimum.

The first to notice this problem intrinsic property was Swami who reported that, surprisingly, lesser sophisticated optimization strategies like Iterative Improvement are often superior to more complex methods like Simulated Annealing. Swami not only discovered the skew of the cost distribution but also noted its stability across different cost functions: He observed that in experiments with different cost models, an I/O-based one and a Main-memory cost model, performance of optimization algorithms were comparable, suspecting underlying structures common to different cost models [SG88,Swa89].

Ioannidis and Kang for the first time investigated the shape of the cost distribution explicitly finding curves that are best described as Gamma distributions [IK91]. However, they experimented only with one single I/O-based model and therefore attributed their findings to the specific cost model used.

In [WGL00], authors present a sampling mechanism implemented in a commercial database system and extract cost distributions for TPC-H queries using an industrial quality cost function. Furthermore full-blown query optimization and not only join ordering as in previous work was concerned. These finding bear strong resemblance with Ioannidis and Kang's results lending strong support to the abstraction with Gamma distributions.

In contrast to experiments with cost models of increasing complexity we want to complement these observations with experiments using a rudimentary cost function that handles joins only like cartesian products. Such a simplified model is of particular interest for two reasons: Firstly, joins may degenerate to cartesian products, thus the evaluation of cartesian products forms an upper bound of $O(n^2)$ for any join. Secondly, the problem of optimizing the order of cartesian products—though appearing less difficult on first sight—is of the same complexity as join ordering as Scheufele and Moerkotte showed [SM97].

In the cartesian model, costs of each operator compute recursively to

$$c(v) = c(v_l) \cdot c(v_r)$$

where v denotes an operator, i.e., inner node in the query plan, and v_l and v_r its left and right children respectively. If v is leaf, $c(v)$ is the size of the associated base table. The total cost of the plan is the sum of costs per operator.

To extract cost distributions for the cartesian model, we enumerate all non-isomorphic trees of given size, i.e. trees that are not isomorphic under commutative exchange of subtrees. For each tree we generate 1000 configurations of

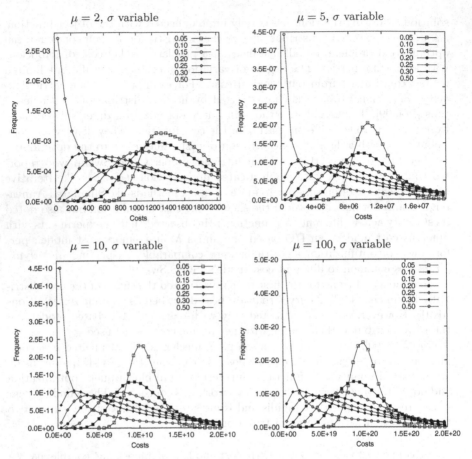

Fig. 1. Cost distributions for cartesian model for $\mu = 2, 5, 10, 100$ and σ as fraction of μ.

base table sizes according to a given distribution and compute the costs. The parameters of the experiment are size of the problem, i.e. number of base tables which translates to the number of leaves in the processing tree, and mean and deviation of the distribution of base tables. Figure 1 shows the resulting cost distributions for trees of size 10. The deviation is given as a fraction of the mean. In this experiment, we used normal distributions for the base tables but experiments with other distributions showed similar results [WP98]. We observe only little skew for a small deviation (0.05) and increasing skew for larger deviation (0.50). The whole range of shapes observed can be abstracted with Gamma distribution of shape parameter ν between 1 and 2 as suggested by Ioannidis and Kang. Moreover, this experiment also confirms the connection between the skew of the cost distribution and the deviation. The higher the deviation—i.e., the variance of the database catalog—the stronger the skew.

The above experiment pinpoints the cause of the skew that has been observed with richer cost models. The tree structure of the plans with its multiplicative costing is responsible for the shape of the cost distributions. When moving from the cartesian model to join ordering the cost distributions become less smooth as not all non-isomorphic trees are valid tree-shapes. Moreover the additional selectivities of the join predicates add further distortions. However, as the sum of experiments—previous work and own ones presented in this paper—suggests further additions to the cost model, including extensions to cover a large variety of operator implementation like different join implementations but also other kinds of operators than joins or cartesian products, do not alter the major characteristic of the cost distributions. Thus, the abstraction proposed by Ioannidis and Kang appears more general than authors first thought.

Before we discuss how to exploit the distributions for optimization purposes, we present some considerations on how to measure the quality of the optimization results.

2.2 Quality Measures

The cost computation in a database system uses statistical data about the state of the database to estimate the execution costs. As natural consequence, the estimates contain errors. While rather precise for small queries, the accuracy of the cost estimation deteriorates with increasing size of the query as estimate errors propagate exponentially through the query plan [IC91]. Plans whose costs differ only by a few percent cannot be distinguished any more reliably; near-optimal results are as good as the optimum itself.

To reach a trade-off between time spent on the optimization and the result quality, Swami proposed a classification according to which query plans can be divided into three groups: *good*, *acceptable* and *bad* plans. Plans are considered *good* if they have costs below twice the minimal costs c_{min}, *acceptable* if they are no more expensive than 10 times c_{min}, and *bad* otherwise. In the following we refer to this classification as *scaling-based classification*.

Note, quality measures of this kind are only of theoretic value in general. When optimizing queries in ad-hoc manner, neither the costs of the optimum nor an approximation is usually available. The same holds for the measure we present below.

Scaling-based classification suffers from the severe drawback to be not invariant under additive translation as the following example shows. Consider a cost distribution of the quality of an exponential distribution

$$\phi_t(x) = \begin{cases} e^{-x+t}, & \text{if } x \ge t \\ 0, & \text{else} \end{cases}$$

t is the additive shift of the distribution. Figure 2 shows ϕ_1 and ϕ_3. The optima are of costs 1 and 3 respectively. We should expect both distributions to have the same ratio of good, acceptable and bad plans as the distribution are of exactly the same shape, only shifted by 2. For ϕ_1 the ratio of good plans computes to

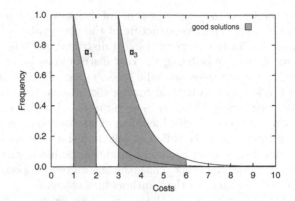

Fig. 2. Classification according to Swami

0.63 (interval $[1,2]$ in Fig. 2). However, for ϕ_3 the ratio of good plans is 0.95 (interval $[3,6]$). Though the distribution actually stayed the same, the ratio of good plans is up 50% at 0.95. The cause for the instability is that only a single reference point, namely c_{min}, is taken into account.

To overcome this drawback, we classify plans with respect to the cost distribution. We denote the quality of a plan by the *relative quantile* Q_x of the cost distribution its costs are in. We say a plan q is of quality Q_x if the following holds for its costs

$$\frac{c(q) - c_{min}}{c_\mu - c_{min}} \le x.$$

Figure 3 shows the exponential distribution of the example above (cf. Fig. 2). For example, Q_1 denotes the quantile from c_{min} up to c_μ. The quantiles Q_1 and $Q_{0.1}$ are highlighted. As the figure shows, quantile-based classification is independent of any translation.

In the following we will use $Q_{0.1}$ as target quantile for the optimization, i.e., we try to find a plan whose costs are in $Q_{0.1}$. Larger quantiles may be justified for larger join queries though.

3   Probabilistic Bottom-Up Join Order Selection

In order to implement an unrestricted sampling mechanism we use a mapping of join predicates to query plans. It might be helpful to outline the idea behind this mapping first: given a sequence of join predicates, we add the corresponding join operators of the query plan one after another. If the predicate involves a base table that is not yet leaf of the query plan, we add a join operator whose children are the new base table and the partial plan that contains the other table. If both tables are already part of the tree, we add only the predicate to

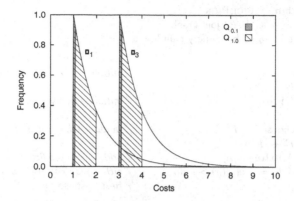

Fig. 3. Quantile-based classification

the deepest possible join. To generate now query plans at random we simply generate random sequences of predicates.

In Figure 4, the algorithm, called QUICKPICK, is outlined in pseudo code. After initializing the variable r that records the cheapest plan found so far with ∞, the candidate set E' is initialized with the set of edges of the join graph, and q with the base relations. Throughout the random bottom-up construction of a tree q holds all partial trees, i.e. q is actually a forest. Generally, only at the very end—earlier only for cyclic join graphs—, q is completed to a single processing tree.

Until the stopping criterion, say a time limit, is fulfilled q is incrementally built-up by choosing and removing an edge e from the candidate set and adding the corresponding join to the tree (ADDJOIN). In doing so, the subtrees that contain the two endpoints of e, i.e. the base relations joined by this edges, are connected with a join operator. If both relations are already leaves to the same sub-plan, only the predicate of e is added to the tree at the deepest possible point. After each such insertion, the costs of the subtrees are computed and summed up. Recall, that q is generally a forest consisting of several disjoint processing trees. If the costs exceed r, the costs of the best plan found so far, we discard q and initialize E' and q again and start assembling a new tree. If the set of candidate edges is empty—i.e. we have completed the processing tree—we check for a new record and in this case copy the plan to q_{best}. After initializing E' and q we start building a new tree.[1]

---

[1] The basic principles of QUICKPICK—without cost-bound pruning—have been described already by Pellenkoft [Pel97]. There, this algorithm is called Random Edge Selection and proofed to be incapable of achieving uniform sampling. However, no further performance analysis is conducted. Others might have probably used similar algorithms to generate initial solutions. However, they also did not evaluate the potential of this elementary technique.

Algorithm   QUICKPICK
Input $G(V, E)$ join graph
Output q_{best} best query plan found

$r \leftarrow \infty$ // initialize lowest costs so far
$E' \leftarrow E$
$q \leftarrow G'(V, \emptyset)$ // initialize query plan
repeat .
    choose $e \in E'$ // random edge selection
    $E' \leftarrow E' \setminus \{e\}$
    ADDJOIN(q, e) // add join or predicate
    if $E' = \emptyset$ **or** $c(q) > r$ **do**   // either plan complete or costs exceed
                                                   // best costs so far

        if $c(q) < r$ **do**   // check for new best plan
          $q_{best} \leftarrow q$
          $r \leftarrow c(q)$
        done
        $E' \leftarrow E$
        $q \leftarrow G'(V, \emptyset)$ // reset query plan
    done
until stopping criterion fulfilled
return q_{best}

Fig. 4. Algorithm QUICKPICK

Essential for the cost bound pruning is the cost computation along the structure in the making. We assume a monotonic cost formula where operators do not influence the costs of their predecessors other than monotonically increasing, i.e. adding an operator later cannot *reduce* the costs of any subtree.

4   Assessment

Before presenting figures on QUICKPICK we investigate the potential of uniform sampling using abstractions for the cost distributions. Afterwards, we compare it to non-uniform sampling and point out the differences and their impact.

4.1   Uniform Sampling

We can put random sampling on solid formal grounds and compute probabilities for a successful search in dependency of the running time invested.

Let A be the random variable

$$A := costs\ of\ a\ query\ plan\ chosen\ at\ uniform\ probability.$$

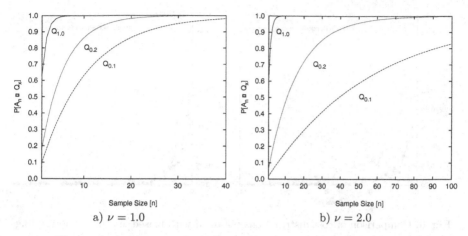

a) $\nu = 1.0$ b) $\nu = 2.0$

Fig. 5. Probability to select plan with costs below certain threshold

The probability to obtain a plan in Q_x under a cost distribution ξ is

$$P[A \in Q_x] = \int\limits_{c_{min}}^{c_{min} + \frac{x}{c_\mu - c_{min}}} \xi(t)dt.$$

For the random variable A_n

> $A_n :=$ *lowest costs in a sample of n plans chosen at uniform probability*

the following holds:

$$P[A_n \in Q_x] = 1 - \left(P[A \notin Q_x]\right)^n = 1 - \left(1 - P[A \in Q_x]\right)^n$$

In Figure 5, the probability $P[A_n \in Q_x]$ is shown for various x. As cost distribution we use Gamma distributions with shape parameter $\nu = 1, 2$. The sample size is given on the x-axis and the probability is plotted against the ordinate. As both diagrams show, finding a plan better than average $(Q_{1.0})$ is almost certainly achieved by a sample of only as little as 10 plans. For $\nu = 1$ the probability to obtain a plan in $Q_{0.2}$ within a sample of size 20 is already beyond 0.95. For a sample larger than 47 plans, the probability for plans in $Q_{0.1}$ is higher than 0.99 (cf. Fig. 5a). As Figure 5b shows, larger sample sizes are needed to achieve the same quality in case of $\nu = 2$. In particular, to reach into $Q_{0.1}$ with a probability greater than 0.99 requires n to be at least 982. Table 1 shows the necessary values of n to achieve $P[A_n \in Q_x] \geq 0.99$. Note, those figures are by far smaller than the widely accepted limits used for transformation-based probabilistic optimization or even genetic algorithms.

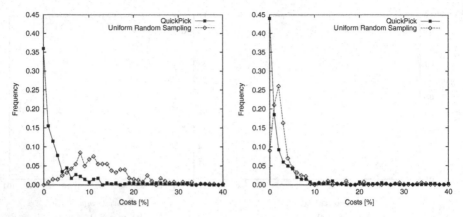

Fig. 6. Comparison of cost distributions obtained with biased and uniform sampling

4.2   Cost Distribution

In order to determine the cost distribution under QUICKPICK, we implemented a cost model comparable to those proposed in [EN94,KS91,Ste96]. Clearly, to be successful, the cost distribution ϕ_B under QUICKPICK must be at least as favorable as the original, i.e. shifted to the left relative to ϕ.

In the following we compare ϕ_B and ϕ under three aspects: (1) selective samples, (2) the correlation coefficient between a larger set of cost distributions, and (3) the shift of ϕ_B relative to ϕ.

In Figure 6, two pairs of cost distributions for high and low variance catalogs are shown. Both samples are of size 5000, the query size used is 50. To obtain cost distributions with QUICKPICK we disabled the cost bound pruning so that complete trees were constructed. In a larger series of test cases ϕ_B was without exception always left of ϕ. Moreover, ϕ_B bore in all cases strong resemblance with exponential distributions.

To test for a connection of ϕ_B and ϕ we compute the correlation coefficient. For two random variables, this coefficient is defined as

$$k = \frac{E[(X - E[X])(Y - E[Y])]}{\sigma_X \sigma_Y},$$

where $E[X]$ denotes the mean of X and σ_X is the deviation. For fully correlated distributions, k approaches 1. The more the distributions differ, the lower k gets. In Figure 7, the correlation coefficient is plotted as a function of the query size.

Table 1. Sample size needed for $P[A_n \in Q_x] \geq 0.99$

	$Q_{0.1}$	$Q_{0.2}$	$Q_{0.3}$	$Q_{1.0}$
$\nu = 1.0$	47	24	16	5
$\nu = 2.0$	982	261	123	16

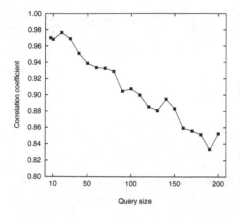

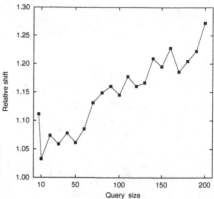

Fig. 7. Correlation of uniform and biased cost distribution

Fig. 8. Relative shift

Each point comprises 50 pairs of randomly generated queries. The plot shows a clear trend of decreasing correlation with increasing query size.

Finally, we determine the relative shift of ϕ_B which is defined as

$$s(x) = \frac{\int\limits_{c_{min}}^{x} \phi_B(x)}{\int\limits_{c_{min}}^{x} \phi(x)}$$

(see e.g. [IK91]). In Figure 8 the shift $s(\mu(\phi))$ is plotted as function of the query size. Again, each data point represents the average of 50 queries. Values above 1 indicate that ϕ_B is relatively shifted to the *left* of ϕ.

Our results clearly exhibit the trend that the biased cost distribution is even more favorable to sampling than the original one. With increasing query size, the difference between the two distributions becomes more distinct, showing the biased one stronger to the left of the original.

4.3   Quantitative Assessment

According to our analysis of the cost distribution, the results reported on by Galindo-Legaria *et al.* in [GLPK94] can immediately be transferred and serve, so to speak, as an upper bound for the result quality.

Like uniform sampling, QUICKPICK is unlikely to find the optimum as sampling works on the premise that all solutions in the top quantile—the size is parameter to the problem—are equally good. Thus "hitting" this quantile in the course of the sampling *is good enough*.

Result Quality Figure 9 shows the quality of the results in terms of quantile-based quality. For the experiments we differentiated the following shapes of query

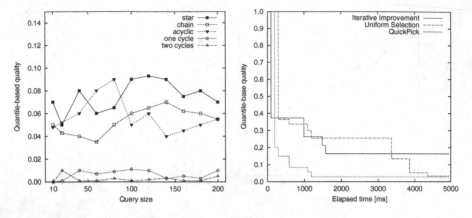

Fig. 9. Performance   **Fig. 10.** Convergence behavior

graphs: *stars*, *chains*, and *tree-shaped* on the one hand, and a type which we call *n-cycle* on the other hand. The first group of three comprises queries that can also be optimized with uniform sampling. The second group exceed the scope of uniform sampling. A graph of type n-cycle contains exactly n cycles, as the name suggests, but the remainder of the graph is unspecified, i.e. we use randomly generated tree-shaped graph and insert n additional edges. Our notion of cyclic graphs reflects real queries better than highly connected graph structures such as grids or cliques. Also the graph theoretic notion of connectivity is little suitable as almost all queries in actual applications are of a connectivity no higher than one.

For acyclic graphs, QUICKPICK delivers results of a quality comparable to that of uniform sampling—for star graphs, QUICKPICK actually implements even uniform sampling. In case of cyclic query graphs, the results are of even higher quality (see Fig. 9).

Convergence Behavior Like with uniform sampling, QUICKPICK's strong point is its quick convergence. Figure 10 shows the costs of the best plan found as function of the elapsed time in comparison with Iterative Improvement and uniform sampling. Due to its biased cost distribution, QUICKPICK converges significantly quicker. With longer running time the competitors catch up. Iterative Improvement sometimes beats QUICKPICK, not significantly though.

To underline the differences between uniform sampling and QUICKPICK, we compute the probability to hit the quantile $Q_{0.1}$ for both algorithms. $Q_{0.1}$ refers to the respective quantile of the original distribution. In Figure 11, these probabilities are plotted as function of the size of the sample. The left plot shows the situation for a high, the right for a low variance catalog. To hit the quantile with more than 90% probability in the high variance case requires a sample size

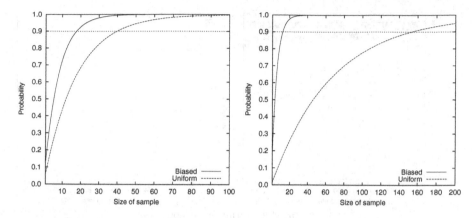

Fig. 11. Probability to hit quantile $Q_{0.1}$ with QUICKPICK and uniform sampling. Left, high variance, right low variance catalog

of 18 and 40 for QUICKPICK and uniform sampling respectively. In case of low variance catalog, the numbers differ even more significantly: 13 and 154.

Cost-bound Pruning Let us finally investigate the impact of cost-bound pruning on QUICKPICK. We introduced the algorithm in the form that partial trees are discarded as soon as their costs exceed the currently best plan's cost.

According to our general considerations about the cost distributions the effectiveness of the pruning depends on the shape of the distributions. The further to the left the distribution is the lower the gains, i.e. the trees are built-up almost to completeness. In Figure 12 this effect is demonstrated with low and high variance catalogs for a query of size 100. The left plot in 12a, shows the number of join predicates inserted with ADDJOIN—referred to as size of tree in the figure. As a stopping criterion we used 100000 insertions which made in this example for 1286 explored trees in total. For each (partial) tree we indicate the size when it was discarded (see Fig. 12a, left), 100 being the maximum. Note, not every tree completed is a new record since the last join can still exceed the best costs so far, which happens specifically frequent with high variance catalogs. The plot on the right hand side shows the average tree size as function of the number of trees. Starting at 100 it drops quickly to about 80 (see Fig. 12a, right).

In Figure 12b the same analysis is done for a low variance catalog. Since there is no strong concentration of solutions as opposed to the previous case, pruning kicks in earlier. The average tree size drops to about 40. Consequently, 100000 steps make for a larger number of (partial) trees explored; 2539 in this example.

In the first case savings amount to some 20%, in the second almost 60% on average. As a practical consequence, QUICKPICK with cost-bound pruning inspects a larger sample of trees, 1286 and 2539 in these cases, within the same running time that would be required to build up 1000 plans completely.

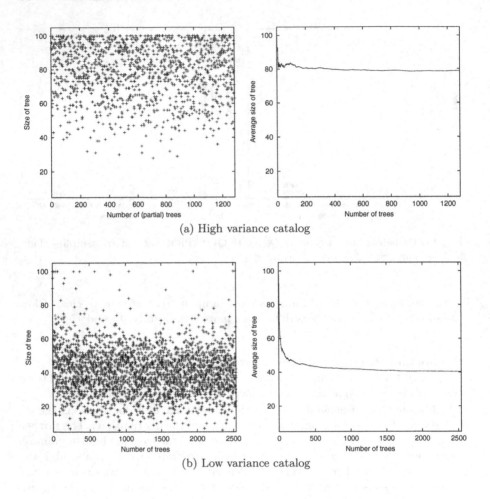

(a) High variance catalog

(b) Low variance catalog

Fig. 12. Effectiveness of cost-bound pruning in QUICKPICK

5   Related Work

The join-ordering problem continuously received attention during the past two decades. Besides enumeration techniques for small query sizes (cf. e.g. [SAC+79, VM96,PGLK97]), heuristics have been developed in order to tackle larger instances [KBZ86,SI93]. However, as Steinbrunn et. al. pointed out, heuristics yield only mediocre results as the queries grow in size [SMK97].

On the other hand, beginning with [IW87], randomized techniques have been introduced and attracted particular interest ever since. Swami and Gupta as well as Ioannidis and Kang proposed transformation-based frameworks where—after creating an initial plan—alternative plans are derived by application of transformation rules. The two most prominent representatives of this class of algorithms *Iterative Improvement* and *Simulated Annealing* can be proven to converge toward the optimal query plan for infinite running time. A theoretical result which is of limited use for practical applications as it does not describe the speed of convergence. As we pointed out above, these algorithms spend most of the running time on escaping local minima and making up for poor intermediate results, reaching high quality results eventually though.

In [GLPK94], Galindo-Legaria *et al.* showed that uniform sampling can achieve results of similar quality but significantly quicker.

In addition, navigating algorithms like Simulated Annealing depend on the quality of the initial query plan which affects the stability of the results obtained and requires careful parameter tuning: if the convergence is urged too firmly, the algorithm may get stuck in a local minimum at an early stage, if the convergence is not forced valuable running time is given away. To mitigate this problem, hybrid strategies like *Toured Simulated Annealing* and *Two-Phase Optimization* were developed [LVZ93,IK91].

Ioannidis and Kang presented a thorough analysis of the search space topology induced by transformation rules. Moreover, according to these studies, navigating algorithms require more than linearly increasing running time with increasing query size.

6   Conclusion

Based on the observation that sampling is a competitive alternative to transformation-based optimization algorithm like Simulated Annealing, we sat out to investigate background and limitations of sampling techniques for query optimization. To date, the problem of uniform random generation of query plans is only solved for acyclic query graphs.

In this paper, we devised a randomized bottom-up join order selection that performs *biased* sampling and is not limited in its application. Our experiments suggest that results for uniform sampling form an upper bound for the new sampling technique underlining its superior performance. The algorithm presented is distinguished by (1) its low complexity of both run time behavior and implementation (2) high quality results and (3) quick convergence.

Our results show that join ordering is, due to its cost distribution, actually "easier" than its property of being NP-complete may suggest. Similar effects are known for other NP-complete problems like graph coloring [Tur88]. The algorithm we presented establishes a well-balanced trade-off between result quality and time invested in the optimization process.

Future Research. Results presented make our algorithm an interesting building block for optimization of more complex queries including aggregates and subqueries. Our future research is directed to investigate ways of integrating sampling and exact methods to speed up the latter. Another direction we are eager to explore is the random generation of plans for complex queries on the lines of the technique presented in this paper.

References

[EN94]   E. Elmasri and S. B. Navathe. *Fundamentals of Database Sytems*. Benja-min/Cummings, Redwood City, CA, USA, 2nd edition, 1994.

[GLPK94]   C. A. Galindo-Legaria, A. Pellenkoft, and M. L. Kersten. Fast, Randomized Join-Order Selection – Why Use Transformations? In *Proc. of the Int'l. Conf. on Very Large Data Bases*, pages 85–95, Santiago, Chile, September 1994.

[GLPK95]   C. A. Galindo-Legaria, A. Pellenkoft, and M. L. Kersten. Uniformly-distributed Random Generation of Join Orders. In *Proc. of the Int'l. Conf. on Database Theory*, pages 280–293, Prague, Czech Republic, Ja-nuary 1995.

[IC91]   Y. E. Ioannidis and S. Christodoulakis. On the Propagation of Errors in the Size of Join Results. In *Proc. of the ACM SIGMOD Int'l. Conf. on Management of Data*, pages 268–277, Denver, CO, USA, May 1991.

[IK91]   Y. E. Ioannidis and Y. C. Kang. Left-Deep vs. Bushy Trees: An Analysis of Strategy Spaces and its Implications for Query Optimization. In *Proc. of the ACM SIGMOD Int'l. Conf. on Management of Data*, pages 168–177, Denver, CO, USA, May 1991.

[IW87]   Y. E. Ioannidis and E. Wong. Query Optimization by Simulated Annealing. In *Proc. of the ACM SIGMOD Int'l. Conf. on Management of Data*, pages 9–22, San Francisco, CA, USA, May 1987.

[KBZ86]   R. Krishnamurthy, H. Boral, and C. Zaniolo. Optimization of Nonrecursive Queries. In *Proc. of the Int'l. Conf. on Very Large Data Bases*, pages 128–137, Kyoto, Japan, August 1986.

[KS91]   H. Korth and A. Silberschatz. *Database Systems Concepts*. McGraw-Hill, Inc., New York, San Francisco, Washington, DC, USA, 1991.

[LVZ93]   R. S. G. Lanzelotte, P. Valduriez, and M. Zaït. On the Effectiveness of Optimization Search Strategies for Parallel Execution Spaces. In *Proc. of the Int'l. Conf. on Very Large Data Bases*, pages 493–504, Dublin, Ireland, August 1993.

[Pel97]   A. Pellenkoft. *Probabilistic and Transformation based Query Optimization*. PhD thesis, Universiteit van Amsterdam, Amsterdam, The Netherlands, 1997.

[PGLK97]   A. Pellenkoft, C. A. Galindo-Legaria, and M. L. Kersten. The Complexity of Transformation-Based Join Enumeration. In *Proc. of the Int'l. Conf. on Very Large Data Bases*, pages 306–315, Athens, Greece, September 1997.

[SAC+79]   P. Selinger, M. M. Astrahan, D. D. Chamberlin, R. A. Lorie, and T. G. Price. Access Path Selection in a Relational Database Management Sy-stem. In *Proc. of the ACM SIGMOD Int'l. Conf. on Management of Data*, pages 23–34, Boston, MA, USA, May 1979.

[SG88]   A. Swami and A. Gupta. Optimizing Large Join Queries. In *Proc. of the ACM SIGMOD Int'l. Conf. on Management of Data*, pages 8–17, Chicago, IL, USA, June 1988.

[SI93]   A. Swami and B. R. Iyer. A Polynomial Time Algorithm for Optimizing Join Queries. In *Proc. of the IEEE Int'l. Conf. on Data Engineering*, pages 345–354, Vienna, Austria, April 1993.

[SM97]   W. Scheufele and G. Moerkotte. On the Complexity of Generating Optimal Plans with Cross Products. In *Proc. of the ACM SIGACT-SIGMOD-SIGART Symposium on Principles of Database Systems*, pages 238–248, Tucson, AZ, USA, May 1997.

[SMK97]   M. Steinbrunn, G. Moerkotte, and A. Kemper. Heuristic and Randomi-
          zed Optimization for the Join Ordering Problem. *The VLDB Journal*,
          6(3):191–208, August 1997.

[Ste96]   M. Steinbrunn. *Heuristic and Randomised Optimisation Techniques in
          Object-Oriented Database*. DISDBIS. infix, Sankt Augustin, Germany,
          1996.

[Swa89]   A. Swami. Optimization of Large Join Queries: Combining Heuristics and
          Combinatorial Techniques. In *Proc. of the ACM SIGMOD Int'l. Conf. on
          Management of Data*, pages 367–376, Portland, OR, USA, June 1989.

[Tra98]   Transaction Processing Performance Council, San Jose, CA, USA. *TPC
          Benchmark D (Decision Support)*, Revision 1.3.1, 1998.

[Tur88]   J. S. Turner. Almost All k-Colorable Graphs are Easy to Color. *Journal
          of Algorithms*, 9(1):63–82, March 1988.

[VM96]   B. Vance and D. Maier. Rapid Bushy Join-order Optimization with Carte-
          sian Products. In *Proc. of the ACM SIGMOD Int'l. Conf. on Management
          of Data*, pages 35–46, Montreal, Canada, June 1996.

[Waa99]   F. Waas. Cost Distributions in Symmetric Euclidean Traveling Salesman
          Problems—A Supplement to TSPLIB. Technical Report INS-R9911, CWI,
          Amsterdam, The Netherlands, September 1999.

[WGL00]   F. Waas and C. A. Galindo-Legaria. Counting, Enumerating and Sampling
          of Execution Plans in a Cost-Based Query Optimizer. In *Proc. of the ACM
          SIGMOD Int'l. Conf. on Management of Data*, Dallas, TX, USA, May
          2000. Accepted for publication.

[WP98]   F. Waas and A. Pellenkoft. Exploiting Cost Distributions for Query Op-
          timization. Technical Report INS-R9811, CWI, Amsterdam, The Nether-
          lands, October 1998.

A User-Centric View of Data Warehouse Maintenance Issues

Henrik Engström[1], Sharma Chakravarthy[2], and Brian Lings[3]

[1]Department of Computer Science, University of Skövde, Sweden
henrik@ida.his.se
[2]Computer Science and Engineering Department, University of Texas at Arlington, US
sharma@cse.uta.edu
[3]School of Engineering and Computer Science, University of Exeter, UK
B.J.Lings@exeter.ac.uk

Abstract. Data in warehouses need to be updated in a timely manner from underlying operational data sources. This is referred to as warehouse maintenance. Not all of the data in the warehouse has the same requirement in terms of staleness (how old can it be with respect to the actual data), or its inverse freshness, and consistency (combining data from autonomous sources may give rise to some inconsistency). Given the requirements and schema information of a data warehouse, identifying policies for change detection and warehouse maintenance is a complex task. In this paper we identify a problem with current specification of user requirements, and suggest a specification scheme that is more general and user-oriented than extant suggestions. We also survey various policies that have been proposed for data propagation and analyse how change detection capabilities of sources influence user, as well as system requirements.

1 Introduction

Data warehousing was introduced in the commercial world in the beginning of the 90s in response to market needs for decision support [Lom95, Cha97, Wu97]. From a usage perspective, a data warehouse can be seen as a database which collects and stores data from different data sources [Gup95, Wid95]. A manager may then, for example, perform extensive and complex analytical queries based on company sales data, without affecting the performance of source databases [Ham95]. Other potential advantages are reduction of response time [Wid95], providing temporal views [Yan98], and to make data continuously available from sources that periodically go off-line [Rou95, Ham95].

Users access the contents of a warehouse (Figure 1) through different tools, such as query languages, spreadsheet programs, web browsers and data mining applications. Data stored in a warehouse is retrieved from sources such as plain files, html-pages, and active and conventional databases [Wid95]. An integrator is responsible for co-ordinating data retrieval from sources and integrating the results into a warehouse. For the sake of generality, we show a wrapper/monitor for each source in Figure 1; in practice some of these may be very thin or even absent.

B. Lings and K. Jeffery (Eds.): BNCOD 17, LNCS 1832, pp. 68-80, 2000.
© Springer-Verlag Berlin Heidelberg 2000

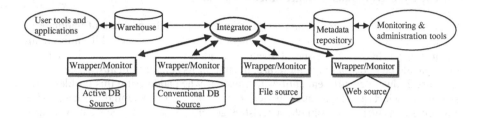

Fig. 1. A typical data warehouse architecture [Wid95, Cha97]

A warehouse may be described as a set of views over its sources [Lom95]. There are a number of factors that make warehouse views special and motivate a separate study of them. A warehouse view is typically materialised, based on distributed, heterogeneous, autonomous sources [Ham95], and is not updated by its users. Heterogeneity implies that sources may have different characteristics, offering different degrees of co-operation. They may use different data models and query facilities, have separate transaction handling and offer different techniques for the detection and propagation of changes. A common transaction mechanism cannot be assumed. Distribution implies that there will be parallel activity in the nodes. The absence of a common clock makes it impossible to obtain a global serialisation of events [Sch96, Yan99]. There is also a communication medium that may introduce additional delays and may be unreliable. Autonomy implies that sources will be updated by applications outside the control of the warehouse environment. Moreover, the integrator may have limited access permissions to sources.

As warehouse maintenance covers a wide spectrum of sources, it is possible that pure relational techniques (which dominate the literature) will not be sufficient in all situations [Jag95]. As a data warehouse supports decision making, its views will be more complex than those typically encountered in relational databases in that they can contain aggregates and statistical operators (moving averages, for example). Explicit updates to warehouse data are rare [Wid95] and even if they do occur are not propagated to sources. In fact, views used in a warehouse may use aggregation or other transformations that make them non-updatable [Day78].

It is important to note that a warehouse consists of several views based on several sources. In addition to views directly based on source data there may also be 'local' warehouse views. This latter kind of view can, for example, be used to optimise the performance of aggregates along different dimensions in a star-schema. How to select and efficiently maintain these internal views has been addressed in several studies [Har96, Lee99, Gup99].

In this paper we clearly define the data warehouse maintenance problem and critically review the literature related to it. From this, we synthesise a clear user view of requirements specification for maintenance and analyse important aspects of system characteristics which impinge on any choice of maintenance strategy.

1.1 The Data Warehouse Maintenance Problem

We define *the data warehouse maintenance problem* to be the problem of maintaining a data warehouse to meet user requirements on quality of service while minimising system impact. In fact, the issue of specifying quality of service is one that has not been considered in detail in the literature, in spite of its centrality in any definition.

Figure 2 illustrates different entities to consider when addressing this problem. The goal is to select a maintenance policy out of a set of potential policies. User requirements as well as system characteristics govern the selection. System evaluation criteria are used to compare candidate policies. We have considered the maintenance problem only for materialised warehouses.

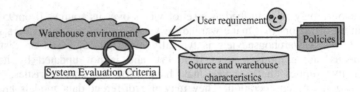

Fig. 2. Components of a data warehouse maintenance problem

User requirement express expected quality of service. This can be explicit or implicit requirements on availability, consistency and response-time, amongst other things. Requirements may differ between different portions of the warehouse. In the same way different views and sources may have different maintenance strategies. The policy selected may in practice be a collection of policies for different warehouse fragments. We define a Source Data Propagation Policy (SDPP) to determine when and how to propagate changes from a source to an integrator. A View Maintenance Policy (VMP) determines when and how to update a warehouse view. This includes SDPPs for each involved source together with information on when and how to join these results. Finally, a data warehouse maintenance policy is the collection of all VMPs for all views in the warehouse that are defined over external sources.

System characteristics capture properties that may affect maintenance activity. This includes capabilities of the sources, the nature of the view, the update and query behaviour etc. All these things affect and constrain the maintenance policies.

System evaluation criteria define yard-sticks for use in the selection process. They include disk I/O, storage and communication requirements. One important characteristic of a data warehouse environment is that there is a distinction between source and warehouse impact. Source impact caused by a policy may be considered more expensive than warehouse impact. One reason for introducing a warehouse is to off-load intensive queries from sources. For these applications, the cost of maintaining a warehouse must not exceed the cost of querying its sources.

2   User Specification

Although materialised data warehouses are motivated by user requirements, little work has been reported on how to specify and utilise such requirements. The goal of this section is to develop a scheme by which user quality of service requirements can be specified.

Several taxonomies and frameworks for view maintenance and data integration have been presented in the literature [Gup95, Zho95, Agr97, Hul96]. None of them specifically addresses the data warehouse maintenance problem and none focuses on user specification. In a small number of approaches the user aspects are explicitly considered in policy selection analysis. As an example, Srivastava et al. [Sri88] assume that user requirement are specified as a number representing the relative importance of the user viewpoint (response-time) to the system viewpoint. Segev et al. utilise a currency and a response-time limit, which are real numbers. Assigning numbers to variables in formulae has a major drawback in that it is hard from a user's perspective to understand their implication. What behaviour will I get if I say that response-time is 45% more important than system impact? Will the system be able to deliver the result of queries within 500 ms if it is specified? We suggest that such balancing primarily should be governed by high-level quality of service specification, avoiding low level parameter settings. If there is no need for fine-grained control, it should be possible to simply specify whether a criterion is important or not. As an example, if consistency and response-time are specified as important but not staleness, it may result in different maintenance activity than if the specification stated that only staleness matters.

2.1   Current Terms

A number of terms related to the user view have been introduced in the literature. Included are: response-time ([Sri88]), availability ([Col96][Qua97]), currency ([Seg90]), freshness ([Hul96B]), staleness ([Hul96]) and consistency ([Zhu99][Agr97][Col96]).

Response-time is defined as the difference between submission of a query and the return of the result [Sri88]. Availability is defined in terms of view-downtime [Col96] e.g. expressed as a percentage.

Currency was introduced in [Seg90] as a measure of the time elapsed since a view last reflected the state of its sources[1]. A zero currency value means that the view is up to date. Segev et al. show that there are potential performance gains by relaxing currency. They note that in practice it is hard to use their definition (source states are not immediately available) and so propose a measure based on last refresh.

A subtle problem with the definition suggested by Segev et al. is that it is defined in terms of the (dynamic) view state, whereas a user is only concerned about the quality of the returned result. Another limitation is that the working definition introduced is only defined for periodic and on-demand policies. This gives rise to two problems:

---

[1] The work related to a distributed environment, not explicitly a data warehousing one.

The currency requirement stated by the user is always met in terms of the time since last refresh, if on-demand maintenance is used. However, the time to refresh the view is not considered. If the user specifies currency to be one second and the maintenance take one minute the requirement is still considered as met.

If an immediate maintenance policy is used, the view currency may be bad (a long time since last refresh), but knowing that changes will be reported when they occur implies that the view can be used to answer queries.

Segev et al. use a response-time constraint to solve the first problem. We claim that this is not an appropriate solution as refresh-time conceptually belongs with currency. If no response-time restriction is specified a view can, in theory, have unbounded refresh delays with results returned being non-current.

Hull et al. [Hul96, Hul96B] introduce definitions of both freshness and staleness. Freshness is defined using a time vector composed of values for each source used in the view definition. A view is considered fresh with respect to the vector if each source state used existed within the indicated period. Staleness on the other hand is defined as the maximum difference between the time a result is returned and (for materialised views) the latest time the view reflected the source. As with freshness, staleness is defined for each source contributing to the view and as with currency, staleness is defined in terms of when a view ceases to reflect its sources. The major difference between currency and staleness is that the latter includes the time to return a result. Freshness and staleness are complementary concepts but Hull et al. give no guidelines when to use either of them.

In a warehousing environment a view may contain data from autonomous and „transaction unaware" sources which may yield inconsistent views if the integration is performed in a straightforward manner. Zhuge et al. [Zhu96] identifies this problem and defines four consistency levels for a warehouse view - convergence, weak consistency, strong consistency and completeness - based on state changes of the view and each of its sources. Zhuge et al. presents several algorithms for different source scenarios (views based on one or more sources with different transaction capabilities) and show how they will guarantee different consistency levels.

2.2 A Proposed Ontology of User Concepts

Based on such work we suggest an ontology of user concepts as shown in Figure 3.

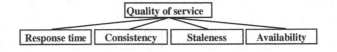

Fig. 3. Quality of service aspects from a user's perspective

The definitions of response time, consistency, and availability are accepted without change in this paper but we propose a new definition for staleness. We believe there is a need to make a clear distinction between quality of service required by users and provided by systems, and the dynamic behaviour of views. Neither currency as defined by Segev et al. nor staleness (or freshness) as defined by Hull et al. has a simple user-oriented definition. We suggest that two distinct measures should be used: view staleness and view age. The former describes the quality of service of the results returned to users, and is defined below. The latter is system-oriented, concerning the view-state and how well it reflects its sources. View age can be used determine when and from where to update views, but is beyond the scope of this paper.

2.3 View Staleness

Assuming that at least weak consistency is provided (or more precisely that the view will use some valid state from each source) we define the measure of staleness of a view informally as follows:

For a view with guaranteed maximum staleness z, the result of any query over the view, returned at time t, will reflect all source changes prior to t-z.

This means that users have an intuitive measure of how recent the information returned by a view can be expected to be. For example, if we have a view containing stock-broker information with a guaranteed staleness of 60 seconds the user knows all changes performed more than a minute ago will be returned. More recent changes may or may not be reflected in the result of queries over the view.

The definition has some nice intuitive properties. When a result is returned the user can easily interpret the associated staleness measure. The definition applies to any maintenance strategy and can be applied to virtual views as well. Moreover, it makes no references to the view-state or the time of query-invocation which means it will not discriminate or favour on-demand maintenance (or immediate for that matter). Finally, if a view guarantees maximum staleness z it will also guarantee maximum staleness z+d, where d>0.

In a real environment it may not be possible to guarantee meeting staleness requirements. This will in practice require that all activities in the system be tightly integrated with a predictable behaviour similar to that provided by a real-time system. In a warehouse scenario this cannot be assumed. The definition of staleness may be altered such that a view guarantees maximum staleness z if the probability of not reflecting changes in time is less than p. The value of p is situation dependent.

2.4 Maintenance Policies

A maintenance policy will be selected to satisfy user requirements whilst minimising system impact. In this section we identify the solution space of the data warehouse maintenance problem in terms of maintenance policies. Several maintenance algorithms have been suggested for view, snapshot and warehouse maintenance. They all relate in that they can be described in terms of when and how maintenance is to be performed. The „how" part of maintenance may be broken down into a number of choices described in the literature. A view could: be maintained incrementally or recomputed; be maintained on-line or off-line; be more or less consistency preserving. It is important to note that a large number of variations and combinations of policies are possible. The set of algorithms is not fixed and more variations can be introduced in the future.

Maintenance timing addresses the question of when to refresh a view. Maintenance activity may be triggered by different types of events [Zho95] such as updates to base data, reading of the view, explicit requests or periodic events. The following are commonly mentioned timings based on these events:

Immediate - maintenance is performed immediately when updates occur. If global transactions are available it might be possible to perform the maintenance as a part of the updating transaction. In a warehousing environment, however, this cannot be assumed. Closely related is eager indicating that updates will be incorporated as soon as they are detected/visible.

Periodic - maintenance is performed on a regular basis (once a second, once an hour, etc.). A view may become „inconsistent" with its base data, representing a snapshot of the sources. Source updates will not be visible in the view until the next refresh. Periodic maintenance is commonly used in commercial systems [Cha97].

On-demand - maintenance is performed when a view is queried. This may reduce overheads if a view is seldom used. On-demand is also referred to as deferred maintenance [Rou86, Han87].

Hybrid - maintenance is triggered by several event types. Segev et al. [Seg91] suggest that on-demand maintenance could be combined with periodic, with the advantage that an update may have been handled when a query is posed, yielding a shorter response time. Hanson [Han87] suggests a hybrid that utilises idle time to refresh on-demand views. In a warehousing environment it may be problematic to detect simultaneous idle time for sources and warehouse.

Random - maintenance is triggered at random. For example, [Seg90] suggests this but gives no details on the rationale for this timing. One potential advantage with random maintenance is that load on the sources may be evenly distributed, avoiding synchronisation of maintenance due to unfortunate periodicity choices.

The maintenance policies in the literature are typically described in terms of SDPP and integrator operation. An SDPP is basically a timing for change propagation. The integrator's part of the VMP is, for example, an algorithm for view update that preserves consistency. For views based on multiple sources it is tacitly assumed that all sources will use the same SDPP. It is, however, important to note that a policy may be more complex, using individual SDPPs. Changes propagated from one source can be cached awaiting another event (periodic or on-demand) which triggers a join with other sources. There is also the potential to use incremental update for one source and recompute for another. Extant approaches do not explore combinations for multi-source views, and have not been considered.

3   System Characteristics

The data warehouse maintenance problem inherits all system parameters impacting on view maintenance in general. This may include system characteristics such as processing capacity, main memory size, I/O and communication capacity. It may also include source-related characteristics such as page size and indexing details. Other important factors which have been shown to impact on maintenance activity include query behaviour (frequency, distribution) and view definition properties such as incrementally maintainable, self-maintainable, key information, duplicates, view selectivity and size. These issues have been thoroughly studied and are taken as given in this paper. In this section we highlight factors which are data warehousing specific.

An important characteristic in warehousing systems is that sources are autonomous and may have a varying degree of service. The absence of some mechanism may have a severe impact on maintenance activity. For example, transaction capabilities impact on consistency preservation as identified by Zhuge [Zhu99]. In this section we will highlight other such characteristics some of which have individually been mentioned in other studies. We show that there are important relationships between these characteristics that may have severe impact on maintenance activity in terms of response-time and staleness.

3.1 Change Detection Capabilities

A limitation with existing work on view and warehouse maintenance (e.g. Han87, Sri88, Seg91, Zho95, Zhu99) is that it assumes that sources are capable of actively participate in maintenance activity. Some authors identify that sources may lack some capabilities but assume that compensation is possible by wrapping sources. There exist source categorisations [Kos98, Wid95] that are aimed at exploring the solution space of wrapping, based on the nature of existing data sources. We, however, claim that isolating wrapping from the rest of the maintenance process may have severe implications on user as well as system performance. As an example, consider a warehouse based on web-sources outside the control of the warehouse administer. A wrapper may provide change detection to enable immediate, incremental maintenance. However, view staleness, storage and processing costs will be greater than by using periodic re-compute.

Instead we suggest that change detection in the wrapper should be made an explicit part of maintenance, and that source characteristics should be used in the policy selection process. Zhou et al. [Zho95] classifies source change detection capabilities as sufficient, restricted, and no activeness. We claim that this classification is too imprecise to be used in policy selection. Instead we suggest three change detection capabilities, shown in Table 1, which a source may have and which affects its ability to participate in view maintenance.

Table 1. Classification of change detection capabilities

Capability	Description
CHAW	Change aware - the ability to, on request, tell when the last change was made
CHAC	Change active - the ability to automatically detect and report that changes have been made
DAW	Delta aware - the ability to deliver delta changes (on request or automatically)

We consider a source to have a certain capability if it provides it to the client without requiring extensive extension or resource-wasting "work-arounds". We claim that these characteristics are orthogonal in the sense that a source can have one, two or three of them in any combination. This is shown through a set of examples:

A source accessed through standard SQL-92 will typically not provide any of these characteristics.

Unix file servers and web servers are examples of sources providing CHAW in that they can, on request, return the time of last modification. All file sources, and the majority of web-sources will, however, not allow the clients to subscribe to change notification, which makes them non-CHAC. This type of source has limited structure and allows textual editing, making change representation non-trivial. There are no obvious DAW capabilities in a file-system.

An active database management system enables users to define rules each specifying an event for which an action should be performed [ACT96]. A typical event might be that a specific entity is altered and the action to send a message to some object. This means that an active database may provide CHAC by using the rule system. Even though it is considered a tractable property, not all ADBMSs enable DAW. A system may, for example, indicate which entity has been changed without delivering the actual change. Moreover, it is entirely possible that a system is unable to deliver CHAW for entities not involved in rule definitions. A relational database equipped with triggers may be unable to provide CHAC due to restrictions of external actions. It is, however, possible that triggers can be used to provide DAW.

The extended query capability of a temporal database can be used to provide DAW. It is, for example, possible to report changes made during the last hour but that does not mean that there is support for automatic change detection (CHAC).

Our next step is to verify that each change detection capability is useful in a policy selection process. For this purpose we present eight maintenance policies and their change detection requirements. The policies we consider are based on four different timings - immediate, on-demand, periodic and hybrid (periodic and on-demand). For each timing we have a policy which recomputes the view and a policy using incremental techniques. Table 2 shows the change detection requirements for each policy.

Table 2. Change detection requirements for different maintenance policies

Policy	Change aware CHAW	Change active CHAC	Delta aware DAW
Immediate incremental		mandatory	mandatory
Immediate recompute		mandatory	
On-demand incremental	desirable		mandatory
On-demand recompute	mandatory		
Periodic incremental			mandatory
Periodic recompute	desirable		
Hybrid incremental	desirable		mandatory
Hybrid recompute	mandatory		

As an example, the table shows that to use immediate incremental maintenance a source needs to be both CHAC and DAW. The former is needed to initiate maintenance and the latter is needed to perform incremental update. On-demand and hybrid have CHAW marked as desirable, indicating that in most cases it will be more efficient to utilise the time of last modification, for example if the staleness requirements are such that slightly outdated data are acceptable. Finally, we observe that on-demand recompute requires CHAW to be able to avoid a full recompute for each query. Otherwise materialisation of the view becomes meaningless. For periodic recompute the requirement is different as the cost of maintenance is independent of query behaviour.

To summarise, we have shown that our suggested classification of change detection capabilities are orthogonal and that each such characteristic may have a crucial impact on the set of eligible policies.

3.2 Extending Sources

As mentioned above, sources that lack a certain service may be extended - wrapped - to provide that service. Other potential extension techniques, e.g. rebuilding a server, are not applicable in a warehousing environment with autonomous sources.

Extending a source to provide, for example, DAW can be achieved by introducing a process which maintains a copy of the source and periodically, or on-demand, queries the source and compares the result with the copy. This process will obviously require system resources such as storage and processing. It may, moreover, have implications for user requirements such as maximum data staleness. In this section we analyse the consequences of extending a source to provide CHAW, CHAC or DAW to a warehouse maintenance activity.

As mentioned previously, the system viewpoint is divided into a source and a warehouse side. A wrapper process may, depending on the nature of the source, be located in either side. If, for example, a web-source external to the warehouse is to be extended to provide DAW it must be queried remotely. This will introduce processing and storage costs in the warehouse and additional communication. If, on the other hand, the extraction process is located in the source, there is no additional communication cost but the source will be penalised with storage and processing costs. The localisation of the extraction process is a trade-off between communication, processing and storage, as illustrated in Figure 4.

Local delta extraction   **Remote delta extraction**

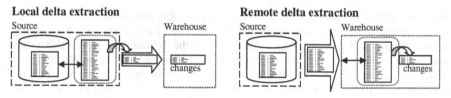

Fig. 4. The difference between local and remote delta extraction

At first glance it may seem obvious that local delta extraction should be used whenever possible, but the cost of storage and processing in the sources may be the most critical criteria, in which case remote extraction will be preferable.

From a user viewpoint the absence of change detection capabilities may affect several criteria. Immediate outperforms on-demand with respect to response time, but requires CHAC. If a source is extended to provide CHAC by periodic polling (with periodicity p) staleness less than p can never be guaranteed. This implies that a view based on a source lacking CHAC can never achieve true immediate maintenance. Polling frequency will, moreover, have a direct impact on processing cost and possibly also on communication. Hence it is not at all obvious that „false" immediate maintenance with polling periodicity p will be found preferable to periodic maintenance with the same periodicity. The usefulness ought to depend on the cost of extracting and incorporating the changes. Figure 5 illustrates the difference between true and false immediate and periodic recompute.

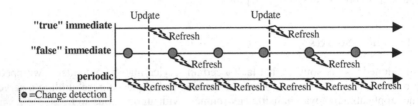

Fig. 5. Comparing maintenance policies „true" immediate (source is CHAC), „false" immediate (source is not CHAC), and periodic

To a user who puts low staleness as the primary optimisation criterion, on-demand may be optimal when no „true" immediate is available. Change awareness (CHAW) can be utilised to avoid unnecessary recomputes. If a source is extended to provide CHAW, a careful analysis is needed to determine whether it is meaningful and not counter-productive. Depending on the source type, CHAW may be achieved in a more or less expensive way. If no other options exist, it may be done through periodic comparisons of snapshots where the processing and storage cost may be motivated by reduction in communication.

4   Conclusions and Future Work

We have defined the data warehouse maintenance problem and, from a critical review of the extant literature, have suggested an ontology for the specification of user service requirements. In so doing, we have refined the definition of view staleness and justified its use in place of the concepts of freshness and currency. We have also identified that existing work is limited by its assumption that sources are capable of participating actively in maintenance activity, either with or without extension. We have suggested a simple classification of source change detection capabilities, and discussed how these impact on maintenance activity.

The results presented form the basis for addressing the data warehouse maintenance problem. This is the subject of current research. The goal is to enable a selection of maintenance strategy based on user specification as well as static and dynamic system characteristics. A general selection algorithm based on the characteristics suggested for user quality of service specification has been developed, and appropriate cost models are being investigated. Preliminary results shows that user quality of service and source characteristics have an important impact on system optimisation.

References

[ACT96] ACT-NET: The Active Database Management System Manifesto: A Rulebase of ADBMS Features. SIGMOD Record 25(3) (1996)

[Agr97] D. Agrawal, A.E. Abbadi, A.K. Singh, T. Yurek: Efficient View Maintenance at Data Warehouses. SIGMOD Conference (1997)

[Cha97] C. Chaudhuri, U. Dayal: An Overview of Data Warehousing and OLAP Technology. SIGMOD Record 26(1) (1997)

[Col96] L.S. Colby, T. Griffin, L. Libkin, I.S. Mumick, H. Trickey: Algorithms for Deferred View Maintenance. SIGMOD Conference (1996)

[Day78] U. Dayal, P.A. Bernstein: On the Updatability of Relational Views. VLDB (1978)

[Gup95] A. Gupta, I.S. Mumick: Maintenance of Materialized Views: Problems, Techniques, and Applications. IEEE Data Engineering Bulletin 18(2) (1995)

[Gup99] H. Gupta, I.S. Mumick: Selection of Views to Materialize Under a Maintenance Cost Constraint. International Conference on Database Theory (1999)

[Ham95] J. Hammer, H. Garcia-Molina, J. Widom, W. Labio, Y. Zhuge: The Stanford Data Warehousing Project. IEEE Data Engineering Bulletin 18(2) (1995)

[Han87] E.N. Hanson: A Performance Analysis of View Materialization Strategies. SIGMOD Conference (1987)

[Har96] V. Harinarayan, A. Rajaraman, J.D. Ullman: Implementing Data Cubes Efficiently. SIGMOD Conference (1996)

[Hul96] R. Hull, G. Zhou: A Framework for Supporting Data Integration Using the Materialized and Virtual Approaches. SIGMOD Conference (1996)

[Hul96B] R. Hull, G. Zhou: Towards the Study of Performance Trade-offs Between Materialized and Virtual Integrated Views. VIEWS'96 (1996)

[Jag95] H.V. Jagadish, I.S. Mumick, A. Silberschatz: View Maintenance Issues for the Chronicle Data Model. PODS (1995)

[Kos98] A. Koschel, P.C. Lockemann: Distributed events in active database systems: Letting the genie out of the bottle. Journal of Data and Knowledge Engineering 25(1-2) (1998)

[Lee99] M. Lee, J. Hammer: Speeding Up Warehouse Physical Design Using A Randomized Algorithm. Design and Management of Data Warehouses, workshop at CAiSE (1999)

[Lom95] D. Lomet (editor), J. Widom (editor): Special Issue on Materialized Views and Data Warehousing. IEEE Data Engineering Bulletin 18(2) (1995)

[Qua97] D. Quass, J. Widom: On-Line Warehouse View Maintenance. SIGMOD Conference (1997)

[Rou86] N. Roussopoulos, H. Kang: Principles and Techniques in the Design of ADMS±. IEEE Computer 19(12) (1986)

[Rou95] R. Roussopoulos, C.M. Chen, S. Kelley, A. Delis, Y. Papakonstantinou: The ADMS Project: Views "R" Us. IEEE Data Engineering Bulletin 18(2) (1995)

[Sch96] S. Schwiderski: Monitoring the Behaviour of Distributed Systems. PhD thesis, University of Cambridge (1996)

[Seg90] A. Segev, W. Fang: Currency-Based Updates to Distributed Materialized Views. ICDE (1990)

[Seg91] A. Segev, W. Fang: Optimal Update Policies for Distributed Materialized Views. Management Science 37(7) (1991)

[Sri88] J. Srivastava, D. Rotem: Analytical Modeling of Materialized View Maintenance. PODS (1988)

[Wid95] J. Widom: Research Problems in Data Warehousing. CIKM (1995)

[Wu97] M.C. Wu, A.P. Buchmann: Research Issues in Data Warehousing. Datenbanksysteme in Büro, Technik und Wissenschaft, Ulm (1997)

[Yan98]   J. Yang, J. Widom: Maintaining Temporal Views Over Non-Temporal Information Sources For Data Warehousing. EDBT (1998)
[Yan99]   S. Yang, S. Chakravarthy: Formal Semantics of Composite Events for Distributed Environments. ICDE (1999)
[Zho95]   G. Zhou, R. Hull, R. King, J.C. Franchitti: Data Integration and Warehousing Using H2O. IEEE Data Engineering Bulletin 18(2) (1995)
[Zhu96]   Y. Zhuge, H. Garcia-Molina, J.L. Wiener: The Strobe Algorithms for Multi-Source Warehouse Consistency. PDIS (1996)
[Zhu99]   Y. Zhuge: Incremental Maintenance of Consistent Data Warehouses. PhD Thesis, Stanford University (1999)

VESPA: A Benchmark
for Vector Spatial Databases

Norman W. Paton[2], M. Howard Williams[1], Kosmas Dietrich[1], Olive Liew[1],
Andrew Dinn[1], and Alan Patrick[1]

[1] Department of Computing and Electrical Engineering
Heriot-Watt University, Edinburgh, UK
howard@cee.hw.ac.uk
[2] Department of Computer Science
University of Manchester, Oxford Road, Manchester, UK
norm@cs.man.ac.uk

Abstract. Facilities for the storage and analysis of large quantities of
spatial data are important to many applications, and are central to geographic information systems. This has given rise to a range of proposals
for spatial data models and software architectures that allow database
systems to be used cleanly and efficiently with spatial data. However, although many spatial database systems have been built, there have been
few systematic comparisons of the functionality or the performance of
such systems. This is probably at least partly due to the lack of a widely used, standard spatial database benchmark. This paper presents a
benchmark for vector spatial databases that covers a range of typical GIS
functions, and shows how the benchmark has been implemented in two
systems: the object-relational database PostgreSQL, and the deductive
object-oriented database ROCK & ROLL extended to support the ROSE
algebra. The benchmark serves both to evaluate the facilities provided
by the systems and to allow conclusions to be drawn on the efficiency of
their spatial storage managers.

1 Introduction

Benchmarks are useful things. There are two principal kinds of benchmark: *functionality* benchmarks, which are targeted at the question 'what can this system
do?'; and *performance* benchmarks, which seek to answer the question 'how fast
is this system?'. In the absence of benchmarks, making detailed comparisons
between alternative proposals concerning their functionality or performance is
generally difficult. An overview of database benchmarks is provided by [6].

The authors became aware of the need for a suitable benchmark for vector-
based spatial databases at an early stage in their design of a spatial extension to
the ROCK & ROLL deductive object-oriented database [3,9]. At this point it was
important to identify a suitable benchmark program that could be used both to
test the functionality of the ROCK & ROLL system and to allow performance
comparisons with alternative approaches. Unfortunately, no existing publicly

B. Lings and K. Jeffery (Eds.): BNCOD 17, LNCS 1832, pp. 81–101, 2000.

available benchmark could be found that was suitable for use with a vector-based spatial database targeted towards spatial querying and analysis.

The best known existing benchmark for spatial databases is SEQUOIA 2000 [20], which has been used in a number of settings [10,4,18]. The SEQUOIA benchmark is explicitly an earth sciences benchmark, and is highly oriented towards raster data. This is reasonable, but makes SEQUOIA inappropriate for use with vector spatial databases. In addition, as SEQUOIA operates with real data sets, it is more difficult to experiment with different data set sizes, as the one data set currently supplied for SEQUOIA stands at around 1Gb. Another performance analysis is provided by [2], but this is more oriented around database population than the time taken for analyses. In some recent work, there has been an emphasis on the generation of spatial data sets (e.g. [11]), but this work has not been followed through into the proposal of complete benchmarks. Other proposals have been narrower in scope than a complete benchmark, for example focusing on spatial join algorithms [14] or indexing [23].

A benchmark which is required to test functionality and assess performance for vector-based spatial databases should ideally satisfy the following requirements:

1. Ease of use. Implementation of the data structures and queries of the benchmark should not be particularly time consuming, and obtaining data sets should be straightforward.
2. Wide ranging functionality: The benchmark should assess as large a range of spatial database features as possible.
3. Scalability: It should be possible to generate data sets that are as small or as large as is required to carry out the performance analyses that are relevant to a particular context.

Due to the absence of any suitable existing benchmark, the benchmark presented in this paper was developed. In terms of the above criteria, it can be seen to satisfy these as follows: *Ease of use* – it has a compact schema, and data for testing purposes is generated synthetically; *Wide ranging* – it has a large number of small test tasks for which performance can be measured; *Scalable* – the data generation software can be used to construct databases that are of a wide range of sizes, from very small, main memory data sets to very large data sets that simulate large scale maps covering a large area. To date, we have used the benchmark to test the functionality and performance of the GIS ARC/INFO [15], the persistent C++ system Exodus [5], the object-relational database PostgreSQL [24], the deductive object-oriented database ROCK & ROLL without built-in spatial extensions [1], and ROCK & ROLL with built-in spatial extensions. The above experiences have shown that the benchmark can be constructed quite rapidly on a range of platforms, although the features it tests can be difficult to support in some environments (e.g. some of the queries did not yield natural implementations in the map-layer oriented ARC/INFO).

The remainder of this paper is structured as follows. Section 2 presents the benchmark. Sections 3 and 4 describe how the benchmark has been implemented in PostgreSQL and ROCK & ROLL, respectively. Section 5 presents and comments on the results of the benchmark, and section 6 presents some overall conclusions.

2 The Benchmark

This section describes the VESPA (VEctor SPAtial) benchmark by describing the data used in the benchmark and the tests that are used to assess the performance of systems.

2.1 Data

Unlike the SEQUOIA 2000 [19] benchmark, VESPA uses synthetic data generated by programs written for that purpose. There are several advantages to this approach: obtaining the data is easier, there is greater control over the size and shape of the spatial objects, and it makes the output of queries more predictable. Working with a single real data set, as in SEQUOIA, ensures that the data is representative of some real world situation, but provides less opportunity for testing software in different scenarios. However, in VESPA, of the many parameters that could potentially be varied in data generation programs, this paper only varies the scale of the data sets generated. Further work on automatic generation of spatial data sets is described in [11,22].

The benchmark is performed on collections of geometric objects representing features on a map. The resulting data sets contain simpler and more regular data than real maps, but are easy to generate and are usable to test a wide range of different cases. The benchmark uses data sets that represent land ownership, states, land use, roads, streams, gas lines and points of interest.

The land ownership data set forms a base for the generated data. Land ownership is represented by an n by n grid of hexagons. The size of all data sets is given relative to the number n of hexagons used to represent land ownership.

Landown The data set *landown* in Table 1 consists of n^2 hexagons arranged in n rows with n columns. Cardinality: n^2

Field Name	Field Definition	Comments
land_nr	integer	external ID
land	polygon	regular hexagon
owner	string[15]	n different names
value	float	generated randomly

Table 1. Data set landown

Field Name	Field Definition	Comments
statename	string[15]	generated randomly
state	polygon	regular hexagon
population	integer	random number < 10,000,000

Table 2. Data set states

States The data set *states* in Table 2 contains hexagons, with $n/3$ rows consisting of $n/3$ hexagons. Cardinality: $(n/3)^2$

Landuse The data set *landuse* in Table 3 consists of triangles, with six triangles placed into each land ownership hexagon. Cardinality: $6 * n^2$

Field Name	Field Definition	Comments
landusename	string[15]	generated randomly
land	polygon	regular triangle
landusetype	string[15]	1 from 5 landuse types enumerated cyclically

Table 3. Data set landuse

Roads The data set *roads* in Table 4 contains lines describing a network. It is built of slanting lines with $n/2$ broadly horizontal and $n/2$ broadly vertical directions. At each intersection point a new line segment starts. Therefore, a road consists of $n/2 + 1$ line segments. Cardinality: $2(n/2)$

Field Name	Field Definition	Comments
roadname	string[15]	randomly generated
road	line	line consisting of n/2 segments
roadtype	string[15]	three roadtypes enumerated cyclically
lanes	int	iterates from 1 to 6
width	float	computed from lanes

Table 4. Data set roads

Streams The data set *streams* in Table 5 consists of lines representing a binary tree. The root of the binary is located in the lower left corner. The depth of the tree is $\sqrt{n}$. Cardinality: $2^{\sqrt{n}+1} - 2$

Gas Lines The data set *gaslines* in Table 6 also contains lines presenting a tree. Its depth is $\sqrt{n+1}$ and therefore it contains about twice as many items as

Field Name	Field Definition	Comments
streamname	string[15]	randomly generated
stream	line	1 segment connecting two points
width	float	

Table 5. Data set streams

the data set streams. The root of this tree is located in the lower right corner of the map. Cardinality: $2^{\sqrt{n}+2} - 2$

Field Name	Field Definition	Comments
gasline_ID	integer	external ID
gasline	line	1 segment connecting two points

Table 6. Data set gasline

Points of Interest   The data set *POI* (points of interest) in Table 7 contains points which are placed on n sloping, parallel lines with consistent distances. Cardinality: n^2

Field Name	Field Definition	Comments
POIname	string[15]	randomly generated
POI	point	
POItype	string[15]	6 types enumerated cyclic

Table 7. Data set POI (points of interest)

Scaling The Benchmark   The scaling of the benchmark is done by two parameters: the size of the map and the size of each data set. Although the data generator can generate data sets of any size, three data sets are used later in the paper with PostgreSQL and ROCK & ROLL, referred to in Table 8 as small, medium and large. For polygons and lines, this table gives both the number of features and the number of segments used to build the features.

Most of the data sets grow by about a factor of 10 with each size step. Exceptions are the data sets gaslines and streams, since they are represented as binary trees. For the data set roads, the number of roads grows about a factor of 3.3, while the number of line segments grows by a factor of 100.

Data Generation   The data is generated by a C++ program which provides classes for all the data sets used. The program has the command line `gen <Scale`

Feature	small	medium	large
scaling factor n	10	33	100
mapsize	1000	10,000	100,000
states polygons	9 (54)	121 (726)	1089 (6534)
landown polygons	100 (600)	1,089 (6,534)	10,000 (60,000)
landuse polygons	600 (1800)	6,534 (19602)	60,000 (180,000)
streams lines	14 (14)	62 (62)	2,046 (2046)
gaslines lines	30 (30)	126 (126)	4,096 (4,096)
roads lines	10 (60)	32(544)	100 (5,100)
POI points	100	1089	10.000

Table 8. Cardinalities. Values in brackets show the number of segments.

`Factor> <mapsize>`, where `<Scale Factor>` is the number n used to describe the cardinalities, and `<mapsize>` specifies the size of the map. For each data set an ASCII file is written, which contains the list of coordinates for each feature.

A sample of the generated spatial data is provided in figure 1.

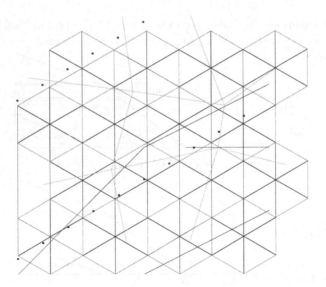

Fig. 1. Drawing of spatial parts of benchmark features

2.2   Tasks

This section provides an informal description of the tasks carried out as part of the benchmark. These tasks include updates to the database, construction of derived spatial values and queries.

Updates

Task 1: Insert new objects: This involves inserting new information into the database, updating all relevant indexes and topological information stored.
 – add a row of hexagons to the data set landown.
 – add the centre points of the hexagons from the data set states to POI.

Task 2: Delete objects: This involves removing the spatial and aspatial data from the database that was inserted by **Task 1**.
 input: landown, poi
 output: modified data sets landown, poi
     Cardinality: $n + n$

Set Operations

Task 3: Union polygons: Union all landuse polygons with neighbours of same landuse type.
 input: landuse
 output: new data set containing the result
     Cardinality: $\approx 0.8 * |landuse|$

Containment Operations

Task 4: Polygon contains point: Retrieve all POI which are inside Scotland
 input: states, POI
 output: POI.poiname, POI.poitype
     Cardinality: $\approx 9 = \frac{|POI|}{|states|} = \frac{n^2}{(\frac{n}{3})^2}$

Task 5: Polygon contains line: Retrieve all streams which are completely inside Scotland.
 input: streams, states
 output: streams.streamname
     Cardinality: ≈ 3

Task 6: Polygon contains polygon: Retrieve all forests which are completely inside Scotland.
 input: landuse, states
 output: landuse.landusename
     Cardinality: $\approx 11 \approx \frac{|landuse|/|landusetype|}{|states|} = \frac{6n^2/5}{(\frac{n}{3})^2}$

Task 7: Line contains Line: Retrieve all gas lines which are completely below a stream (with same location, since map is two dimensional).
 input: gaslines, streams
 output: gaslines.gasline_ID
     Cardinality: $\leq log_2|gaslines|$,

Task 8: Line contains point: Retrieve all points of interest on the road called A1.
 input: roads, POI
 output: POI.poiname, POI.POItype
     Cardinality: ≈ 0

Overlap Operations

Task 9: Polygon overlap line: Retrieve all roads which are at least partly inside Scotland.
input: states, roads
output: roads.roadname, roads.roadtype
      Cardinality: ≈ 4

Task 10: Polygon overlap polygon: Retrieve all forests which are at least partly inside Scotland.
input: states, landuse
output: landuse.landusename
      Cardinality: $\approx 11 \approx \frac{|landuse|/|landusetype|}{|states|} = \frac{6n^2/5}{(\frac{n}{3})^2}$

Task 11: Line overlap line: Retrieve all gas lines which are at least partly below a stream.
input: gaslines, stream
output: gaslines.gasline_ID
      Cardinality: $\leq log_2|gaslines|$, as in Task 10

Intersect Operations

Task 12: Line intersect line: Retrieve all streams crossed by a road
      input: streams, roads
output: streams.streamname
      Cardinality: $\leq |streams|$

Task 13: Line intersect polygon: Retrieve all roads which go through a forest.
input: landuse, roads
output: roads.roadname
      Cardinality: $\leq |roads|$

Adjacent Operations

Task 14: Polygon adjacent polygon: Retrieve all states which border the state Scotland.
input: states
output: states.statename
      Cardinality: 6

Task 15: Polygon adjacent line: Retrieve all polygons from landuse that are adjacent to the stream Dee.
input: landuse, streams
output: landuse.landusename
      Cardinality: ≈ 0

Task 16: Line connection: Retrieve all streams connected directly to the Dee.
      input: streams
output: streams.streamname
      Cardinality: 4

Search inside area

Task 17: Buffer search: Retrieve all polygons from landuse which are less than 200m from a stream.
input: landuse, streams
output: landuse.landusename, landuse.landusetype
    Cardinality: $\leq |landuse|$

Task 18: Window search: Retrieve all the POI, which are inside a rectangle of 10 km $\times$ 10 km with the tourist information in the center of the rectangle.
input: POI
output: POI.poiname
    Cardinality: ≈ 1

Measurement Operations

Task 19: Size of polygon: Compute the size of all polygons in landuse.
input: landuse
output: landuse.landusename, area(landuse.land)
    Cardinality: $|landuse|$

Task 20: Length of line: Compute the length of all streams.
input: streams
output: streams.streamname, length(streams.streamname)
    Cardinality: $|streams|$

Task 21: Distance to constant: Compute for all POI the distance to a specific tourist information office.
input: POI
output: POI.poiname, distance(Constant, POI.POI)
    Cardinality: $|POI|$

Analysis Operations

Task 22: Spatial aggregation: Compute the size of the area overlapped by the polygons from landuse and states.
input: landuse, states
output: area(landuse $\bigcup$ landown)
    Cardinality: 1

Task 23: Transitive closure: Find all the streams that might be affected by salmon nets at the mouth of the river Dee.
input: streams
output: streams.streamname
    Cardinality: $4|streams|$

Aspatial operations

Task 24: Aspatial selection: Retrieve all roads of type motorway with at least 3 lanes.
   input: roads
   output: roads.roadname, roads.lanes
       Cardinality: $\frac{4}{6}|roads|$
Task 25: Aspatial join: Select all stream and roads that have the same width.
   input: streams, roads
   output: streams.streamname, roads.roadname, streams.width
       Cardinality: $\frac{n}{3}\frac{2^{\sqrt{n+1}-2}}{3}$
Task 26: Aspatial aggregation: Compute the sum of values of land for each owner.
   input: landown
   output: landown.owner, Σlandown.value
       Cardinality: $\sqrt{|landown|}$

3   The Benchmark in PostgreSQL

PostgreSQL is an object-relational database developed at the University of California at Berkeley [24] [1]. It is a derivative of the influential POSTGRES system [21], which pioneered work on the extension of the relational model with abstract data types and active rules. In this context, it is the abstract data type (ADT) facility that is of most interest, in that it has been used to extend the primitive types of PostgreSQL with vector spatial data types. The ADTs supported by PostgreSQL are not unlike those that are beginning to be supported by relational database vendors.

The ADTs in PostgreSQL allow programmers to introduce new types into the kernel of the database by:

1. Defining *input* and *output* functions that map from an external (string) representation of an instance of the type to the internal, stored form of the instance. For example, a point that is represented to the user as the string *(1.0,2.0)* could be represented internally as a pair of reals stored in an R-tree.
2. Defining a collection of functions that take the user defined types as arguments and/or return them as results. This would allow, for example, a *polygon_area* function to take as input a value of type *polygon* and to return a real.

The functions that define new types are written in C, and are dynamically linked into the PostgreSQL system at runtime. There is also an interface that allows the indexing facilities of the basic system to be extended to support indexing of ADTs, for example, to allow spatial indexes to be used with spatial data types. The ADTs of PostgreSQL can be considered to provide low-level and

---

[1] The URL of the current release of PostgreSQL is http://www.postgresql.org

potentially dangerous facilities for adding efficient extensions to the database for particular domains. They are potentially dangerous because incorrect ADT definitions can easily corrupt a database. However, they help to overcome the limited programming facilities that have traditionally restricted the use of the relational model for storing complex data types, such as those associated with spatial databases.

3.1 Data Model

The implementation of the benchmark exploited extensions to a collection of spatial data types that are supplied with the PostgreSQL system. The spatial types introduced into PostgreSQL are: *point*, which consists of a pair of real numbers; *lseg*, which consists of a pair of points; *path*, which consists of a list of points; and *polygon*, which consists of a list of points. All spatial types are indexed using an R-tree, and algorithms are largely derived from those provided in [17]. The PostgreSQL tables used by the benchmark are defined in figure 2.

```
CREATE TABLE landown (              CREATE TABLE streams (
        land_nr    int4,                   streamname  char16,
        land       polygon,                stream      lseg,
        owner      char16,                 width       float8);
        value      float8);
                                    CREATE TABLE gaslines (
CREATE TABLE states (                       gasline_ID  int4,
        statename  char16,                  gasline     lseg);
        state      polygon,
        population int4);           CREATE TABLE pois (
                                            poiname     char16
CREATE TABLE landuse (                      poi         point,
        landusename char16,                 poitype     char16);
        land        polygon,
        landusetype char16);

CREATE TABLE roads (
        roadname   char16,
        road       path,
        roadtype   char16,
        lanes      int4,
        width      float8);
```

Fig. 2. Table definitions for benchmark in PostgreSQL

3.2 Tasks

All interaction with the database in the benchmark is carried out using SQL, which was always used embedded in C programs. For the sake of conciseness, only a few representative tasks are presented here, and only the SQL and not the surrounding C programs, are presented.

Task 4: Polygon contains point: This is a spatial join operation, where points of interest are retrieved when they are inside the polygon that is the state attribute of Scotland.

```
SELECT pois.poiname, pois.poitype
FROM pois, states
WHERE states.statename = "Scotland"
AND pt_in_poly(pois.poi, states.state)
```

Task 9: Polygon overlap line: This is similar to Task 7, except that the spatial join is based on the overlap operation involving paths and polygons.

```
SELECT roads.roadname, roads.roadtype
FROM roads, states
WHERE states.statename = "Scotland"
AND path_ovr_poly(roads.road, states.state)
```

Task 14: Polygon adjacent polygon: This is a topological self join using the adjacency relationship on states.

```
SELECT S1.statename
FROM states S1, states S2
WHERE S2.statename = "Scotland"
AND poly_adj_poly(S2.state, S1.state)
```

4   The Benchmark in ROCK & ROLL

The ROCK & ROLL deductive object-oriented database is built around three components:

The object model OM: The underlying data model is an object-oriented semantic data model that supports a conventional set of object modelling concepts – object identity, inheritance, sets, lists, aggregates, etc.

The imperative language ROCK: The language ROCK allows OM objects to be created, retrieved and manipulated. It provides a conventional set of programming constructs (loops, if statements, etc), and can be used to define methods on OM types.

The deductive language ROLL: The language ROLL allows deductive rules to be defined that express derived properties of the objects stored in the database in a declarative manner. ROLL can be used to express both queries and methods, but contains no facilities for describing control flow or updates. This latter feature makes ROLL amenable to optimisation using extensions of earlier deductive query optimisation techniques [7].

The fact that ROCK and ROLL share the same type system, namely OM, means that they can be integrated without manifesting the impedance mismatches that are characteristic of other multi-language systems [3].

In the ODESSA (Object-oriented DEductive Spatial Systems Architecture) project [9], the kernel of ROCK & ROLL has been extended to provide support for the ROSE algebra [13]. The ROSE algebra is a vector spatial algebra that maps all spatial values onto a finite resolution grid called a realm. The operations of the ROSE algebra have desirable computational complexity[12], and ODESSA exploits a novel implementation strategy whereby the realm is not explicitly stored [16]. The implementation of ODESSA also corrects aspects of the original ROSE algebra proposal, in which problems arose with certain geometries.

The ROSE algebra provides three spatial data types: `points` – a set of point values; `lines` – a set of paths connecting realm points; `regions` – a set of areas, possibly containing holes. All operations on the ROSE algebra are closed – they return values that are themselves either scalar or points, lines or regions values.

The benchmarked implementation of ROCK & ROLL uses the commercial object database ObjectStore for persistence.

4.1 Data Model

In ODESSA, `points`, `lines` and `regions` have been added to the OM data model as primitive types. This means that OM objects can have attributes that take on spatial values. The benchmark builds upon the straightforward class hierarchy given in figure 3.

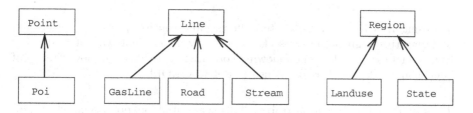

Fig. 3. Inheritance hierarchy for benchmark

The OM classes `Point`, `Line` and `Region` each have an attribute of type `points`, `lines` and `regions` respectively. For example, the definition of `Region` is illustrated in figure 4. These classes are used as placeholders for generic functionality, such as that used to populate the database from text files. These classes are then subclassed by the domain classes used by the benchmark. For example, `State` is defined as in figure 5.

4.2 Queries

All interaction with the database takes place using ROCK & ROLL programs. In practice, any task that can be carried out using ROLL can also be carried

```
type GEO.Region:
    properties:
      public:
        RegionsRep : regions;
    ROCK:
        new();
        readData();
        print();
        ...
end_type;
```

Fig. 4. Type definition for **region**

```
type GEO.State:
    specialises: Region;
    properties:
        public:
            Name: string,
            Number: int;
    ROCK:
        new();
        readData();
        print();
end_type
```

Fig. 5. Type definition for `State`

out using ROCK, but ROLL often allows more concise query expression and is declarative – an optimiser seeks to identify an efficient way of evaluating ROLL queries and rules. The following code fragments illustrate how a range of benchmark tasks are carried out using ROCK & ROLL.

Task 4: Polygon contains point: This is a spatial join operation, where points of interest are retrieved if they are inside a region. This can be expressed in either ROCK or ROLL. The first version illustrated below uses ROLL to obtain in s the object identifier of the `State` with name equal to `Scotland`, and then uses a ROCK `foreach` loop to iterate through the points of interest, checking to see if they are `inside` s.

```
var s:= [ any S | get_Name@S:State == "Scotland" ];

foreach p in Poi do begin
    if (get_PointsRep@p inside get_RegionsRep@s)
        write get_Name@p, nl;
end
```

The following version relies more on the embedded ROLL query, and the way in which the query is evaluated is implicit; an explicit ROCK loop is used only to generate the results:

```
var ps:= [ all P | get_Name@S:State == "Scotland",
                   get_RegionsRep@S == SR,
                   get_PointsRep@P == PR,
                   PR inside SR ];


foreach p in ps do
begin
    write "Point ", get_Name@p, " lies inside Scotland", nl;
end
```

Task 9: Polygon overlap line: The following ROLL query retrieves all Roads that either **intersect** with Scotland or that are **inside** Scotland.

```
[ all R | get_Name@S:State == "Scotland",
          get_RegionsRep@S == SR,
          get_LinesRep@R == RR,
          RR intersects SR
        ;
          get_Name@S:State == "Scotland",
          get_RegionsRep@S == SR,
          get_LinesRep@R == RR,
          RR inside SR ];
```

Task 14: Polygon adjacent polygon: Self joins are straightforward to express in logic languages, as can be seen from the following:

```
[ all A | get_RegionsRep@A:State == AR,
          get_RegionsRep@S:State == SR,
          AR adjacent SR,
          get_Name@S == "Scotland" ];
```

5   Results

This section presents the results of running the benchmark on the PostgreSQL and ODESSA platforms, with a view to allowing comparison of the different implementations and scaling of the specific approaches. The figures were obtained on a 143 Mhz Sun UltraSPARC1 with 64Mbytes of RAM. All figures are elapsed times, and are the average of three distinct runs.

Tables 9, 10 and 11 give the times obtained for PostgreSQL, ROCK and ROLL, respectively, so that the scalability of the individual approaches can be assessed. The following can be observed:

Task	Small	Medium	Large
1	2.50	3.20	4.20
2	1.50	5.50	55.90
3	33.20	3803.50	20419.20
4	0.95	1.33	4.30
5	0.90	0.95	1.85
6	1.13	3.08	20.95
7	1.00	3.00	2176.03
8	0.93	1.33	6.67
9	0.97	1.25	3.67
10	1.10	2.75	17.77
11	1.30	3.38	2118.10
12	1.30	3.50	622.63
13	1.75	13.97	317.50
14	0.90	1.25	3.67
15	1.10	3.50	24.98
16	0.90	0.98	1.90
18	0.90	1.38	5.23
19	1.45	6.70	98.71
20	0.90	1.08	2.80
23	1.00	1.90	4.50
24	0.90	0.95	0.98
25	0.90	1.50	63.77
26	1.00	1.50	5.40

Table 9. Benchmark results for PostgreSQL for all data sets.

Task	Small	Medium	Large
1	15.83	43.50	130.57
2	4.89	60.65	637.19
3	3.09	129.27	806.86
4	0.74	6.54	113.15
5	0.03	0.08	8.66
6	2.52	95.89	163.15
7	0.05	1.05	944.60
8	0.08	2.86	144.12
9	0.10	10.47	23.66
10	8.15	80.61	195.18
11	0.21	1.22	1077.11
12	0.48	52.15	4142.08
13	0.22	103.12	1252.53
14	0.01	0.07	7.12
15	0.10	42.29	209.14
16	0.01	1.53	22.96
19	4.53	128.84	1522.61
20	0.00	0.01	0.04
23	0.41	4.59	37.98
24	0.00	0.15	11.56
25	0.01	0.12	14.20
26	1.09	51.36	1261.26

Table 10. Benchmark results for ROCK for all data sets.

Task	Small	Medium	Large
1	6.68	85.55	1769.32
2	20.99	785.20	4135.72
4	1.10	7.22	232.88
5	0.06	0.08	16.30
6	2.78	148.55	669.63
7	0.01	1.15	972.16
8	0.10	4.86	284.31
9	0.14	4.99	30.84
10	0.17	307.35	1098.68
11	0.39	1.12	1195.64
12	0.57	69.87	4365.22
13	5.23	96.48	570.53
14	0.01	0.02	4.30
15	0.09	124.97	589.70
16	0.01	2.56	27.92
19	2.40	89.28	1055.25
20	0.01	0.30	7.73
23	1.50	48.20	255.72
24	0.00	0.16	12.76
25	0.01	0.41	18.57
26	0.94	44.25	1139.89

Table 11. Benchmark results for ROLL for all data sets.

PostgreSQL: Most of the benchmark tasks are supported rather well by Post-greSQL. The current ADTs do not support buffer search (*Task 17*). The transitive closure query (*Task 23*) has been carried out using the recursive facilities of PostgreSQL.

The performance of PostgreSQL is generally good, and most tasks scale well across the different data sets. This stems from the fact that PostgreSQL is able to make good use of its spatial index during query evaluation to restrict the number of pairwise comparisons of spatial values carried out. Where PostgreSQL scales less well in query tasks, for example in Tasks *7, 11* and *12*, this is probably because the minimum bounding rectangles around streams are often quite large, and thus are not very effective at narrowing the search space.

ROCK: Most of the benchmark tasks have been supported in ROCK. Those that are absent include buffer search (*Task 17*) and measurement operations (*Tasks 21,22*), as these are problematic in the ROSE algebra due to the distortions associated with the finite resolution geometry.

The implementations of most tasks in ROCK involve explicit loops, some-times nested, through stored collections, testing for spatial properties. This means, broadly speaking, that the best ROCK can hope to do is scale in pro-portion with the number of times that the most nested statement is executed. For example, in *Task 4*, the containment test is executed approximately 100 times in the small data set, 1000 times in the medium data set and 10000 times in the large data set. The increase in task time for small to medium of *0.74* to *6.54* seconds is broadly in line with the number of loop iterations, while the increase for the large data set to *113.15* seconds is slightly slower than might have been hoped for. The implementation of the ROSE algebra, in which intersections are computed and stored explicitly at insertion time, means that the more intersections exist in a data item, the slower will be the algorithms that run over the data item. Changes to the number of segments that intersect with the boundary of Scotland could have the effect of slowing the intersection test, but this should not explain the jump in execution time on its own, as initial intersection tests involve minimum bounding rectangles. Where the ROCK times deteriorate rapidly with growing data sets, this is where the number of inner loop executions is also large. For example, in *Task 11*, the number of iterations in the small, medium and large data sets are, respectively, (14×30) 420, (62×126) 7812 and (2046×4096) 8,280,416, so the time taken to perform individual membership tests shows no sign of increasing as the data set grows.

ROLL: To keep its logical semantics straightforward, ROLL is not able to up-date the underlying database (as in *Task 1*) or to construct new spatial values (as in *Task 3*). Thus where figures are included for ROLL for such activities, ROLL is used to carry out only part of the relevant task.

The implementations of the tasks in ROLL do not make explicit how the tasks should be carried out. In practice, query planning is carried out by the optimiser described in [7]. This optimiser has been extended so that it is aware of the spatial operators that can appear in queries, but currently does no query planning that takes account of the semantics of spatial constructs. For example, it does not make use of the R-tree that is used to store ROSE algebra constructs (and which is used extensively when the database is updated). As a result, ROLL queries, like their ROCK counterparts, essentially execute nested loop joins over collections of spatially referenced objects, and scale broadly in line with the number of spatial operations in the inner loop. An extension to the ROLL optimiser could therefore have a significant effect on the time taken to evaluate most of the example queries.

Comparing ROLL with ROCK in the benchmark, ROLL queries are occasionally faster than their ROCK counterparts, but most perform similarly, or up to 5 times slower, for larger data sets. This is largely due to the fact that ROLL uses a set-oriented evaluation strategy, and thus allocates and deallocates significant amounts of store during query processing. The set-oriented semantics turn out not to be particularly effective in avoiding repetition of effort in this benchmark.

The following can be observed in terms of the relative merits of the different approaches:

1. Inserting new data into the database and deleting existing data from the database is generally quicker in PostgreSQL than in ODESSA. This is to be expected, as considerable effort is expended at insertion time in the ROSE algebra to resolve interactions between values that are being updated and other spatial values. This up-front effort in the ROSE algebra is central to the clean semantics that it supports, and allows other spatial operations to be supported efficiently [12].
2. The effective use of spatial indexes at query time is generally much more important than the performance of pairwise operations on spatial values. The fact that the ROSE algebra operations have attractive complexity measures compared with those implemented in PostgreSQL makes little difference in most of the query tasks, and in most cases PostgreSQL scales much better than ODESSA. The only task in which the complexity of the pairwise operations seems to dominate is *Task 3*, where ODESSA scales much better than PostgreSQL.
3. The poor performance of ROLL in the benchmark stems largely from the failure of the optimiser to exploit the R-tree that exists in the ODESSA system. This in turn is because the ROLL optimiser is largely a logical optimiser [7], and a key requirement here is for a range of physical optimisations.

6   Conclusions

This paper has presented a vector based spatial benchmark that can be used to test both the functionality and performance of spatial database systems. The benchmark includes a range of query and update tasks over synthetic data sets, and can be implemented with moderate effort on different platforms. The intention in providing a fairly large number of test queries and programs has been to allow fine grained analysis of the performance of systems. This was important to us in the development of the ODESSA system, and we believe should be of interest to the developers of future spatial database systems.

The comparison presented in this paper, between PostgreSQL and ODESSA, shows that the benchmark can be used to differentiate between the performance of different spatial database systems, and that the tests stretch the different systems in different tasks. The benchmark can also be used as a test suite for evaluating the reliability of new database systems and implementation techniques. For example, it was implementing the VESPA benchmark on ODESSA that revealed to us an error in the underlying geometry on which the ROSE algebra builds; the resolution of this problem is described in [8].

Acknowledgements: This work is supported by the UK Engineering and Physical Sciences Research Council, whose support we are pleased to acknowledge. We are also grateful for the contribution of Reto Hafner, who implemented most of the benchmark in ROCK & ROLL.

References

1. A.I. Abdelmoty, N.W. Paton, M.H. Williams, A.A.A. Fernandes, M.L. Barja, and A. Dinn. Geographic Data Handling in a Deductive Object-Oriented Database. In D. Karagiannis, editor, *Proc. 5th Int. Conf. on Databases and Expert Systems Applications (DEXA)*, pages 445–454. Springer-Verlag, 1994.
2. D. Arctur, E. Anwar, J. Alexander, S. Charkravarthy, Y. Chung, M. Cobb, and K. Shaw. Comparison and benchmarks for import of VPF geographic data from object-oriented and relational database files. In *Proc. SSD 95*, pages 368–384. Springer-Verlag, 1995.
3. M.L. Barja, N.W. Paton, A.A.A. Fernandes, M.H. Williams, and A. Dinn. An Effective Deductive Object-Oriented Database Through Language Integration. In J. Bocca, M. Jarke, and C. Zaniolo, editors, *Proc. 20th Int. Conf. on Very Large Data Bases (VLDB)*, pages 463–474. Morgan-Kaufmann, 1994.
4. P.A. Boncz and M.L. Kersten. Monet: An Impressionist Sketch of an Advanced Database System. In *Proc. Basque Int. Wshp. on Information Technology*, pages 240–251. IEEE Press, 1995.
5. M. Carey, D. DeWitt, G. Graefe, D. Haight, J. Richardson, D. Schuh, E. Shekita, and S. Vandenberg. The EXODUS Extensible DBMS Project: An Overview. In S. Zdonik and D. Maier, editors, *Readings in Object-Oriented Databases*, CA 94303-9953, 1990. Morgan Kaufman Publishers, Inc.
6. S.W. Dietrich, M. Brown, E. Cortes-Rello, and S. Wunderlin. A Practitioners Introduction to Database Performance Benchmarks and Measurements. *The Computer Journal*, 35(4):322–331, 1992.
7. A. Dinn, N.W. Paton, M.H. Williams, A.A.A. Fernandes, and M.L. Barja. The Implementation of a Deductive Query Language Over an Object-Oriented Database. In T.W. Ling, A.O. Mendelzon, and L. Vieille, editors, *Proc. 4th Intl. Conf. on Deductive Object-Oriented Databases*, pages 143–160. Springer-Verlag, 1995.
8. A. Dinn, M.H. Williams, and N.W. Paton. Ensuring Geometric Consistency in the ROSE Algebra for Spatial Datatypes. In *submitted for publication*, 1997.
9. A.A.A. Fernandes, A. Dinn, N.W. Paton, M.H. Williams, and O. Liew. Extending a Deductive Object-Oriented Database System with Spatial Data Handling Facilities. *Information and Software Technology*, 41:483–497, 1999.

10. K. Gardels. SEQUOIA 2000 amd Geographic Information: The Guernewood Ge-oprocessor. In T. Waugh and R. Healey, editors, *Proc. SDH*, pages 1072–1085. Taylor & Francis, 1994.
11. O. Gunther, V. Oria, P. Picouet, J-M Saglio, and M. Scholl. Benchmarking Spatial Joins A La Carte. In *Proc. SSDBM*, pages 32–40. IEEE Press, 1998.
12. R.H. Guting, T. de Ridder, and M. Schneider. Implementation of the ROSE Alge-bra: Efficient Algorithms for Realm-Based Spatial Data Types. In M.J. Egenhofer and J.R. Herring, editors, *Proc. 4th Int. Symposium on Large Spatial Databases (SSD)*, pages 196–215. Springer-Verlag, 1995.
13. R.H. Guting and M. Schneider. Realm-Based Spatial Data Types: The ROSE Algebra. *VLDB Journal*, 4(2):243–286, 1995.
14. E.G. Hoel and H. Samet. Benchmarking Spatial Join Operations with Spatial Output. In *Proc. VLDB*, pages 606–618, 1995.
15. S. Morehouse. ARC/INFO: A Geo-Relational Model for Spatial Information. In *Proceedings of 7th Int. Symposium on Computer Assisted Cartography*, pages 388–398, Washington, DC, 1986.
16. V. Muller, N.W. Paton, A.A.A. Fernandes, A. Dinn, and M.H. Williams. Virtual Realms: An Efficient Implementation Strategy for Finite Resolution Spatial Data Types. In M.J. Kraak and M. Molenaar, editors, *Proc. 7th SDH*, pages 697–709. Taylor & Francis, 1996.
17. J. O'Rourke, editor. *Computational Geometry in C*. Cambridge University Press, New York, 1994.
18. J. Patel. Building a Scalable Geo-Spatial DBMS: Technology, Implementation, and Evaluation. In *Proc. SIGMOD Conf.*, pages 336–374. ACM Press, 1997.
19. M. Stonebraker, R. Agrawal, U. Dayal, E. Neuhold, and A. Rueter. DBMS Research At A Crossroads: The Vienna Update. In *Proc. of the 19th VLDB*, pages 688–692, Dublin, Ireland, 1993. R. Agrawal et al (Eds).
20. M. Stonebraker, J. Frew, K. Gardens, and J. Merideth. The sequoia 2000 storage benchmark. In *Proc. ACM SIGMOD*, pages 2–11, 1993.
21. M. Stonebraker and G. Kemnitz. The POSTGRES Next-generation Database Management System. *Communications of the ACM*, 34(10):78–92, October 1991.
22. T. Theodoridis, R. Silva, and M. Nascimento. On the Generation of Spatiotempo-ral Datasets. In *Proc. 6th Int. Symposium on Spatial Databases*, pages 147–164. Springer Verlag, 1999.
23. Y. Theodoridis, T. Sellis, A.N. Papadopoulos, and Y. Manolopoulos. Specifications for Efficient Indexing in Spatiotemporal Databases. In *Proc. SSDBM*, pages 123–132. IEEE Press, 1998.
24. A. Yu and J. Chen. The Postgres95 User Manual. Technical report, Computer Science Division, Dept of EECS, University of California at Berkeley, 1995.

Collection Views: Dynamically Composed Views Which Inherit Behaviour

Peter M.D. Gray, Graham J.L. Kemp, and Patrick Brunschwig, and Suzanne Embury *

Department of Computing Science, University of Aberdeen, King's College, Aberdeen, Scotland, AB24 3UE

Abstract. Collection Views provide a means of coercing an object (or set of objects) of one type into an equivalent set of objects of another, more useful type. For example, in some circumstances it may be more convenient to view a shape object as a set of coordinate objects — in order to use a method to display the shape on the screen, for example. Collection views provide the DBMS with information on how to perform this coercion automatically. The DBMS can then adapt sets of values retrieved from some level of an is-part-of hierarchy, so that they are usable by pre-defined method functions defined on collections of parts. This adaptation is performed by composing a series of functions at runtime, rather than requiring the user to anticipate the queries that will be asked and create many stored classes to support them. Collection views thus allow stored data to inherit method behaviour defined in external applications, withour requiring the user to modify that behaviour or to store modified copies of the data. We have extended the P/FDM system to support collection views, and have demonstrated their utility by a bioinformatics example.

Keywords: Views, OODB, Bioinformatics, Inheritance

1 Introduction

In our research with scientific databases we have found the need to adapt external method code to work with sets of stored data values which are not at the chosen level of aggregation in an `is-part-of` hierarchy. In the course of doing this we have found the need for a kind of view over collections of objects at various such levels of aggregation. This *collection view* is distinguished by a particular kind of transitivity (or inheritance) based on the abstract `is-part-of` relationship. At first sight it fits the usual kind of subtype inheritance used in databases, but this turns out not to be so.

Consider, for example, a hierarchy of geographic entities at various levels, associated with spatial regions each of which encloses a collection of non-overlapping regions at the next level. For example, we could have countries related to their provinces, within which are districts within which are towns. On an E-R

---

* Present address: Dept. of Computer Science, Cardiff University, PO Box 916, Cardiff, Wales, UK CF2 3XF

B. Lings and K. Jeffery (Eds.): BNCOD 17, LNCS 1832, pp. 102–121, 2000.

diagram these correspond to distinct entity classes joined together by a hierarchy of one-many relationships. Suppose we want a view that gives us aggregate data for all the towns in a district, or all the provinces in a country, in order to compute demographic statistics or the economic profile of a region. In each case the relationship is implied by the transitivity of existing relationships. Thus, before applying the aggregate function which expects a set of towns as its argument, we make use of the "part-of" relationships to turn a province or a country into a set of towns. Unlike normal views, where we derive virtual (non-persistent) objects as instances of classes, here we derive relationships to sets of existing objects. We wish to avoid storing these derived relationships persistently, since they are based on transitivity, with many possible combinations that can quickly be derived at runtime.

As a related example, consider the case where we abstract down from a town to a geometric point representing the town centre. Once again, we might wish to form a view representing a derived relationship to a bag of such points.

The same considerations apply to the well known bill-of-materials hierarchy, based on `is-part-of` relationships between components at different named levels of sub-assembly, ranging from aircraft wings down to fasteners. This is, of course, very similar to the way in which large protein molecules are made up of chains of residues which are made up of atoms. We wish to define methods on sets of components that are related to a common higher-level assembly. These methods could compute bulk properties such as average cost or total weight, or else print frequency histograms, etc.

From a conceptual modelling viewpoint, the important idea is that we can define various methods on the derived sets to compute or display aggregate values. For example, a method could compute the centroid of a set of points. By exploiting the transitivity of the part-of relationships, it could be applied to a whole county or country. Alternatively, a weighted centroid could be defined on a set of town, with towns weighted according to population. Thus these methods are defined on abstract *collection classes* which are populated by derived relationships from different starting classes (see Figure 1). Thus the methods define a formal interface to the abstract class (in the OOP sense), specifying behaviour.

We have found this representation to be a great improvement on alternatives. Firstly, we have simplified the ER diagram by separating collection class interfaces clearly off to the side and avoiding many extra subtype arrows. Next, we have used runtime generation of composed functions to reduce the number of view definitions that have to be stored (for example adapted definitions of the centroid function for each level of the view hierarchy). Also, by using composed views to adapt the data at run-time, we have avoided having to have many stored subtypes containing derived data. These would have taken up space and needed specialised updates whenever the base data was changed. We also feel that this insight is a valuable contribution to E-R modelling. It arose first in a real protein database application, which we explain below, where our partners were scientists with a strong background in OOP techniques, but not in schemas!

We have implemented this on the P/FDM object database [11], which has a schema founded on the E-R Model with SubTypes. It uses functions to hide the distinction between derived and stored properties. In consequence, it is good at computing over collections of scientific data stored according to an E-R model. Functions are defined on classes, and thus behave like methods that do not change state. By integrating collection views with the query language we are able to use normal selection predicates to compute particular starting sets from which the collection class instances can be derived. Thus we can take advantage of the database software for processing large collections, and use the optimiser to plan use of indexes as appropriate.

We believe that the ideas set forward below could also be introduced into a well structured object query language such as OQL, or else through classes that pre-process calls to JDBC. However, it is not essential to do this. The real need is for a clear conceptual separation of this kind of view class in an E-R diagram, even when the classes are implemented in an *ad hoc* fashion as interfaces to Java or C++, or else to legacy code through CORBA object wrappers [13]. They are applicable where the data are structured around part-whole relationships, with various levels of repeated subunits, which is not uncommon.

Below, we shall introduce the protein schema from which the examples in this paper are drawn. Next, we compare and contrast the class/type hierarchies seen in OOP and object databases. We then describe the concept of collection views and how they relate to a particular kind of OO Design Pattern [8]. We then see how they are formally described and the rules for their use. Finally, we show how these have been implemented in the P/FDM object database, and we give examples of their use.

2   Protein Structure Domain: Motivation for Collection Views

The idea of collection views presented in this paper was motivated by our participation in a collaborative bioinformatics project. As part of this, the project partners had several meetings to agree a schema for protein structure data. Of particular interest is the three-dimensional structure of proteins for which the basic data are available as atomic coordinates and distributed by PDB [2] on behalf of scientists world-wide. These data are of great importance to a large number of scientists in different disciplines, working on drug design, or understanding a new protein, or on its relationship to genome sequences.

Proteins are molecules which are found in all living organisms and perform a variety of biochemical functions. Each protein contains at least one polypeptide chain, which is made up of hundreds of amino-acid residues. The twenty different kinds of amino-acid residues found in proteins differ in size, charge, and various other properties. The order in which the residues occur in the sequence determines how the protein chain will fold in three dimensions, and it is the resulting three dimensional shape which gives a protein its particular biochemical activity.

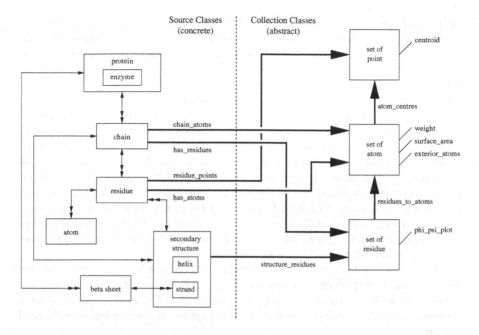

Fig. 1. Extract from the protein structure database. Thick arrows represent collection view adapter functions which populate collection classes, shown as the boxes they point to. Thin arrows represent relationships named in the schema. Nested boxes represent specialised subtypes of the enclosing box.

Protein structure can be viewed at different levels. The *primary structure* is the sequence of amino-acid residues in a protein chain, and is often represented as a string of characters with different letters standing for different residue kinds. At the next level, sections of protein chains fold into regular shapes (*secondary structure elements*) which are stabilised by hydrogen bonds between backbone atoms. Alpha-helices and strands are the most common examples of such structures. Each strand will lie adjacent to one or more others to form a beta-sheet. The *tertiary structure* of a protein is a description of its conformation in terms of the coordinates of its individual atoms. An extract from the schema diagram for our protein structure database is shown on the left side of Figure 1. A more complete description is given in [5,10].

From the object-oriented viewpoint, one of the most significant aspects is that the same set of objects may be viewed at different levels of abstraction, ignoring differences of detail that are important at lower levels. Thus a helix object may be viewed as an ordered sequence of residues (ignoring 3-D coordinates) which may in turn be viewed as a set of residues (unordered) which can be viewed as a merged set of atoms with some derived property (weight, surface area). However, it is also meaningful to ask for the weight of a chain, or the weight of an individual residue. In designing the schema, we wanted to capture the notion of kinds of protein fragment to which functions such as weight or surface area could be applied. Therefore, our early schema diagrams included classes like *set-of-residue* and *set-of-atom*, and in order to inherit functions defined on these classes we found ourselves over-using *is-a* inheritance arrows. This confused the schema diagram. It was also inappropriate since it was only *behaviour*, and not *structure*, that we wanted to inherit from classes like *set-of-atom*.

One thing that shows that the view hierarchy is not inheriting structure, is that the means of identifying instances changes as we proceed through the hierarchy, since we are looking at objects (sets of residues, sets of atoms) at different levels of aggregation. By contrast, in an *is-a* hierarchy, the means of identifying instances is the same at all levels and all specialised classes inherit the key definition defined at the top of that hierarchy. For example, a *student* instance is completely identified by virtue of being a person, as also is a more specialised *foreign student*. Thus, while our early schema diagrams showed classes like *chain* and *residue* related by an *is-a* relationship to *set-of-atom*, these classes were not in fact related in that way.

This led us to introduce a special kind of inheritance hierarchy for collection views which would clarify the schema diagram by considering collection view inheritance as if in "another dimension" (see right of Figure 1). This also saves one from a combinatorial explosion of subtype inheritance arrows, as explained earlier.

2.1   Objects in Object Databases and OOP: Classes and Class Hierarchies

Another way to see the difference between the two kinds of inheritance is to look at how they are used by OO programmers and in OODB. Class declarations in an object-oriented programming language are used by the programmer to describe the structures of temporary objects holding evanescent (non-persistent) variables. They are needed to describe the computations performed using those variables; thus they emphasise procedural *behaviour* which may be inherited. For example, a C++ programmer will often introduce extra *slots* into an object which act as instance variables holding extra state information, to be used by a group of methods (procedures) that use these variables as a kind of shared workspace in their computations.

In contrast, a semantic data modelling approach leads to class declarations which describe data values which are of interest long term, emphasising their *structure*, i.e. the attributes and relationships of concepts in the domain which are to be stored. This structure may be inherited. We believe that a semantic data modelling approach leads to subclass-superclass relationships which are better suited to the integration of long term persistent data. The importance of the introduction of collection views is that it allows one to add extra functionality without confusing the subclass hierarchies.

We believe it helps to be aware of the difference between these two kinds of relationships, and we have a built a system in which we can formalise the difference. Thus, in this paper, we describe an investigation of *collection views*, through which behaviour is inherited, in addition to having *is a subclass of* relationships through which both structure and behaviour are inherited. It turns out that *collection views* are another kind of *user-defined transitive relationship* with its own kind of transitivity, to add to those studied by [17].

3 Views in Database Schema Architecture

The original notion of views in databases comes from the definition of *external schema* or *subschema* in the ANSI-SPARC document of 1975. This described a database architecture with a central conceptual schema defining all data items, their types and constraints and relationships. The conceptual schema was viewed through alternative subschemas suited to different applications.

The ANSI-SPARC idea of a sub-schema was twofold. Firstly it only showed an application a subset of the available entity classes and data item names, which helped to provide privacy and access control. Secondly and more importantly, it served to isolate an application program from minor changes to the conceptual schema as it evolved. It might be that some of the data item names were changed. More significantly, some data items that were stored in an early version of the schema might be derived items in later versions. This might be because of a change in units used to record a value, or because the schema now stored more precise details from which the value could be derived. In this case the job of the subschema was to convert and map from the conceptual schema item values onto values expected by the application. We should now say that it helped to provide a *constant interface protocol*, much as an object presents to the outside world. It is this latter aspect that collection views are providing.

We consider a *collection view* to be a kind of adapter or coercion mechanism that takes any object of a given class or type and derives on demand a collection of objects of an adapted type, so as to fit a desired tool or method. It thus presents a constant interface, as just described, to a method which is possibly legacy code, adapting it to an evolving collection of objects. Each such "view" is basically a derived relationship, without the privacy aspects of a subschema.

Views in OODB

Early proposals for parametrised views were made by Abiteboul and Bonner [1]. A review of these and other kinds of object views is given by Chan and Kerr [3]. A commercial implementation of View expressions in OQL is described by Florescu *et al.* [6]. View expressions are queries which can use the full expressivity of OQL and which can derive subsets of an existing class, or else sets of constructed tuples which may contain object identifiers. They are intended to help in reusing cached results of OQL queries, and do not define their results as members of derived classes with method interfaces. In the MultiView system [14] a view is formed by applying a query operator to a source class (or classes) that restructures the source class's type and/or extent membership in order to form a virtual class with a type and extent derived from its source class(es).

A similar concept is *application views*, introduced by Fowler [7]. Similar types of view are provided in OPM [4] which is in use for genome databases. The essential point is that an application view is based on a one-to-one mapping from a subset of a persistent source class, selected by a predicate, onto a derived class. The selected objects form the extent of a new derived class with new methods. Thus the view perceives a subset of the database objects, for example proteins with no helices. Methods can be selectively chosen ("inherited") from those applicable to the source class, or derived methods added. However, the examples given concentrate on methods applying to individual instances and not to collections as a whole.

The advantage of the one-to-one mapping is that it makes it possible to have methods that appear to update objects in a view but which actually apply the update to the corresponding stored objects. This is not suitable for collection views, since the methods are intended to apply to the results of a one-to-many mapping. Also it is much more straightforward to make updates direct to the source class, or else through a separate application view.

It would be possible to integrate collection views with application views. For example, we could derive a collection view starting from a particular class in an application view. However, this is future work and it would be much harder to represent clearly in an E-R diagram.

Of course, it may be desirable to cache a derived view, where this takes a considerable effort to compute and many clients wish to access it. This then leads to interest in triggered rules to update the cached view following small changes to the underlying database. This is an active area of research [16] but it is largely orthogonal to this paper. Instead, we are concerned with uses of inheritance in views which support OOP interfaces to collections at different levels of aggregation taken from persistent object-oriented data, and we are aware of very little other work on this.

4   Collection Views as Adapters in OOP

Once one has the idea of a view as an adapter which puts a new face on the class and provides it with a desired interface then one can see a corresponding framework used in object-oriented programming. Figure 2 is based on the well known text on Design Patterns [8]. Using standard OM/T notation, it shows how a `TextView` class member is adapted to look like a **Shape** class member. More precisely, it acquires an *interface* like a Shape member. This is done by defining a sub-type `TextShape` which inherits the interface, but also includes an extra slot `text` pointing to the `TextView` member. Method definitions in the sub-type override those in the supertype and compute the desired interface values by calling up methods on the TextView member. Thus the data items (slot values) in the Shape object are filled in by calculation or copying from the TextView object and any other related objects, as defined in the body of the adapter method.

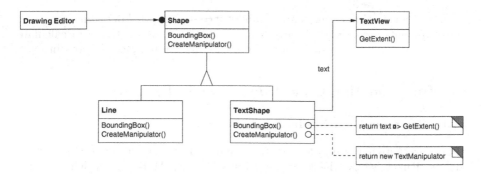

Fig. 2. Adapter pattern. BoundingBox requests, declared in class Shape, are converted to GetExtent requests defined in TextView. Since TextShape adapts TextView to the Shape interface, the drawing editor can reuse the otherwise incompatible TextView class. (Adapted from [8])

The interesting thing about this technique is that it can create the derived or adapted object of class Shape at run-time and the object need not persist after the running of the application. This contrasts with objects of the persistent class TextView, from which it is derived. This class will have all of its instances held in persistent storage (a database). We do not wish to store the derived adapter objects persistently, since they take up space and would need maintaining.

Thus we want to include classes like **TextShape** on the ER diagram, as shown on the right of Figure 1. Just as **TextShape** is not simply a supertype of **TextView**, so **set-of-atom** is not simply a supertype of **residue**. Instead, they are classes used to describe computational behaviour, where the behaviour is encapsulated in method definitions (operations). The important missing links are filled in by *adapter functions* (shown by thick arrows) which complete the connection to data stored in the persistent classes. (These hide the implementation of the adapter, which differs in detail from that in Figure 1). We must not read these arrows as *is-a*, instead we read them as *can be viewed as*. For example, "a chain can-be-viewed-as a set of residues", states that the collection class **set-of-residue** is derivable by adapters from the persistent class **chain**. It can also be derived by different adapters from other classes storing various segments of chain in the form of helices, strands, turns and loops.

Once we have used a collection view to derive an object of the collection class set-of-residue then we can of course apply to it any *method* defined on the class. Thus this class and its methods and adapters enable us to view helices and chains as a set of residues and thus to present a *constant interface* to a display method such as phi-psi-plot (shown in Figure 1).

Likewise, consider the collection class set-of-atom. This is obtainable by an adapter from an individual residue or from a chain. It is also derivable indirectly from helices by viewing them as set-of-residue! Thus we can have a view on a view, forming an interesting kind of inheritance path (see below). Once again the view presents a consistent interface to application methods that can calculate either the weight or the total surface area of any adapted piece of protein.

5   Implementing Collection Views in P/FDM

5.1   Semantic Data Modelling Approach

In our work we have taken a semantic data model database as our starting point. In particular, we use the Functional Data Model (FDM) [18], which was proved on the MultiBase project [15] for heterogeneous data integration, because of its ability to capture data semantics independently of storage details. We have implemented a database management system called P/FDM, which is like the original FDM and is used for data integration [12]. We continue to improve and extend it because of its solid theoretical foundation and amazing adaptability [9]. Its data manipulation language (Daplex) strongly influenced early OODBMS such as IRIS. In fact our current version of Daplex is very similar to the ODMG language OQL both in syntax structure, and in how it handles and passes object identifiers as values. It is recursively defined and strongly typed (see *http://www.csd.abdn.ac.uk/~pfdm/*).

Following FDM principles, we declare a class to be a subclass of another only if it truly is a special kind of the same general concept, e.g. an "enzyme" might be declared as a special kind of "protein". Even then, we only declare a new subclass if there are additional attributes or relationships which are meaningful for the subclass (e.g. enzyme classification number) but which are not meaningful for instances of the superclass in general. All attributes, relationships and methods defined on the superclass are also defined on all its subclass(es), including the key attributes which we use to identify object instances.

5.2   Schema Definitions for Collections on Concrete Classes

A collection view can be defined on any of the concrete classes or subclasses described in the database schema, or on another collection view. It takes any object of the given class or view type and derives on demand a collection of objects of an adapted type, so as to fit a desired tool or method. It may return a set of concrete instances declared in the database schema, or else a set of primitive values or tuples of such values (such as `point(x,y,z)`).

We have implemented this scheme on the P/FDM object database by adapting and generalising the system code (written in Prolog) that handles inheritance. Because P/FDM represents relationships as functions, which may be stored or derived, it is easy to represent adapter functions directly as P/FDM functions. In order to do this we identify the adapter functions F by introducing extra schema declarations with the keywords:

```
using F, an Atype can be viewed as a set of Btype
```

Schema Extract

```
declare protein ->> entity                  % Class declaration
declare protein_name(protein) -> string     % Function declaration

declare chain ->> entity
declare chain_id(chain) -> string
declare num_residues(chain) -> integer
declare chain_protein(chain) -> protein
define has_residues(chain) ->> residue       % Adapter function

declare residue ->> entity
declare position(residue) -> integer
declare name(residue) -> string
define has_atoms(residue) ->> atom           % Adapter function

declare structure ->> entity
declare structure_chain(structure) -> chain
declare structure_residues(structure) ->> residue
declare helix ->> structure

declare atom ->> entity

define weight(set of atom) -> float          % Function defined on a set
define surface_area(set of atom) -> float    % Function defined on a set
```

Collection View Declarations

```
using has_residues, a chain can be viewed as a set of residue
using structure_residues, a structure can be viewed as a set of residue
using has_atoms, a residue can be viewed as a set of atom
using atom_centres, a set of atom can be viewed as a set of point
```

Fig. 3. Schema extract and collection view declarations.

Example declarations are given in Figure 3. In one example we are able to use an existing stored relationship called *has_residues* as an adapter function, relating a protein chain to its many residues. In the general case an adapter function would be defined as a stored method, written in Daplex or in Prolog (possibly with callouts to C).

5.3   Composition of Adapter Functions

There is a kind of transitivity between adapter functions that allows us to compose them. Many people will look on this as a kind of *view inheritance*, so that a method defined on a more abstract view is applicable to an object belonging to a view lower down in the hierarchy. Thus for example the method centroid

Queries

```
for each c in chain such that
    weight(c) >= 1000 and weight(c) =< 2000
print(protein_name(chain_protein(c)), weight(c));


print(chain_id(any c in chain such that weight(c) > 1000));


for each h in helix such that surface_area(h) > 1000
print(chain_id(structure_chain(h)), surface_area(h));


for each c in chain
print(average(over r in has_residues(c) of weight(r)));
```

Extract from Typescript

```
| ?- daplex.
|: for the c in chain such that protein_code(chain_protein(c)) = "1CRN"
|:    for each r in has_residues(c)
|:    print(name(r), weight(r));

ASN 23.6
ALA 15.4
GLY 12.0      % more result values have been omitted

|: for each c in chain
|: print(chain_id(c), weight(c));

A 1006.2      % more result values have been omitted
```

Fig. 4. Example queries on collection views.

can be applied to a set of points, but it can also be applied to a set of residues, or even to a helix further down the hierarchy of thick arrows.

In order to implement this we use the adapters to perform what in programming language theory is a coercion or *type cast*. For example:

   y := sqrt(2) is coerced to y := sqrt(float(2))

Thus if h is a variable holding an instance of type helix then centroid(h) really stands for (see Figure 1):

   centroid(atom_centres(residues_to_atoms(structure_residues(h))))

Here structure_residues is an adapter function defined on class secondary-structure-element that delivers an object of class set-of-residue. In this way the various adapter functions are composed together into a derived relationship which will construct a set of objects to which centroid is applicable.

Where only a single coercion is needed, we can determine it from a knowledge of the source and destination classes, since we allow at most one adapter function (or arrow) between any two classes. However, where arrows form a path, there may be alternative paths, and we explain how to resolve this later. Note that adapter functions are often multi-valued (i.e. deliver a set or bag) and that two such functions can be composed and will deliver a single flattened set as result. This is in accordance with Shipman's original Functional Data Model, because if instead they delivered a set of sets then it would not fit the next adaptor function.

We must stress the difference from normal method inheritance in C++ or Smalltalk, where the method that is inherited simply works on those slots in the object that are defined at its level. There is no question of adapting the values before applying the method. Likewise if one applies a method defined on a secondary structure to an instance of a helix (one of its subtypes) then the method just works on that part of the data structure which is common to all secondary structure objects and not specialised to a helix. This is subtype inheritance, and once again there is no notion of adapting values.

5.4   Collection Views in an Object-Relational Database

Let us consider how the examples in Figure 4 would look in an object-relational syntax, which may be more familiar. A syntax for Object-Relational DBMS with examples is defined in the well known text [19]. Here they introduce user-defined functions with arguments and discuss their inheritance behaviour. For example, they give the function *overpaid(employee_t)*, which can be overloaded to work on the more specialised argument type *student_employee_t*. Thus they give:

```
select  e.name
from    emp e
where   overpaid(e);
```

What we are proposing looks similar, with the same syntax of a user-defined function applied to an entity type, but here we interpret it as a dynamically composed view by adaptation, instead of as an inherited function. Using this syntax we could write analogous queries to those in Figure 4:

```
select  r.name
from    residue r
where   weight(r) > 20.0
```

Here **weight** does not apply directly to **residue**, which needs adapting via the adapter function **has_atoms** to generate a setof(atom). Similarly we could have:

```
select  c.chainid
from    chain c
where   weight(c) > 220.0
```

Here the collection view mechanism would compose **has_residues** with **has_atoms** to make a suitable adaptor. Another example from the figure, this time adapting to surface_area, can be done using dot notation:

```
select h.structure_chain.chainid, h.surface_area
from   helix h
where  h.surface_area >1000
```

The examples with nested loops are awkward in SQL-3, and it is easier to separate the loops using auxiliary functions. Trying these examples makes one realise the great advantages of the referentially transparent FDM syntax which is so easily substitutable.

5.5 Extending Adapter Functions

Where an adaptor function maps a single item A onto a set of items of type B it is always possible to define a corresponding adapter that maps a set of A onto a flattened set of B. For example, when A = residue and B = set of atom, then the adapter from A to B is has_atoms. We now define the adapter residues_to_atoms to take a set of residue S and deliver the union of the results of has_atoms applied to each residue in turn: union(map(has_atoms,S)).

This is often what is needed when an operation (such as centroid) is defined over a set of values of one type (B), but is given a set of values of another type (A). Thus, an end-user may provide a specific adaptor for this set-to-set case (usually for efficiency) but where they do not the system will automatically extend the item-to-set adapter, as just described.

6 Checks on a Collection View Definition

We give below a series of checks on a syntactically well-formed view definition that enforce the rules and conditions discussed earlier.

```
using <adapter-name>, a <etype> can be viewed as a set of <rtype>
using <adapter-name>, a set of <etype> can be viewed as a set of <rtype>
```

- The result type <rtype> applies to each instance of the set formed by the collection view. Here *etype* must be a defined entity class name, or a named subtype of such a class, and *rtype* must be likewise, or else a tuple type (such as point) or scalar type. For any given *etype* there can be at most one collection view mapping onto a particular *rtype*. However, there may be other collection views, as long as they map onto different *rtypes*.
- The set expression forming the body of the definition of the adapter must compute a set of tuples or scalars or pre-existing object identifiers of type *rtype*, determined from the instance(s) of type *etype*. It must do this without updating any stored values.
- The form of view definition that starts from set of <etype> is used to define an adapter to coerce a set of values. It is needed for adapters between two collection views, as in the right of Figure 1. However, note that this set of values may just be the results of a Daplex expression or query delivering results of the right type. It does not have to be the output of applying another adapter function. For example:

```
for each c in chain
print(surface_area(r in has_residues(c) such that name(r)="TYR"));
```

- All of the collection view mappings on the database can be drawn as a graph G whose nodes are the entity types and whose arcs are directed from the etype node to the rtype node. Considered as a whole, the graph must be acyclic, and any newly defined arc that would make it cyclic must be disallowed (unless other arcs that make it so are first removed). Where the graph is not a pure tree, then any alternative paths between two nodes should be flagged, with a warning to the user to ensure these are equivalent.
- Where an adapter arrow joins collection view V1 to V2, then if it is composed with an adapter joining V0 to V1, we must ensure that the derived relationship between V0 and V2 is semantically meaningful. This will happen automatically if the individual adapters are based on is-part-of relationships in the physical world. If not, and we have not yet seen an example of this, then it could be overridden by another adaptor directly joining V0 to V2, with the desired meaning. Alternatively, it would be better to remove the adapter between V1 and V2 if it is not useful.

7 Formal Description

The introduction of collection views into P/FDM requires a modification of the standard method evaluation procedure. It is easiest to present the modified semantics of method evaluation by first presenting the standard semantics, followed by the new cases which must be added for collection views.

Without collection views, method evaluation in P/FDM is a simple two stage process:

- Bind to the correct method definition, following subtype inheritance links where appropriate.
- Evaluate that method definition.

With collection views, this process is extended by modifying the first step and adding an additional second step:

- Bind to the correct method definition, following subtype inheritance links and collection view links where appropriate.
- Coerce the arguments supplied to the method so that they are of the required type.
- Evaluate the method definition using the coerced arguments.

The third step is unaffected by the introduction of collection views.

We will now give a formal description of the semantics of method binding and coercion of arguments under collection views. The following definitions will be used as the basis for this presentation.

- A relation MS containing details of the methods known to the database. The tuples contain the method name, the first argument type, the remaining argument types, the result type and the unique identifier for the method definition:

$$MS \equiv \{< m, t, ts, rt, d >\}$$

- A relation SLs describing the subtype links known to the database. The tuples contain the subtype and the supertype respectively:

$$SLs \equiv \{< t_i, t_j >\}$$

- A transitive relation $subtype$ over SLs:

$$(\forall t_i, t_j) \; subtype(t_i, t_j) \Leftrightarrow$$
$$(< t_i, t_j > \in SLs \vee ((\exists t_k) \; < t_i, t_k > \in SLs \wedge \; subtype(t_k, t_j)))$$

- A relation CLs describing the collection view links known to the database. The tuples contain the two types linked by the view and the definition identifier for the function which links them:

$$CLs \equiv \{< t_i, t_j, d >\}$$

This relation is extended as explained in section 5.5, so that for any t_i which denotes a simple entity type there will also be a corresponding tuple $< set\_of(t_i), t_j, d' >$ adapting the set of that type.
- For each function d_i, a relation D_i which represents the extent of that function.

7.1 Method Binding

In P/FDM, method binding occurs based on the type of the first argument supplied to the method call. The method definition used will either be that which is defined directly on the first argument type (where it exists) or that which is defined on the "lowest" supertype of that type. Formally, the relationship between a method f with first argument of type t and a method definition d is given by the expression:

$$(\forall f, t, d) \; binds(f, t, d) \Leftrightarrow$$
$$(< f, t, \_, \_, d > \in MS \vee (< f, t, \_, \_, d > \notin MS \wedge \; inherited(f, t, d)))$$

where $inherited(f, t, d)$ is defined as:

$$(\forall f, t, d) \; inherited(f, t, d) \Leftrightarrow ((\exists t_k) \; subtype(t, t_k) \wedge \; < f, t_k, \_, \_, d > \in MS \wedge$$
$$\neg((\exists t_l) \; subtype(t, t_l) \wedge \; subtype(t_l, t_k) \wedge \; < f, t_l, \_, \_, \_ > \in MS))$$

These two definitions describe a common form of method inheritance for object databases. Note that we have included the negations of some of the conditions for bindings in later branches of the disjunction to indicate the relative precedences between the binding options. We never bind to an inherited function when a directly defined function is available.

The possibility of binding to method definitions through collection view links adds a third branch to the disjunction:

$$(\forall f, t, d) \ binds(f, t, d) \ \Leftrightarrow \ (< f, t, \_, \_, d > \in MS \ \vee$$
$$(< f, t, \_, \_, d > \notin MS \ \wedge \ inherited(f, t, d)) \ \vee$$
$$(< f, t, \_, \_, d > \notin MS \ \wedge \ \neg inherited(f, t, d) \ \wedge$$
$$((\exists t_k, p) < f, t_k, \_, \_, d > \in MS \ \wedge \ best\_coercion\_path(t, t_k, p)))$$

In other words, a function f with definition d can be applied to a value of type t if the "best" available coercion path exists from t to the type that the function f is defined on (t_k). We define the notion of a *coercion path* from type t_1 to type t_{n+1} as a sequence of collection view function definitions which can be composed to transform values from one type to another:

$$(\forall t_1, t_{n+1}, d_1, \dots, d_n) \ cpath(t_1, t_{n+1}, < d_1, \dots, d_n >) \ \Leftrightarrow$$
$$((\exists t_2, \dots, t_n) \ clink(t_1, t_2, d_1) \ \wedge \ clink(t_2, t_3, d_2) \ \wedge \ \dots \ \wedge \ clink(t_n, t_{n+1}, d_n))$$

where *clink(t_i, t_j, d)* is defined to allow inheritance of collection view functions as follows:

$$(\forall t_i, t_j, d) \ clink(t_i, t_j, d) \ \Leftrightarrow \ (< t_i, t_j, d > \in CLs \ \vee$$
$$((\exists t_k) \ subtype(t_i, t_k) \ \wedge \ < t_k, t_j, d > \in CLs)^1$$

The process of binding to a function through a coercion path is complicated by the fact that there may be several possible paths leading from the starting type to a type on which a function f is defined. Where this is the case, the question arises as to which path should be followed, since this determines the result of the binding process.

A number of different options exist for selecting the "best" coercion path from a type. For example, it is possible to concoct complicated schemes which favour directly defined collection view functions over inherited ones. However, all such schemes contain an element of arbitrary choice and none are wholly satisfactory. We have chosen to follow a compromise approach in which the shortest path to an appropriate function definition is chosen. Collection view definitions which result in more than one "shortest" path should be flagged at compile-time, to warn the user that they need to be equivalent. For our purposes, therefore, we define the "best" coercion path from a type as follows:

$$(\forall t_i, t_j, p) \ best\_coercion\_path(t_i, t_j, p) \ \Leftrightarrow \ (cpath(t_i, t_j, p) \ \wedge$$
$$\neg((\exists p_k) \ cpath(t_i, t_j, p_k) \ \wedge \ \#p_k < \#p))$$

Here, the length of a sequence p is denoted by the expression $\#p$.

7.2   Coercion of Arguments

Once we have identified that a method can be "inherited" through collection view links, it is necessary to transform the arguments that have been given in

---

[1] We believe it is possible to extend this definition to include the case where the collection link is followed by a sub-type link instead of preceded by it but have had no demand for it.

the method call using the collection view functions so that they match the types required by the function.

Essentially, this stage in the process is one of identifying and evaluating a composed function which will perform the necessary coercion for each argument. Since it is possible that more than one, or even all, of the arguments to the method call may require some coercion, we must be ready to find a coercion path for each of them. By this stage, we have already identified the function definition to which the method call binds, and we can use this information to extract the required argument types from the metadata. That is, the relationship between a method call m, applied to argument types $< at_1, \ldots, at_n >$, and the coercion paths $< p_1, \ldots, p_n >$ necessary to transform those arguments for method evaluation is given by the following expression:

$$(\forall m, at_1, \ldots, at_n, p_1, \ldots, p_n) \; coercion\_paths(m, < at_1, \ldots, at_n >, < p_1, \ldots, p_n >) \Leftrightarrow$$
$$((\exists d, rt_1, \ldots, rt_n) \; binds(m, at_1, d) \wedge \; < m, rt_1, < rt_2, \ldots, rt_n >, \_, d > \in MS \wedge$$
$$best\_coercion\_path(at_1, rt_1, p_1) \wedge \ldots \wedge best\_coercion\_path(at_n, rt_n, p_n))$$

In other words, the coercion paths are given by finding the identifier (d) of the method to which the call to m binds, and then extracting the expected argument types $(rt_1, \ldots, rt_n)$ for this method from the metadata. A coercion path must then be found (as defined by $best\_coercion\_path$) from each at_i to each rt_i, $1 \leq i \leq n$.

Each coercion path must now be applied to its respective argument value, to transform it into a value of the type required by the method that has been called.

The application of a coercion path $< d_1, d_2, d_3 >$ to a value x denotes the composed function:

$$d_3(d_2(d_1(x)))$$

Note that the first adapter function d_1 will always deliver a set of items, and that subsequent adapters will adapt sets of items to sets of items, as explained in Section 5.5. Here d_1 must be compatible with the type of the expression x, which may be a single entity or a set.

7.3   Implementation Strategies for Collection Views

We have defined the semantics of a function call involving one or more collection view links. In fact, there are two complementary ways in which this semantics can be implemented, corresponding to the two different levels of access to a P/FDM database. In P/FDM, queries may be written directly in Prolog, by including calls to database primitives to evaluate methods, create data, etc. This kind of access requires run-time handling of collection views. Alternatively, queries may be written in the Daplex data manipulation language and then compiled into the equivalent Prolog programs for execution. This kind of access allows the possibility of compile-time handling of collection views.

Run-Time Handling To implement the collection view mechanism at the Prolog level, we have modified the behaviour of the database primitives handling method evaluation. These primitives attempt to determine whether a collection view link can be used to bind the method call to its definition at run-time. The coercion paths required to transform the argument values are then identified and *interpreted* as a series of instructions for transforming the arguments.

Compile-Time Handling At the Daplex level, we handle collection views at compile-time by replacing method calls which require coercion with the calls that will perform that coercion at run-time. Effectively, we are *compiling* the coercion path, rather than interpreting it as we have described above. This approach requires a set of rewrite rules for queries which will insert the necessary additional function calls.

8   Persistence

It is important to realise that collection views are transitory and computed on demand in order to provide a set of objects with an appropriate interface to one or more utility methods (such as phi-psi-plot). They may look like persistent classes (which also have methods) on a schema diagram, but they do not persist. The only changes that can persist are those arising from allowable updates on the underlying objects of the view. It is possible to enlarge the definition of the view by adding extra functions to compute other derived properties; this is a form of schema evolution. However, it is not possible for a view class to have *stored* properties, because it is just an abstract class defining an interface. Furthermore, if the view class derives `set of <etype>` then the result must belong to the powerset of the stored values of `<etype>` in the current database state. Thus, if you compute a collection of of residue objects forming a set-of-residue, it cannot contain any new residue objects.

9   Conclusions and Discussion

Different people involved in designing a schema can have different ideas on the role and importance of inheritance, and this can impede progress in agreeing a common schema. By separating out the different ways in which inheritance is used, we can focus on the structural relationships among the data and think about what subtype-supertype relationships are needed for long-term persistence.

In the case of collection views there may be more than one path leading to the same desired target class (for example forming sets of atoms from helices). One is faced with the usual problem as to choice of path. One can trap the path at definition time and warn of ambiguity or disallow it if it is cyclic. We have chosen to put an ordering on the paths based on length, by using a breadth-first search. We currently prefer subtype "steps" in the path to adapter "steps". All this has been concisely and systematically implemented in Prolog. We also require that paths between the same pairs of types should yield equivalent sets as results (but we have no automatic way to check this). More work is needed, but these problems are commonly encountered and do not invalidate the basic concept of collection views.

This description obviously raises some questions about possible improvements. In particular, is it possible to *lazily evaluate* the adapter functions so that they produce the members of a set (of atoms or residues etc.) one by one on demand instead of all at once, to save on storage allocation. The usual difficulty arises where an intermediate or final bag is generated from which it is necessary to remove duplicates, thus holding up the process. However, one often knows beforehand (from the definition of the adapters) that this cannot happen, and it would be nice to make use of this knowledge.

We have seen the value of being able to define views on object databases that return collections of objects. These collections can then be processed by an object-oriented program (possibly wrapping legacy code). The view is valuable in providing a consistent interface to this application code. It provides automatic casts which are commonly used and appreciated in programming languages, for example when working with mixed integers, reals and fractions. By defining collection views through inheritance of adapter functions in the schema we avoid a combinatorial explosion of view classes. This will also allow the schema to evolve while continuing to provide a consistent interface to the application, by modifications to the adapter functions. This is the proper role of a schema in supporting views.

Acknowledgements

We are grateful to our partners in the EC-funded BRIDGE project [10] for originally bringing this problem to our attention in discussions on a standard protein database schema from which sets of protein fragments could be derived. We are also grateful to the EU ERASMUS scheme for funding Patrick Brunschwig who was able to implement the design while visiting from Univ. of Zurich.

References

1. S. Abiteboul and A. Bonner. Objects and Views. In J. Clifford and R. King, editors, *SIGMOD 91 Conference*, pages 238–247, Denver, Colorado, May 1991. ACM Press.
2. F.C. Bernstein, T.F. Koetzle, G.J.B. Williams, E.F. Mayer, M.D. Bruce, J.R. Rodgers, O. Kennard, T. Shimanouchi, and M. Tasumi. The Protein Data Bank: a Computer-Based Archival File for Macromolecular Structures. *J. Mol. Biol.*, 112:535–542, 1977.
3. D.K.C. Chan and D.A. Kerr. Improving one's views of object-oriented databases. Technical report, Glasgow University, Dept. of Computing Science, 1994.
4. I.A. Chen and V.M. Markowitz. *An Overview of the Object-Protocol Model (OPM) and OPM Data Management Tools*. Information Systems, Pergamon Press, 1995.

5. S. M. Embury and P. M. D. Gray. The Declarative Expression of Semantic Integrity in a Database of Protein Structure. In A. Illaramendi and O. Díaz, editors, *Data Management Systems: Proceedings of the Basque International Workshop on Information Technology (BIWIT 95)*, pages 216–224, San Sebastían, Spain, July 1995. IEEE Computer Society Press.

6. D. Florescu, L. Raschid, and P. Valduriez. Answering queries using oql view expressions. In Mumick and Gupta [16].

7. M. Fowler. Application Views: another technique in the analysis and design armoury. *Journal of Object-Oriented Programming*, 12, 1993.

8. E. Gamma, R. Helm, and J. Vlissides. *Design Patterns*. Addison-Wesley, 1994.

9. P.M.D. Gray, S.M. Embury, K.Y. Hui, and G.J.L. Kemp. The Evolving Role of Constraints in the Functional Data Model. *J. Intelligent Information Systems*, 12:113–137, 1999.

10. P.M.D. Gray, G.J.L. Kemp, C.J. Rawlings, N.P. Brown, C. Sander, J.M. Thornton, C.M. Orengo, S.J. Wodak, and J. Richelle. Macromolecular structure information and databases. *Trends in Biochemical Sciences*, 21:251–256, 1996.

11. P.M.D. Gray, K.G. Kulkarni, and N.W. Paton. *Object-Oriented Databases: a Semantic Data Model Approach*. Prentice Hall Series in Computer Science. Prentice Hall International Ltd., 1992.

12. G.J.L. Kemp, J. Dupont, and P.M.D. Gray. Using the Functional Data Model to Integrate Distributed Biological Data Sources. In P. Svensson and J.C. French, editors, *Proceedings Eighth International Conference on Scientific and Statistical Database Management*, pages 176–185. IEEE Computer Society Press, 1996.

13. G.J.L. Kemp, C.J. Robertson, and P.M.D. Gray. Efficient access to biological databases using CORBA. *CCP11 Newsletter (http://www.hgmp.mrc.ac.uk/CCP11/newsletter/vol3_1/kemp/)*, 3, 1999.

14. H. A. Kuno and E. A. Rundensteiner. The MultiView OODB View System: Design and Implementation. *TAPOS*, 2:202–225, 1996.

15. T. Landers and R. L. Rosenberg. An Overview of MULTIBASE. In H.-J. Schneider, editor, *Distributed Data Bases*. North-Holland Publishing Company, 1982.

16. I. S. Mumick and A. Gupta, editors. *Proc. Workshop on Materialised Views: Techniques and Applications(Montreal)*. ACM SIGMOD, 1996.

17. A. Sathi, M.S. Fox, and M. Greenberg. Representation of Activity Knowledge for Project Management. *IEEE Transactions on Pattern Analysis and Machine Intelligence*, 7:531–552, 1985.

18. D. W. Shipman. The Functional Data Model and the Data Language DAPLEX. *ACM Transactions on Database Systems*, 6(1):140–173, 1981.

19. M. Stonebraker and D. Moore. *Object-Relational DBMSs: The Next Great Wave*. Morgan Kaufmann Publishers Inc., 1996.

Global Transaction Termination Rules in Composite Database Systems

Can Türker[1], Kerstin Schwarz[2], and Gunter Saake[3]

[1] Swiss Federal Institute of Technology (ETH) Zürich
Institute of Information Systems, ETH Zentrum
CH-8092 Zürich, Switzerland
tuerker@inf.ethz.ch
[2] UBS AG
Flurstrasse 62
CH-8098 Zürich, Switzerland
kerstin.schwarz@ubs.com
[3] Otto-von-Guericke-Universität Magdeburg
Institut für Technische und Betriebliche Informationssysteme
Postfach 4120, D–39016 Magdeburg, Germany
saake@iti.cs.uni-magdeburg.de

Abstract. In composite database systems, global transactions are decomposed by the global transaction manager into several global subtransactions that are executed at the corresponding component database systems. This paper shows that the execution and termination of a global transaction depend on the specified extensional assertions on the local classes as well as on the given kinds of global requests. In some cases, a global transaction is supposed to be successful if exactly one global subtransaction is successfully executed. In other cases, all global subtransactions have to be successful in order to commit the global transaction. We discuss various termination rules for global transactions and thus provide new insights into a complex problem.

Keywords: global transactions, composite database systems, extensional assertions, termination dependencies.

1 Introduction

A *composite*[1] *database system* provides a homogeneous interface to possibly heterogeneous component database systems. This homogeneous interface consists of a global schema which is the result of a logical integration of the schemata of the corresponding component database systems [1,15]. The integration is based on the *extensional assertions* [17,19] which are specified by the database

---

[1] Here, we explicitly do not use the notion of *federated database systems* because we are interested in integration scenarios in which the component database systems are willing/cooperating to achieve global consistency. In contrast, as argued by many authors, the component database systems of a federated database system are assumed to be autonomous and thus not primarily interested in supporting global consistency.

B. Lings and K. Jeffery (Eds.): BNCOD 17, LNCS 1832, pp. 122–139, 2000.

integrator. These extensional assertions determine the relationships among the extensions of related local classes, e.g. extensional containment or equivalence. Extensional assertions as well as the global schema itself are stored in the global (meta) database managed by the composite database system.

Since these extensional assertions are integration constraints, they always have to be valid, i.e., the composite database system has to maintain these constraints; otherwise the global schema is based on false assumptions and thus it is incorrect. Using the global schema, *global transactions* are able to *transparently* access and manipulate data located in different component database systems [2]. Depending on the given global schema and particularly on the specified extensional assertions, a global transaction is decomposed into a set of *global subtransactions* that operate on the component database systems.

Figure 1 depicts a scenario in which two local classes **Employee** are integrated into one global class **Employee**. For simplicity, we assume that both classes have the same attributes. During schema integration the designer of the global schema has specified that the local classes are extensionally equivalent, i.e., these classes have to contain the same (semantically equivalent) objects in each database state. In consequence, a global insertion transaction t_g must be transformed into two global subtransactions t_1 and t_2 which try to perform the insertions in the corresponding component database systems. Due to the extensional assertion, both global subtransactions have to be successful in order to commit the global transaction. In case one global subtransaction commits while the other one aborts, the requirement that both classes are extensionally equivalent is violated. In order to correctly terminate a global transaction, a global transaction termination protocol is needed.

Besides extensional equivalence, there are further extensional assertions. Depending on the extensional assertions, different *global transaction termination rules* are needed to correctly terminate a global transaction. For instance, in some cases a commit of only one global subtransaction is sufficient to commit the global transaction, i.e., a global transaction can commit although some of the global subtransactions are aborted. In order to get a grasp of the meaningful global transaction termination rules, we analyze the underlying transaction termination dependencies. For that, we use the transaction closure framework [12,13] which provides a complete set of the possible termination dependencies.

In particular, we show that a global transaction cannot always be executed by exactly one global subtransaction per corresponding component database system — which however is assumed by most approaches to transaction management in multidatabase systems. Based on our investigation of the effects of global insert, update, and delete transactions, we will show that in some cases several global subtransactions operating on the *same* component database system are required to correctly perform a global transaction.

The paper is organized as follows: Section 2 introduces transaction termination dependencies. In Section 3 we analyze termination dependencies of global transactions and derive meaningful global transaction termination rules. Section 4 discusses strategies for executing global transactions. Depending on the

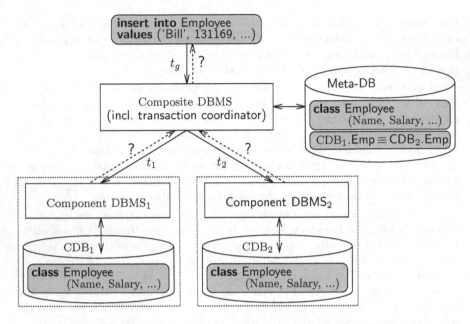

Fig. 1. Global Insertion into Extensionally Equivalent Classes

extensional assertions on the local classes, we investigate the underlying dependencies among the related transactions. In Section 5 we sketch a general protocol that captures the different global transaction termination rules. Section 6 concludes the paper.

2   Transaction Termination Dependencies

As formal framework for specifying and reasoning about dependencies between transactions we use the concept of a transaction closure which provides a complete set of termination dependencies [11,13]. *Termination dependencies* are used to specify constraints on the occurrence of the significant termination events commit (c) and abort (a) of related transactions. For instance, if the global transaction aborts, then its global subtransactions have to abort, too.

We have identified a small set of binary and ternary termination dependencies being sufficient to specify any n-ary termination dependency among several transactions [12]. The binary dependencies are summarized in Table 2. For a dependency, a valid termination event combination of the related transactions is denoted by '$\checkmark$' whereas the invalid ones are represented by '—'.

The termination dependency between the transactions t_i and t_j is **vital**(t_i, t_j) if the abort of t_i leads to the abort of t_j ("t_i is vital for t_j"). If this dependency holds in both directions, i.e., if the abort of t_i leads to the abort of t_j and vice versa, we say t_i and t_j are vital-dependent on each other, denoted **vital_dep**(t_i, t_j). The termination dependency **exc**(t_i, t_j) disallows that both

	a_{t_i} a_{t_j}	a_{t_i} c_{t_j}	c_{t_i} a_{t_j}	c_{t_i} c_{t_j}
vital(t_i, t_j)	✓	—	✓	✓
vital_dep(t_i, t_j)	✓	—	—	✓
exc(t_i, t_j)	✓	✓	✓	—

Fig. 2. Binary Termination Dependencies

transactions t_i and t_j commit together. In the default case, when no dependency is specified between two "independent" transactions, clearly all termination event combinations are valid. The formal specification of the termination dependencies is as follows ($\Rightarrow$ denotes implication):

$$\mathbf{vital}(t_i, t_j) :\Leftrightarrow (a_{t_i} \Rightarrow a_{t_j})$$

$$\mathbf{vital\_dep}(t_i, t_j) :\Leftrightarrow \mathbf{vital}(t_i, t_j) \wedge \mathbf{vital}(t_j, t_i)$$

$$\mathbf{exc}(t_i, t_j) :\Leftrightarrow (c_{t_i} \Rightarrow a_{t_j}) \vee (c_{t_j} \Rightarrow a_{t_i})$$

There are termination dependencies among more than two transactions that cannot be expressed by conjunctions of binary dependencies alone. We identified three fundamental ternary dependencies that, in combination with the binary dependencies **vital** and **exc**, enable us to specify every possible n-ary termination dependency using conjunctive formulae only [12]. The ternary dependency **vital**(t_i, t_j, t_k) states that transaction t_k has to be aborted if both transactions t_i and t_j abort. The dependency **dep**(t_i, t_j, t_k) expresses that a commit of transaction t_i and an abort of transaction t_j leads to the abort of transaction t_k. In case of **exc**(t_i, t_j, t_k), the transaction t_k has to abort, if both transactions t_i and t_j commit:

$$\mathbf{vital}(t_i, t_j, t_k) :\Leftrightarrow (a_{t_i} \wedge a_{t_j}) \Rightarrow a_{t_k}$$

$$\mathbf{dep}(t_i, t_j, t_k) :\Leftrightarrow (c_{t_i} \wedge a_{t_j}) \Rightarrow a_{t_k}$$

$$\mathbf{exc}(t_i, t_j, t_k) :\Leftrightarrow (c_{t_i} \wedge c_{t_j}) \Rightarrow a_{t_k}$$

As depicted in Table 3, ternary termination dependencies disallow exactly one termination event combination of the three related transactions.

	a_{t_i} a_{t_j} a_{t_k}	a_{t_i} a_{t_j} c_{t_k}	a_{t_i} c_{t_j} a_{t_k}	a_{t_i} c_{t_j} c_{t_k}	c_{t_i} a_{t_j} a_{t_k}	c_{t_i} a_{t_j} c_{t_k}	c_{t_i} c_{t_j} a_{t_k}	c_{t_i} c_{t_j} c_{t_k}
vital(t_i, t_j, t_k)	✓	—	✓	✓	✓	✓	✓	✓
dep(t_i, t_j, t_k)	✓	✓	✓	✓	✓	—	✓	✓
exc(t_i, t_j, t_k)	✓	✓	✓	✓	✓	✓	✓	—

Fig. 3. Ternary Termination Dependencies

3   Global Transaction Termination Rules

Depending on the nature of a global transaction, different termination dependencies among the global transaction t_g and its global subtransactions t_1, ..., t_n are possible and meaningful. Nevertheless, the following general rules always hold:

Rule 1: Since a transaction cannot be forced to commit, the common abortion of all transactions should be always possible.

Rule 2: The abortion of the global transaction implies the abortion of all global subtransactions:

$$a_{t_g} \Rightarrow (a_{t_1} \wedge a_{t_2} \wedge \cdots \wedge a_{t_n})$$

This fact can be expressed by the following conjunction of binary dependencies:

$$\mathbf{vital}(t_g, t_1) \wedge \mathbf{vital}(t_g, t_2) \wedge \cdots \wedge \mathbf{vital}(t_g, t_n)$$

Rule 3: The global transaction can only commit if at least one of the global subtransactions commits. In other words, the global transaction cannot commit if all global subtransactions abort:

$$c_{t_g} \Rightarrow (c_{t_1} \vee c_{t_2} \vee \cdots \vee c_{t_n})$$
$$\equiv (a_{t_1} \wedge a_{t_2} \wedge \cdots \wedge a_{t_n}) \Rightarrow a_{t_g}$$

This fact can be expressed by the following n-ary dependency:

$$\mathbf{vital}(t_1, t_2, \ldots, t_n, t_g)$$

For brevity, but without loss of generality, our following considerations are restricted to a global transaction t_g with two global subtransactions t_1 and t_2. However, the results can easily be extended to the n-ary case.

Figure 4 represents the effects of the Rules 1–3 on the set of possible termination event combinations:

- The first rule states that each valid dependency must allow that all transactions may abort together. Thus, the first termination event combination must be always valid.

- The second rule forbids the termination event combinations where the global transaction t_g aborts and at least one of the global subtransactions t_1 or t_2 commits. Therefore, the second, third, and fourth termination event combinations are invalid.

- The third rule forbids the termination event combinations where the global transaction t_g commits and none of the global subtransactions t_1 or t_2 commit. Therefore, the fifth termination event combination is disallowed.

t_g	t_1	t_2	1	2	3	4	5	6	7	8	
a_{t_g}	a_{t_1}	a_{t_2}	✓	✓	✓	✓	✓	✓	✓	✓	Rule 1
a_{t_g}	a_{t_1}	c_{t_2}	—	—	—	—	—	—	—	—	Rule 2
a_{t_g}	c_{t_1}	a_{t_2}	—	—	—	—	—	—	—	—	Rule 2
a_{t_g}	c_{t_1}	c_{t_2}	—	—	—	—	—	—	—	—	Rule 2
c_{t_g}	a_{t_1}	a_{t_2}	—	—	—	—	—	—	—	—	Rule 3
c_{t_g}	a_{t_1}	c_{t_2}	✓	—	✓	✓	—	—	✓	—	
c_{t_g}	c_{t_1}	a_{t_2}	✓	✓	—	✓	—	✓	—	—	
c_{t_g}	c_{t_1}	c_{t_2}	✓	✓	✓	—	✓	—	—	—	

Fig. 4. Termination Event Combinations

Finally, three termination event combinations are free in that sense that they are not fixed by these rules. In consequence, there are eight possible dependency combinations which have to be considered.

Let us now discuss these eight cases which represent different *global transaction termination rules*:

1. **at least one**: This first case allows to commit the global transaction t_g if at least one of the global subtransactions t_1 or t_2 commits. That is, this global transaction termination rule does not require further restrictions in addition to that defined by the Rules 1-3:

$$\textbf{vital}(t_1, t_2, t_g) \wedge \textbf{vital}(t_g, t_1) \wedge \textbf{vital}(t_g, t_2)$$

2. **at least t_1**: Here, the global transaction t_g may only commit if the global subtransaction t_1 commits. This restriction is expressed by strengthening the dependency $\textbf{vital}(t_g, t_1)$ to $\textbf{vital\_dep}(t_g, t_1)$. Altogether, the following dependencies are given:

$$\textbf{vital}(t_1, t_2, t_g) \wedge \textbf{vital\_dep}(t_g, t_1) \wedge \textbf{vital}(t_g, t_2)$$

3. **at least t_2**: In contrast to the previous case, here the global transaction t_g may only commit if the global subtransaction t_2 commits. This restriction is expressed by strengthening the dependency $\textbf{vital}(t_g, t_2)$ to $\textbf{vital\_dep}(t_g, t_2)$:

$$\textbf{vital}(t_1, t_2, t_g) \wedge \textbf{vital}(t_g, t_1) \wedge \textbf{vital\_dep}(t_g, t_2)$$

4. **exactly one**: In this case, the global transaction t_g may only commit if exactly one of the global subtransactions t_1 or t_2 commits. Thus, it is not allowed that both global subtransactions commit together. This condition is expressed by an additional dependency $\textbf{exc}(t_1, t_2)$:

$$\textbf{vital}(t_1, t_2, t_g) \wedge \textbf{vital}(t_g, t_1) \wedge \textbf{vital}(t_g, t_2) \wedge \textbf{exc}(t_1, t_2)$$

5. **all**: This termination rule is well-known from distributed database systems. The global transaction t_g may only commit if all global subtransactions

commit. In other words, if one transaction aborts, then the other transactions have to abort, too. This fact is described by restricting the dependencies $\textbf{vital}(t_g, t_1)$ and $\textbf{vital}(t_g, t_2)$ to the dependencies $\textbf{vital\_dep}(t_g, t_1)$ and $\textbf{vital\_dep}(t_g, t_2)$, respectively:

$$\textbf{vital}(t_1, t_2, t_g) \wedge \textbf{vital\_dep}(t_g, t_1) \wedge \textbf{vital\_dep}(t_g, t_2)$$

Note that the ternary dependency is implied by the binary dependencies.

6. **only** t_1: The global subtransaction t_2 does not need to be started because it always has to abort. Thus, the consideration can be reduced to the global transaction t_g and the global subtransaction t_1 that are connected by the dependency $\textbf{vital\_dep}(t_g, t_1)$.

7. **only** t_2: The global subtransaction t_1 does not need to be started because it always has to abort. Therefore, the consideration can be reduced to the global transaction t_g and the global subtransaction t_2 that are connected by the dependency $\textbf{vital\_dep}(t_g, t_2)$.

8. **None**: This case is not meaningful since all transactions always have to abort.

Note that the **at least one** rule corresponds to the "weakest" dependency combination. The other dependency combinations restrict this dependency combination either by strengthening some of the dependencies or by adding further dependencies. Also, note that the **only** rules corresponds to the **all** rule on a reduced set of related transactions. Here, the involved transactions either commit or abort together.

4   Relationships between Extensional Assertions and Global Transactions Termination Rules

In this section, we consider global insert, update, and delete transactions. Again, we consider a scenario in which the composite database system relies on two component database systems. A global transaction t_g is executed on a global class C_g that is composed by the union of the local classes C_1 and C_2. This global transaction is decomposed into two global subtransactions t_1 and t_2. The global subtransaction t_1 works on the local class C_1 whereas the global subtransaction t_2 operates on the local class C_2 (of another database system). The termination dependencies between these transactions depend on the extensional assertions on the local classes as well as on the global update strategy.

4.1   Extensional Assertions on Classes

The *extension* of a class is the set of instances of this class in a given database state. $Ext_{C_1}^S$ denotes the extension of the class C_1 in a database state S. Let C_1 and C_2 be two semantically related classes. Then, the database integrator may define one of the following binary *extensional assertions* [17,20] on the classes C_1 and C_2:

$$\text{Disjointness:} \quad C_1 \oslash C_2 :\Leftrightarrow \forall S \colon Ext_{C_1}^S \cap Ext_{C_2}^S = \emptyset$$
$$\text{Equivalence:} \quad C_1 \equiv C_2 :\Leftrightarrow \forall S \colon Ext_{C_1}^S = Ext_{C_2}^S$$
$$\text{Containment:} \quad C_1 \supset C_2 :\Leftrightarrow \forall S \colon Ext_{C_1}^S \supseteq Ext_{C_2}^S$$
$$\text{Overlap:} \quad C_1 \text{ⱖ} C_2 :\Leftrightarrow true$$

Two classes are extensionally disjoint if there are no common objects in the extension of these classes in any database state. Extensionally equivalent classes have the same extensions in each database state. One class extensionally contains another class if the extension of the first class is a superset of the extension of the other class in any database state. Finally, in case of overlap there are no restrictions on the relationship between the extensions of the two related classes.

4.2   Global Insert Transactions

From the global point of view, an object can be seen as (globally) inserted if at least one of the global subtransactions is successful, i.e., the object is inserted into at least one local class. In this case, the object is inserted into the composite database. However, this insertion must satisfy the extensional assertions specified on the related local classes. Since in general it is not known in advance in which local class(es) the globally created object may be inserted, for each corresponding local class an insertion operation has to be started.

Insert into $C_g = C_1 \cup C_2$ with $C_1 \oslash C_2$

In case of extensionally disjoint classes exactly one of the global subtransactions is allowed to commit. Thus, in this scenario the **exactly one** rule has to be applied for the transactions t_g, t_1, and t_2.

However, if the global class contains a *discriminant attribute* [3] whose value corresponds to an individual local class, then only one global subtransaction t_i is started to perform the insertion. In this case, the **only** t_i rule is used.

Insert into $C_g = C_1 \cup C_2$ with $C_1 \equiv C_2$

Extensionally equivalent classes require that a globally created object is inserted either into all related local classes or into none of them. From this follows that the abort of one of the transactions t_g, t_1, and t_2 leads to the abort of the other transactions. The **all** rule corresponds to this scenario.

Insert into $C_g = C_1 \cup C_2$ with $C_1 \supset C_2$

In this case, an insertion into class C_2 requires that the same object is member of the class C_1. On the other hand, if an object is inserted into class C_1, the object must not necessarily be inserted into class C_2. Thus, different insertion strategies are possible:

- The strongest requirement on the global level is called the *maximum strategy*. This strategy requires that a globally created object has to be inserted into all related local classes. We can guarantee this requirement only by using the **all** rule.

- Following the *flexible strategy*, the globally created object has to be inserted into as many local classes as possible. However, the containment assertion requires that the object has to be inserted at least into class C_1. Inserting the object into class C_2 is optional. This refers to the **at least** t_1 rule.

- The *minimum strategy* inserts the globally created object using a minimal number of global subtransactions such that the extensional relationships between the local classes are maintained. Since the class C_1 extensionally contains the class C_2, the object has to be inserted only into class C_1. The subtransaction t_2 does not need to be executed. This corresponds to the **only** t_1 rule.

Insert into $C_g = C_1 \cup C_2$ with $C_1 \sqcap C_2$

In case of extensionally overlapping classes the globally created object may be inserted into only one or both related local classes. As above, different insertion strategies are possible:

- The *maximum strategy* requires that the globally created object is inserted into all related local classes. Thus, we have to use the **all** rule.

- The *flexible strategy* tries to insert the globally created object into as many local classes as possible. Thus, all global subtransactions are submitted to the local systems. In order to commit the global transaction, at least one of them has to finish successfully. In case all global subtransactions abort, the object is not inserted. This strategy corresponds to the **at least one** rule.

- The *minimum strategy* requires that the globally created object is inserted by a minimal number of global subtransactions. For instance, in case of extensionally including classes the object is only inserted into the class which extensionally contains the other class. For extensionally overlapping classes the insertion can be done in both classes. Therefore, one of the candidate classes has to be chosen:

  - *Statically*: The administrator of the composite database system identifies the class during schema integration.

  - *Dynamically*: Depending on different values, such as the load of the system or the amount of local objects, the global transaction coordinator dynamically chooses a local class.

  - *Randomly*: The global transaction coordinator randomly chooses one of the local classes.

In all cases, only one of the global subtransactions is initiated to execute the global transaction. The other global subtransaction is not started. This refers to the **only** t_i rule.

- Finally, we can use a mixture of the strategies above which is called *flexible strategy with priorities*. In this case, we follow the flexible strategy, and thus insert the globally created object into as many classes as possible. Furthermore, one of the classes obtains priority. This means that the object has to be inserted into this class. As described above, the priority can be given by a static, dynamic, or random method. For example, if the priority is given to class C_1, then the related transaction t_1 has to be executed successfully. This refers to the **at least** t_1 rule. If class C_2 has priority, the system must follow the **at least** t_2 rule.

4.3   Global Update and Delete Transactions

Objects may also be globally updated or deleted. An object is considered as globally updated or deleted, respectively, if all corresponding objects in the local classes are updated or deleted. However, we cannot always deduce from the extensional assertions in which classes the object to be updated or deleted participates. For example, in extensionally overlapping classes the object may be in one of the classes or in both of them. Due to possible local insert operations submitted by local transactions, we even cannot conclude from the global insert strategy in which local classes an object appears. Thus, we always have to submit both global subtransactions t_1 and t_2 to the local systems. A global subtransaction aborts only if the object to be updated or deleted is member of the related classes but cannot be updated or deleted successfully. We follow the **all** rule to successfully update and delete global objects. A transaction that does not find an object to update or delete is considered as executed successfully. Otherwise, we could not deduce the correct reason for the abortion of a global subtransaction.

Figure 5 summarizes the rules for global inserts, updates, and deletes.

	at least one	at least t_1	at least t_2	exactly one	all	only t_1	only t_2
insert $(C_1 \oslash C_2)$	—	—	—	✓	—	—	—
insert $(C_1 \equiv C_2)$	—	—	—	—	✓	—	—
insert $(C_1 \supset C_2)$	—	✓	—	—	✓	✓	—
insert $(C_1 \cap C_2)$	✓	✓	✓	✓	✓	✓	✓
update / delete	—	—	—	—	✓	—	—

Fig. 5. Termination Rules for Global Operations

4.4   Combining Transaction Termination Rules

In the previous subsections we have considered global transactions with a single operation. However, transactions usually consist of several operations. These operations may also concern different global classes.

Traditional approaches [2,7,5] supporting global transactions in federated or multidatabase systems assume that for each global transaction there is *at most one* global subtransaction per component database system. In the following, we show that under this assumption certain kinds of global transactions cannot be executed (terminated) correctly.

As a counterexample we consider the following scenario. The global transaction t_g consists of the following insert and delete operations (where the classes C_1 and C_3 are managed by one component database system while the classes C_2 and C_4 are managed by another component database system):

Insert into $C_{g_1} = C_1 \cup C_2$ with $C_1 \oslash C_2$;
Delete from $C_{g_2} = C_3 \cup C_4$ with $C_3 \equiv C_4$;

The global transaction is decomposed into two global subtransactions t_1 and t_2. The transaction t_1 performs the insertion into the local class C_1 and deletion from the local class C_3 whereas the transaction t_2 executes the insertion into the local class C_2 and the deletion from the local class C_4. The question is now:

> *In which cases can the global transaction be said to have executed successfully? If both global subtransactions commit or if exactly one global subtransaction commits?*

A commit of both global subtransactions means that the insertion is performed on the local classes C_1 and C_2 and the deletion is executed on the local classes C_3 and C_4. However, in this case the extensional relationship between the classes C_1 and C_2 is not disjoint anymore, i.e., the extensional assertion cannot be guaranteed. Therefore, both global subtransactions cannot commit together. On the other hand, if both global subtransactions cannot commit together, the deletion cannot be executed successfully.

> *Thus, under the usual assumption that global subtransactions do not communicate with each other, this global transaction cannot be performed by two global subtransactions only.*

A possible solution to the example discussed above is to initiate two global subtransactions for each global operation. The global subtransactions t_1 and t_2 execute the local insert operations whereas the global subtransactions t_3 and t_4 perform the local delete operations. According to the rules presented in Figure 5, the insertion transactions are terminated using the **exactly one** rule whereas the deletion transactions are terminated using the **all** rule.

The ternary dependency between the transactions t_g, t_3, and t_4 is eliminated because it is already expressed by the binary dependencies **vital_dep**(t_g, t_3) and

vital_dep(t_g, t_4). In summary, we have the following dependencies:

$$c_{t_g} \Rightarrow ((c_{t_1} \wedge a_{t_2}) \vee (a_{t_1} \wedge c_{t_2})) \wedge c_{t_3} \wedge c_{t_4}$$
$$\equiv (a_{t_1} \wedge a_{t_2}) \vee (c_{t_1} \wedge c_{t_2}) \vee a_{t_3} \vee a_{t_4} \Rightarrow a_{t_g}$$
$$\equiv \mathbf{vital}(t_1, t_2, t_g) \wedge \mathbf{vital}(t_g, t_1) \wedge \mathbf{vital}(t_g, t_2) \wedge$$
$$\mathbf{exc}(t_1, t_2) \wedge \mathbf{vital\_dep}(t_g, t_3) \wedge \mathbf{vital\_dep}(t_g, t_4)$$

Thus, here we have a mixture of the rules **exactly one** and **all**. In the sequel, the generalization of this rule will be denoted as the **mixed**$_i$ rule. The index i states that only one of the transactions $t_1, ..., t_i$ and all of the transactions $t_{i+1}, ..., t_n$ have to commit in order to commit the global transaction t_g. More formally:

$$\mathbf{mixed}_i(t_1, ..., t_n, t_g) :\Leftrightarrow \left(c_{t_g} \Leftrightarrow \biguplus_{j=1}^{i} c_{t_j} \wedge \bigwedge_{k=i+1}^{n} c_{t_k} \right), \text{where}$$

$$\biguplus_{j=1}^{i} c_{t_j} :\Leftrightarrow (c_{t_1} \wedge a_{t_2} \wedge ... \wedge a_{t_i}) \vee (a_{t_1} \wedge c_{t_2} \wedge ... \wedge a_{t_i}) \vee ... \vee (a_{t_1} \wedge a_{t_2} \wedge ... \wedge c_{t_i})$$

As depicted in Figure 5, each global operation corresponds to a global rule. Global operations can be combined into one global subtransaction if the corresponding rules are compatible. In Figure 6 the combinations of all rules are summarized. Due to space restrictions, we use abbreviations: **a** stands for **at least**, **e** for **exactly one**, and **o** for **only**.[2]

	a one	a t_1	a t_2	e one	all	o t_1	o t_2
a one	a one	a t_1	a t_2	e one	all	o t_1	o t_2
a t_1	a t_1	a t_1	a $t_1 \wedge t_2$	o t_1	all	o t_1	a $t_1 \wedge t_2$
a t_2	a t_2	a $t_1 \wedge t_2$	a t_2	o t_2	all	a $t_1 \wedge t_2$	o t_2
e one	e one	o t_1	o t_2	e one	—	o t_1	o t_2
all	all	all	all	—	all	all	all
o t_1	o t_1	o t_1	a $t_1 \wedge t_2$	o t_1	all	o t_1	o $t_1 \wedge t_2$
o t_2	o t_2	a $t_1 \wedge t_2$	o t_2	o t_2	all	o $t_1 \wedge t_2$	o t_2

Fig. 6. Combining Transaction Termination Rules

For brevity, we do not discuss all combinations. Rather we mention some general rules and interesting cases:

---

[2] **a** $t_1 \wedge t_2$ stands for **at least** t_1 **and** t_2; analogously **o** $t_1 \wedge t_2$ stands for **only** t_1 **and** t_2. In our case — we only consider two global subtransactions t_1 and t_2 — these rules correspond to the **all** rule. The distinction between these rules becomes essential when considering more than two global subtransactions.

- The **at least one** rule represents the weakest requirement, i.e., this rule is always strengthened by another one. For example, **at least one** and **exactly one** are combined to **exactly one**.

Please note that this strengthening may lead to termination rules that are too strong in some cases — these rules are depicted by light gray colored boxes in Figure 6. Suppose, there is a global transaction with the following two operations:

> Insert into $C_{g_1} = C_1 \cup C_2$ with $C_1 \cap C_2$ using the flexible strategy;
> Insert into $C_{g_2} = C_3 \cup C_4$ with $C_3 \cap C_4$ using the flexible strategy;

Both operations correspond to the **at least one** rule. However, the following situation may occur: In the global subtransaction t_1, the insertion into C_1 fails while the insertion into C_3 could be performed successfully if the former operation would have not been failed. In the global subtransaction t_2, the insertion into C_4 fails while the insertion into C_2 could be performed successfully if the former operation would have not been failed. In consequence, both global subtransactions, and thus the global transaction, fail.

> *Consequently, a global transaction may fail although, from a global point of view, there is a way to successfully perform the operations of this transaction.*

- Combining **at least** t_i with **exactly one** results in **only** t_i because in this case the global transaction can only commit if t_i commits. However, if t_i commits, then the other global subtransaction has to abort.

- The **all** rule depicts the strongest requirement, i.e., a combination with the **all** rule always leads to the **all** rule. One exception is the incompatible combination **all** and **exactly one** (which was already discussed by the example before). This incompatibility has a fundamental consequence:

> *The corresponding global operations must be performed by different global subtransactions.*

- The rules **all** and **only** t_1 can be combined if the global subtransaction t_1 contains both operations whereas the global subtransaction t_2 only contains the operation corresponding to the **all** rule. To illustrate this case, suppose that the global transaction consists of the following two operations:

> Insert into $C_{g_1} = C_1 \cup C_2$ with $C_1 \equiv C_2$;
> Insert into $C_{g_2} = C_3 \cup C_4$ with $C_3 \supset C_4$ using the minimal strategy;

The first operation requires the **all** rule whereas the second one needs the **only** t_1 rule (under the assumption that the global subtransaction t_1 performs the insertion into the local class C_3). The global transaction can be performed by two global subtransactions t_1 and t_2 such that t_1 executes the insertions into the local classes C_1 and C_3 and t_2 performs the insertion into the local class C_2. The global transaction may only commit if both global subtransactions commit. Thus, the resulting rule is **all**.

The dark gray colored boxes in Figure 6 refer to such kinds of combinations where the global operation is not executed in both global subtransactions, i.e., using the minimal semantics.

In summary, we can state that the combinations in the "white" and dark gray colored boxes (except the ones with '—') are the "good" ones which always satisfy the given dependencies and perform all global operations in a correct way. In contrast, the combinations in the light gray colored boxes are the "potentially too strong" ones. These combinations might lead to executions that are rejected due to a violation of the given dependencies although there is an execution that would satisfy the given dependencies and perform all global operations in a correct way. Note that these combinations unfold a fundamental problem of executing global transactions under dependencies: To avoid unnecessary rejections of a global transaction, all possible executions have to be considered in the worst case.

5   Global Transaction Termination Protocol

Atomic commitment protocols such as the *two-phase commit (2PC)* protocol [6] and its variants *presumed abort/commit* [8] have been studied extensively in the context of distributed database systems. As pointed out in [9], the problem of the atomic commitment in federated database systems cannot be solved without locally participating in an atomic commitment protocol. There are several approaches to ensure global transaction atomicity, e.g. [10,16,7,14,21,18,4]. All these approaches focus on *atomic commitment* of global transactions. As we have shown in this paper, global atomic commitment alone is not sufficient to correctly deal with the termination of global transactions.

Following our previous discussion, a global transaction termination rule corresponds to a boolean formula. As we have seen before, atomic commitment is a special case. Therefore, a generalization of the two-phase-commit (2PC) protocol is needed to capture the various transaction termination rules. Figure 7 sketches such a global transaction termination protocol (that does not consider site failures). The circles denote the states and the dashed lines indicate messages between the *coordinator* (global transaction) and the *participants* (global subtransactions).

The traditional 2PC protocol has been modified as follows (the modified parts are denoted by the thick lines in Figure 7). In the **WAIT** state, originally the coordinator waits for the votes from *all* participants. In the generalized protocol, the coordinator evaluates the formula corresponding to the given termination rule immediately after having received a vote from a participant. As soon as the formula yields true, the coordinator decides for a "global commit". A global commit does not necessarily imply that all participants that have voted for commit will receive a global commit message. For instance, in case of the **exactly one** rule, only one participant may commit even if several participants may have voted for commit.

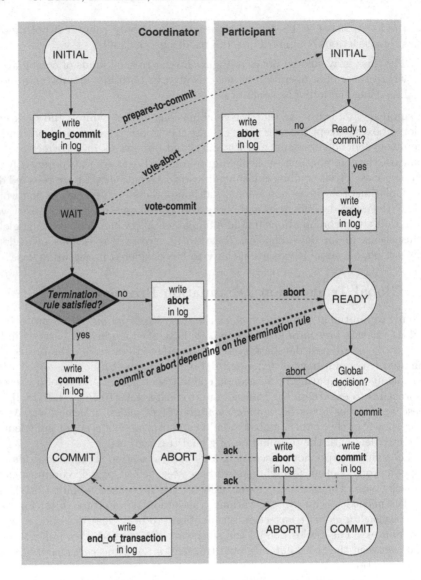

Fig. 7. The Generalized Transaction Termination Protocol

Note that the participant part of the 2PC protocol does not need to be modified. A participant that has voted for commit remains in the state **READY** until it receives the global decision message. In contrast to the traditional 2PC protocols, here a participant cannot infer from a commit message that all other participants have committed, too. Analogously, an abort message does not imply that no other participants has committed.

6   Conclusions

The contributions of this paper can be summarized as follows:

1. We have systematically investigated possible and meaningful global transaction termination rules and their correspondence to global operations. Especially, we pointed out the impact of extensional assertions on the correct termination strategy for global transactions. We have shown that atomic commitment is not necessary in all cases. In the **exactly one** case atomic commitment is even the wrong choice because only one global subtransaction is allowed to commit in order to commit the global transaction.

2. Moreover, we have shown that there are cases in which it is not possible to (correctly) perform a global transaction by executing at most one global subtransaction per component database system. This, however, is the general assumption on which most approaches to transaction management in composite (federated) database systems rely on. From our analysis we can conclude which operations can be combined within a global subtransaction.

3. Finally, we sketched a generalized protocol that supports the various global transaction termination rules. As an important issue, this protocol requires only changes of the 2PC coordinator protocol. Therefore, this generalized protocol can be used in a composite database system environment (without further restricting the local autonomy) if the component database systems support the standard 2PC participant protocol.

The knowledge about the correct decomposition and termination of global transactions is essential for maintaining globally consistent databases. This also includes that local transactions have to observed and necessary actions triggered when extensional assertions are violated. In this way, a local transaction becomes a global one.

Acknowledgments: Thanks to Ingo Schmitt for helpful comments on an earlier draft of this paper. We are also thankful to the anonymous referees for their valuable suggestions.

References

1. C. Batini, M. Lenzerini, and S. B. Navathe. A Comparative Analysis of Methodologies for Database Schema Integration. *ACM Computing Surveys*, 18(4):323–364, December 1986.
2. Y. Breitbart, H. Garcia-Molina, and A. Silberschatz. Overview of Multidatabase Transaction Management. *The VLDB Journal*, 1(2):181–240, October 1992.
3. S. Conrad, I. Schmitt, and C. Türker. Considering Integrity Constraints During Federated Database Design. In S. M. Embury, N. J. Fiddian, A. W. Gray, and A. C. Jones, editors, *Advances in Databases, 16th British National Conf. on Databases, BNCOD 16, Cardiff, Wales, July 1998*, Lecture Notes in Computer Science, Vol. 1405, pages 119–133. Springer-Verlag, Berlin, 1998.

4. A. K. Elmagarmid, J. Jing, W. Kim, O. Bukhres, and A. Zhang. Global Commit-tability in Multidatabase Systems. *IEEE Transactions on Knowledge and Data Engineering*, 8(5):816–824, October 1996.
5. D. Georgakopoulos, M. Rusinkiewicz, and A. Sheth. Using Tickets to Enforce the Serializability of Multidatabase Transactions. *IEEE Transactions on Knowledge and Data Engineering*, 6(1):166–180, February 1994.
6. J. Gray. Notes on Data Base Operating Systems. In R. Bayer, R. M. Graham, and G. Seegmüller, editors, *Operating Systems, An Advanced Course*, Lecture Notes in Computer Science, Vol. 60, pages 393–481. Springer-Verlag, Berlin, 1978.
7. S. Mehrotra, R. Rastogi, Y. Breitbart, H. F. Korth, and A. Silberschatz. En-suring Transaction Atomicity In Multidatabase Systems. In *Proc. of the 11th ACM SIGACT-SIGMOD-SIGART Symposium on Principles of Database Systems, PODS'92, San Diego, CA*, pages 164–175. ACM Press, New York, 1992.
8. C. Mohan, B. Lindsay, and R. Obermarck. Transaction Management in the R* Dis-tributed Database Management System. *ACM Transaction on Database Systems*, 11(4):378–396, December 1986.
9. J. G. Mullen, A. K. Elmagarmid, W. Kim, and J. Sharif-Askary. On the Impos-sibility of Atomic Commitment in Multidatabase Systems. In P. A. Ng, C. V. Ramamoorthy, L. C. Seifert, and R. T. Yeh, editors, *Proc. of the Second Int. Conf. on System Integration, ICSI'92*, pages 625–634. IEEE Computer Society Press, Los Alamitos, CA, 1992.
10. P. Muth and T. Rakow. Atomic Commitment for Integrated Database Systems. In N. Cercone and M. Tsuchiya, editors, *Proc. of the 7th IEEE Int. Conf. on Data Engineering, ICDE'91, April 8–12, 1991, Kobe, Japan*, pages 296–304. IEEE Computer Society Press, Los Alamitos, CA, 1991.
11. K. Schwarz. *The Concept of Transaction Closure for the Consistent Specification of Dependencies in Complex Applications*, Dissertationen zu Datenbanken und In-formationssystemen, Vol. 65. infix-Verlag, Sankt Augustin, 1999. (In German).
12. K. Schwarz, C. Türker, and G. Saake. Extending Transaction Closures by N-ary Termination Dependencies. In W. Litwin, T. Morzy, and G. Vossen, editors, *Ad-vances in Databases and Information Systems, Proc. Second East-European Sym-posium, ADBIS'98, Poznań, Poland, September 1998*, Lecture Notes in Computer Science, Vol. 1475, pages 131–142. Springer-Verlag, Berlin, 1998.
13. K. Schwarz, C. Türker, and G. Saake. Integrating Execution Dependencies into the Transaction Closure Framework. *International Journal of Cooperative Information Systems (IJCIS)*, 8(2–3):111–138, June/September 1999.
14. A. Sheth, M. Rusinkiewicz, and G. Karabatis. Using Polytransaction to Manage Interdependent Data. In A. K. Elmagarmid, editor, *Database Transaction Mo-dels for Advanced Applications*, pages 555–581, Morgan Kaufmann Publishers, San Mateo, CA, 1992.
15. A. P. Sheth and J. A. Larson. Federated Database Systems for Managing Dis-tributed, Heterogeneous, and Autonomous Databases. *ACM Computing Surveys*, 22(3):183–236, September 1990.
16. N. Soparkar, H. Korth, and A. Silberschatz. Failure-Resilient Transaction Mana-gement in Multidatabases. *IEEE Computer*, 24(12):28–36, December 1991.
17. S. Spaccapietra, C. Parent, and Y. Dupont. Model Independent Assertions for Integration of Heterogeneous Schemas. *The VLDB Journal*, 1(1):81–126, July 1992.
18. A. Tal and R. Alonso. Integration of Commit Protocols in Heterogeneous Databa-ses. *Distributed and Parallel Databases*, 2(2):209–234, 1994.

19. C. Türker. *Semantic Integrity Constraints in Federated Database Schemata*, Dissertationen zu Datenbanken und Informationssystemen, Vol. 63. infix-Verlag, Sankt Augustin, 1999.
20. C. Türker and G. Saake. Consistent Handling of Integrity Constraints and Extensional Assertions for Schema Integration. In J. Eder, I. Rozman, and T. Welzer, editors, *Advances in Databases and Information Systems, Proc. Third East-European Symposium, ADBIS'99, Maribor, Slovenia, September 1999*, Lecture Notes in Computer Science, Vol. 1691, pages 31–45. Springer-Verlag, Berlin, 1999.
21. J. Veijalainen and A. Wolski. Prepare and Commit Certification for Decentralized Transaction Management in Rigorous Heterogeneous Multidatabases. In F. Golshani, editor, *Proc. of the 8th IEEE Int. Conf. on Data Engineering, ICDE'92, Tempe, Arizona, USA, February 2–3, 1992*, pages 470–480. IEEE Computer Society Press, Los Alamitos, CA, 1992.

A Review of Multidatabase Transactions on the Web: From the ACID to the SACReD

Muhammed Younas[1], Barry Eagelstone[1], and Rob Holton[2]

[1] Department of Information Studies, University of Sheffield, UK
{M.Younas, B.Eaglestone}@sheffield.ac.uk
[2] Department of Computing, University of Bradford, UK
DRW.Holton@scm.brad.ac.uk

Abstract. This paper analyses the characteristics of Web-multidatabase transactions and associated transaction management issues. Current Web-database transaction management solutions are reviewed. Conclusions drawn are that these are currently too restrictive. Flexibility is required through nested flexible transaction strategies, with compensation, and contingency or alternative subtransactions. Furthermore, the classical ACID test of transaction correctness is over-restrictive and unrealistic in the Web context. A relaxation of the ACID test is proposed, based on semantic atomicity, local consistency, and durability, for resilient transactions, i.e., the SACReD properties. These conclusions motivate the authors ongoing research and development of a prototype CORBA-compliant middleware Web-multidatabase transaction manager based upon a hybrid configuration of open and closed nested flexible transactions.

1. Introduction

The World Wide Web (Web) dramatically extended roles and applications of database technology but poses new problems for the database community. The Web is important because it provides low cost ready-made global infrastructure for integrated information systems. However, it currently provides unsatisfactory support for certain associated requirements. This paper reviews a facility that is a pre-requisite to successful operation of such systems, i.e., effective transaction management (TM). Section 2 charts the evolution of multidatabase applications, through to current Web-based federated information systems, and identifies a mismatch between classical TM and characteristics of Web-multidatabase applications. Current TM solutions for Web applications are reviewed in Section 3. Section 4 then examines TM protocols and correctness criteria with respect to Web-multidatabase transactions. Finally, Section 5 gives a summary and conclusions, as well as identifying ongoing work towards a Web Transaction Model (WebTraM) motivated by those conclusions.

2. Web-Database Transactions

Exploitation of multiple database sources has been a focus prior to the spread of the Web. Initially, related problems of TM were scoped to operate within single

B. Lings and K. Jeffery (Eds.): BNCOD 17, LNCS 1832, pp. 140–152, 2000.
© Springer-Verlag Berlin Heidelberg 2000

distributed database systems [OV91]. This made TM a tractable problem. For example, workable solutions for traditional ACID (Atomic, Consistent, Isolated, Durable) transactions on distributed databases have been implemented using two phase commit protocol (2PC) [BHG87, OV91] and are used in proprietary distributed database systems. In the mid-1980s the focus moved from database distribution to the mulitidatabase problem, i.e., integrating separate, pre-existing, autonomous and heterogeneous database systems [BGS92]. These characteristics of the component databases necessitated that the multidatabase system „sits on top of" component systems and appear to them as just another user. A consequence was removal from the multidatabase TM mechanisms of direct control over local TM, such as locking protocols or awareness of the local „ready to commit" status. Also, rather than recovery through local transaction aborts, multidatabase TM must often rely on compensating [LKS91, GS87, CR94], and alternative (or contingency) transactions [Zha+94, MR97, NM97, JK97, EB97]. Compensating transactions remove effects of committed subtransactions if the associated transaction aborts. Alternative transactions are executed, in case of failure, to perform the same or an alternative task. Since Web transactions are more vulnerable to abortion due to the unreliable nature of the Internet and stronger requirements for local systems autonomy, alternative transactions can play a vital role. However, they have limited applications, since certain tasks are non-reversible or mandatory.

Multidatabase systems also introduce conflicts between requirements for integrated global access, and the autonomous operation and administration of component systems. This makes mapping between global and local schemas volatile and uncertain in the presence of semantic and schematic heterogeneities. Many workable multidatabase systems succeed because compromises are made between these requirements, in environments where central administrative control can be imposed and local autonomy and heterogeneity restricted, e.g., in certain healthcare and engineering applications [CEH97]. However, this restriction is harder to achieve within the open and libertarian environment of the Web.

Characteristics of Web-multidatabase applications determine new requirements for Web TM. According to [EB97], commercial Web-based transactions are characterised by large transactional computations, complex data accessing patterns, invocation (direct or indirect) of computations at other sites by a unit of transaction (a subtransaction), active capabilities, and support for heterogeneous and autonomous environments. The potential for integration of existing information systems also introduces other characteristics. Consider a hypothetical booking service for the Euro 2000 Football Competition, which integrates subsystems for transport, accommodation and match tickets. This type of application illustrates the following:

Openness and non-prescription. The Web is a more open and less prescriptive environment within which users operate. Note that the above application provides integrated access to a number of component information systems, i.e., for accommodations, transport and tickets. However, Web browsers will also allow ad hoc navigation outside of this integrated environment, for example, to search tourist information pages. This contrasts with pre-Web applications, within which the scope, functionality and access paths were tightly prescribed and controlled by the application. This complicates TM, since either transactions must be scoped dynamically, or users must be allowed to navigate in and out of pre-defined transaction boundaries.

Long duration and complexity. A transaction may require access to many database systems and Web servers, with frequent user interaction, both with the system and possibly other users. Transactions are therefore complex, and can be decomposed into subtransactions for component sub-systems. These characteristics are typical of Web applications, and are partly a consequence of the enabling, rather than prescriptive, function of Web browsers. This becomes problematic if a consequence is the locking of data resources for long periods, as would be the case with conventional TM.

User cooperation. In the example, there is potential for interaction and co-operation between users, for instance, if a party makes a group booking. This conflicts with the assumptions of conventional ACID transaction technology, which requires that transactions are isolated from each other. User activities and actions for collaborative work in the Web environment are defined in [MGN97]. (The authors suggest these can be implemented using the CORBA Transaction Service, but do not clarify how the actions can be used as transactions or how recovery is provided for those actions in case of failures.)

Web TM is also made problematic by characteristics of the Web technology, itself. Basic Web communications support is based on HTTP and TCP/IP protocols. HTTP [Ber92] is used by the Web to retrieve information from the servers distributed across the Internet, and is built on the top of TCP/IP. HTTP is a stateless protocol, since its basic working mechanism is that a client establishes a connection to the remote server and then issues a request. The server then processes the request, returns the response to the client and closes the connection. For each additional request of the client, HTTP must establish a new connection with the server. The Web therefore has a natural granularity of the point-to-point message and response, rather than the session or transaction. This necessitates ad hoc higher level mechanisms (such as cookies, hidden variables [OH98] and URL rewriting [EKR97]) for maintaining connections. Also, since the Web is largely unregulated, it is unrealistic to base a TM solution on the assumption that a higher-level TM mechanism based upon multi-message sessions will be widely adopted and supported. Further, Web TM must compensate for negative aspects of Web-based applications, such as poor performance, variability in the quality of Web services, a lack of an underlying information structure, and varying levels of support for Web-services at different browsers, so as to ensure acceptable levels of performance and reliability.

3. Current Approaches

The Web offers a range of architectural choices for Web-systems designers. As in [KRR99], we use these to classify current Web TM approaches as follow.

- *Client-side* refers to the technique where the databases are accessed directly from the browser, e.g., using browser plug-ins, and Java applets.

- *Server-side* refers to the technique where browsers access databases through Web servers, e.g., SSI, CGI, or Java servlets.
- TM can also be implemented within *middleware*, whereby servers act as intermediary processes, interfacing clients to 'back-end' database systems. (See [PS98, OH98, TK98] for reviews of associated technologies, e.g., Java RMI, DCOM, and CORBA.)

The *client-side* approach potentially improves performance. The Web application is executed locally, rather than as a shared service, and TM can be implemented straightforwardly through the existing DBMS mechanisms [KRR99] (this approach has been adopted by DBMS providers to support Web access to their products). A penalty is the need to transmit application code and the dependency on the client's resources. A disadvantage is lack of flexibility to accommodate underlying systems, as it needs dedicated clients and servers for supporting transactional features. Examples of client-side TM are in [Bil98], [LS+97], and [LS98].

ITM [Bil98] serves a single user's requests directed to multiple databases, in contrast to traditional approaches that serve multiple users' transactions. It implements 2PC but with modification for the preservation of privacy and loyalty. For example, if a transaction spans two servers, the loyalty property requires that these are known to each other, via the authentication scheme. However, within ITM, servers cannot communicate. Therefore, if a failure occurs, the recovery mechanism must operate outside of ITM [BHG87]. Moreover, responsibility of concurrency control is left to participating DBMS. The author assumes that deadlock will be very rare, and when it does occur, a time-out strategy can be used to resolve it. The innovative feature of ITM is its handling of transactions that are not prescribed a priori. Within ITM, database systems have no knowledge about the existence of each other, and there is no global transaction manager. Instead, transactions are self-managed. There are some discrepancies in the description of the ITM [Bil98]. For instance, though it is stated that participating sites may not communicate with each other, it is recommended that they should communicate for recovery purposes. Also, modification to 2PC is proposed in order to preserve privacy and loyalty properties, but the nature of these modifications is not defined, and is problematic if sites are not allowed to communicate with each other. Moreover, ITM excludes a global transaction manager, but suggests that one should perform resolution of deadlocks between transactions.

The TM model proposed in [LS+97] is interesting because it illustrates an approach to coping with the heterogeneous nature of Web resources. Transactional gateways and browser proxies are used to enable browsers to take part in transactional applications. The purpose of a gateway is to make the browser capable of accessing the transactional applications. These can be accessed through different gateways that can be configured according to browser-specific requirements. That is, if a browser is transactional, then the gateway downloads transactional application objects for the relevant browser. For a non-transactional browser, the gateway creates a transactional browser proxy. The latter enables non-transactional browsers to take part in transactional application activities, and consists of code that resides in the browser as well as in the gateway. The above approach allows application-specific tailoring, by providing an object-oriented toolkit, W3OTrans, with which programmers develop

Web applications using possibly nested atomic actions. These applications can distribute over multiple Web servers, multiple browsers, or execute locally within a single browser [Ing+95].

The JTSArjuna system for 'Java Transactions for the Internet' [LS98] also implements client side TM. JTSArjuna is a CORBA Transaction Service compliant system that provides users with facilities to develop Internet transactional applications using Java. In addition, it ensures end-to-end transactional integrity between browsers and transactional applications and supports nested transactions. The system can be considered as an alternative to W3Otrans [LS+97], described above. Whereas W3OTrans uses transactional gateways and browser proxies to make the browser transactional, JTSArjuna uses Java applets and also maintains the security policy of a particular browser.

Of the above client-side TM systems, those in [LS+97] and [LS98] have the advantage of not requiring modifications to the clients. However, the use of applets causes problems. Concurrency and recovery by browsers require some persistently stored information about transaction status, but Java applets are constrained by the Java Security Manager from writing to the local disk. Both systems circumvent this problem by routing status data writes to a (possibly remote) writable disk. However, writing to a remote disk causes lack of reliability and performance, because of unreliable Internet communications and delays incurred. The situation becomes worse when a „forced-write" is made, since the transaction execution must then be suspended until transfer to persistent storage is completed [CP87].

Server-side TM is applicable to large-scale applications, since it removes the need to transmit code to the client and reliance on the clients' resources. Again, this approach is implementation specific and suffers from autonomy and heterogeneity problems [KRR99]. The former occurs because neither Web servers nor database servers are designed to support Web transaction applications. The classic use of Web servers is to maintain Web pages while database servers support the database applications. However, Web transactions demand co-ordination among different servers in order to meet reliability and execution correctness criteria. For example, if a Web transaction spanning multiple Web servers fails, then there should be a mechanism to correctly terminate the transaction. Similarly when competing Web transactions give rise to deadlock, co-ordination between the Web servers becomes of importance to resolve it. Heterogeneity creates problems for Web transactions, since, for example, database servers involved may follow different transaction models.

Our literature search identified the TIP model [LEK98, EKL97] as the sole example of server-side TM. TIP uses 2PC, as is typical of current Web TM systems. TIP is instructive because of its limitations and consequential dependencies on other systems, as highlighted by the Internet Engineering Task Force (IETF). These make TIP at best a partial solution to the Web TM problem. For example, TIP requires compatibility and reliance on existing security systems, such as Transport Layer Security, to authenticate TIP commands, and TCP to establish connections between transaction managers. Also, it is assumed that TIP will use some private mechanisms to detect connection failure and to provide transaction recovery [LEK98]. In addition, there are problems if the transaction managers, such as database transaction managers on TP monitors (e.g., Tuxedo [Tuxedo96]) are client-only systems. This is because these provide application interfaces for demarcating TIP transactions, but lack access to local recoverable resources (e.g. databases), which may result in unreliability. Consequently, they cannot be appropriately used as transaction co-ordinators. Therefore transaction co-ordination and failure recovery must be delegated to other subsystems. There is also the problem of adoption, which is always problematic for solutions to generic Web related problems. Although TIP Internet-Drafts are intended to pave the way for the implementation of 2PC on the Internet for transaction-based electronic commerce applications, this requires that the TM of participating systems must comply with the TIP specification. TIP compliant TM should offer a set of APIs that are to be used by local applications to import and export TIP transactions. Clearly, TIP requires modifications to the underlying servers (e.g. Web or database servers). Consequently, autonomy of Web and database servers is violated, and flexibility to support heterogeneous data sources (whose modification is not feasible) is reduced. In addition, the 2PC supported by TIP creates other problems such as poor performance and a lack of advanced transaction support. Despite the above reservations, the work on the TIP model [LEK98, EKL97] does contributes to the development of Internet transaction processing (especially in electronic commerce applications) by describing the main aspects required for the implementation of 2PC in the Internet.

The third approach is to implement TM within *middleware*. According to [Ber96], „middleware is a term that captures so many concepts and architectures and thus its meaning remains often unclear. However, at the broadest level it can be defined as a generic system that provides platform independence, and supports standard interfaces and protocols in addition to distribution". Within the context of Web TM, middleware is an approach where clients, transaction services, and underlying database systems are implemented as independent system components. Unlike the previous approaches, middleware factors out transactional features into a third component. A consequence is the prescription of architectures and interfaces to which participating systems must conform. De-coupling TM from the application and database support provides a basis for reuse of TM solutions in different contexts. TM middleware differs according to host technology and level of transaction support. Advantages claimed of this approach [Ber96] include, flexibility, since it provides a way to link existing legacy systems to newer applications based on Internet, intranet, and object-oriented technology without having to totally rewrite these applications. It can also improve the performance by reducing the load on underlying Web or database servers. Examples of TM middleware include X/Open Distributed Transaction Processing (DTP) Model [Atz+99], Object Transaction Service (OTS) [OMG97], and JPernLite: Extensible Transaction Services for WWW [YK98].

X/Open DTP is not a Web TM system, but has become a de facto standard for distributed database systems. DTP has been adapted for Web TM by OMG within the OTS. However, DTP-based products are limited, since DTP does not have any support for advanced transactions and is limited to ACID transaction models. In fact, current middleware TM solutions predominantly apply 2PC protocol and ensure ACID properties. They do this by restricting the environments within which TM takes place. However, as has been shown in the previous discussion, ACID properties can not be guaranteed in the Web environment. Some middleware systems are extensible, such that application specific solutions can be constructed, e.g., the JpernLite system which can be extended to provide concurrency control for extended transactions through the use of plug-in codes.

4. Protocols and Correctness Properties

Current Web TM solutions are predominantly based upon 2PC (e.g., [LEK98, Bil98, LS⁺97]) or its variants (e.g., [OMG97]). The latter improve performance by making early assumptions which reduce message costs, e.g., *presumed abort* [OV91, MLO86] and *presumed commit* [MLO86, CP87], or by exploiting the capabilities of high performance communications links, e.g., *Implicit Yes Vote (IYV)* [HC95]. However, these do not address key characteristics of the Web database applications discussed in section 2.

[EB97] addresses the problem of Web transaction complexity, and suggests use of a closed nested transaction (NT) model. The authors argue that an NT approach is necessary to support large transactional computations, complex data accessing patterns, invocation of remote computations, active capabilities, and support for heterogeneous and autonomous environments. This complexity requires decomposition of transactions into possibly nested subtransactions. The authors suggest concurrency control algorithms of distributed transaction models are applicable to the Web environment with little or no modifications. Their analysis is based upon the observation that the multidatabase framework (where each database is autonomous) characterises electronic commerce and therefore provides a framework for reasoning using formal specification.

An advantage of NT models is that they can control complex transactions using hierarchical decomposition. Transactions are nested by allowing each to be constituted from other transactions (subtransactions) in addition to primitive read and write operations. Thus transactions are tree structured. Subtransactions can execute atomically with respect to the other sibling subtransactions and their parent transaction as well. The subtransactions can abort unilaterally without causing abortion of the entire transaction. The commit of the subtransactions can be performed in two ways: (i) subtransactions can not commit before the commit of the root (or parent) transaction, (ii) subtransactions can commit unilaterally, irrespective of the commitment of other subtransactions and the (root) transaction. A nested transaction is called a *closed-nested* transaction if it follows (i), and an *open-nested* transaction if it follows (ii), for the commitment of subtransactions [CR94]. Closed-nested transactions guarantee ACID properties, as a subtransaction transfers all resources to its root transaction at the commit time, and no other transaction can access its intermediate results. Open-nested transactions relax the ACID properties. For example, *atomicity* is relaxed by allowing subtransactions to commit unilaterally, and *isolation* is violated by exposing the results of the committed subtransactions to other transactions.

We see the close-NT model as having only limited applications. Depending on the nature of particular Web applications, both the closed-nested and open-nested transactions have strengths and weaknesses. The former are appropriate for applications where the maintenance of the ACID properties is crucial and where the transaction is of short duration, performing simple calculations. However, close-nested transactions fall short of the requirements of advanced applications, especially in the Web environment. Consider the Euro2000 example where a transaction makes arrangements for a football supporter. A closed-nested transaction cannot be used, as it causes subtransaction to hold resources, e.g., ticket and flight data, of the respective Web-database systems until the termination of the whole transaction. For such applications, open-nested transactions are more appropriate, so that subtransactions can release resources unilaterally after finishing their specified tasks.

Another development in TM that better suits the Web environment is the flexible transaction. Flexibility is provided by compensating and alternative (or contingency) transactions. The use of flexible transactions is also favoured in [EB97] for electronic commerce applications. Compensating transactions have been defined, by [GS87, LKS91], as separate global transactions, which undo the effects of particular transactions. However, in reality, a Web transaction can be composed of different kinds of subtransactions that may or may not be compensatable and this limits transaction flexibility. Thus the structure of the Web transaction does not always allow the definition of a separate global compensating transaction. Furthermore, the execution correctness criterion in [LKS91] for a compensatable global transaction is very restrictive, since it is based on the assumption that all the underlying DBMS should follow the two-phase locking (2PL) protocol. This cannot be applied generally to Web transactions because they can access DBMS of any kind, whether using 2PL or timestamp method for concurrency control. However, the concept of flexible transactions has been generalised [Zha+94] to describe subtransactions that provide compensation or alternatives for a particular subtransaction within the context of a global transaction, thus providing multiple pathways to completion of a global transaction. The advantage is therefore a greater resilience to failure.

In general, we believe that classical transaction technology badly serves the Web environment. This is because this environment is largely unregulated and therefore the assumptions of classical TM cannot be guaranteed to hold. In particular, the ACID test of transaction correctness must be re-assessed as the criteria for transaction correctness, since ACID properties are unrealistic for Web transactions in the majority of situations. This is the case specifically where local „ready to commit" states cannot be determined globally or where long duration makes postponement of local commit until global commit unacceptable. TM solutions therefore include variants of the 2PC, such as *Optimistic 2PC* [LKS91] which relax the ACID condition by allowing unilateral local commit of subtransactions, and to avoid excessive resource blocking in long duration transactions. Also the use of compensating transactions (rather than transaction abort with traditional undo operation [BHG87]) complicates the notions of transaction correctness. [LKS91] therefore proposes additional correctness properties, namely, atomicity of compensation (i.e., a transaction can read a database state affected by a subtransaction or the corresponding compensation transaction, but not both) and serialisability when subtransactions are not aborted, but taking into account affects of compensations. Also, [Zha+94] defines flexible transactions based upon representative partial orderings that show the execution of alternative sets of subtransactions. Based upon these the authors defined semi-atomicity of transactions as the property where: i) all the subtransactions in one partial ordering commit and all other attempted (active) subtransactions in another partial orderings are either aborted or have their effects undone, and ii) no partial effects of its subtransactions remain in local databases.

Furthermore, the classical *atomicity* property requires an „all or nothing" ethos. An atomic transaction must either appear to execute in its entirety or not at all. Other transactions can not be exposed to a database state caused by a partially completed transaction (atomicity is achieved using deferred update or immediate update with write-ahead log protocol techniques [CBS96]). Within a Web-multidatabase system, atomicity can be assured at the local database level for subtransactions, using the TM of the participating DBMS. However, in cases where the local „ready to commit" state cannot be determined at the global level, atomicity cannot be enforced for the (global) Web transaction. A relaxed atomicity property is therefore appropriate in which unilateral committing of subtransactions is accepted, and where as a consequence, intermediate states of local databases are accessible. This relaxed atomicity is known as *semantic atomicity* of a transaction [WS92, BE96, GS87, BK91]. In this context, the term, „semantic" refers to the consequence of relaxing the atomicity of transactions by exploiting the semantics of their operations. To preserve the property of semantic atomicity, a Web transaction is required to commit either all of its subtransactions, or if any of the subtransaction is aborted then the effects of the committed subtransactions must be compensated for via compensating transactions. Clearly, a Web transaction must execute in its entirety to preserve the semantic atomicity property. Note that compensating a completed subtransaction requires that both the actual subtransaction and its compensating subtransaction are atomic. Semantic atomicity is interpreted as the „all-or-nothing" effects of a transaction on a shared systems state in terms of Web level details. In other words, semantic atomicity is the way of masking the existence of aborted subtransactions (of a Web transaction) to all applications that will be subsequently executed.

The *consistency* property requires that a transaction should transform the respective databases from one consistent state, i.e., one that satisfies the integrity constraints, to another consistent state [CBS96]. This property, where subtransactions are allowed to unilaterally commit, can be enforced only at the component database level. Inter-database consistency cannot be enforced (and cannot generally be specified). Furthermore, preservation of consistency by a transaction can not guarantee the validity of database states. For example, in the Euro2000 example, if a flight seat reserved by a subtransaction is cancelled due to the unavailability of match ticket, its state remains consistent but invalid between commit and compensation. Maintenance of the integrity of component databases is a function of the component DBMS, rather than the Web TM system.

Violation of the *isolation* property is a consequence of semantic atomicity, since the partial effects of subtransactions that unilaterally commit are then exposed to other transactions. In practice isolation may not be desirable when transactions involve co-operation and negotiation between users.

The final ACID property, *durability*, requires that the effects of a committed transaction must not be erased and should be made permanent in the respective databases. Durability must be exercised for the committed Web transactions even in the case of failures. Recovery techniques are used to achieve the property of durability. Persistency of transactions is necessary for human-oriented systems where operations such as editing and debugging takes a long time, and rolling back those operations may lead to a significant loss of work [YK98].

The ACID properties, can also be supplemented by additional properties that are desirable, and essential in certain Web transactions. For example, in [Bil98] the properties of *privacy* and *loyalty* are defined as tests for assessing the security of transactions, (thus ACID becomes PLACID). Privacy is defined for the transmission of confidential information (e.g., credit card numbers). Loyalty is defined for authenticity and non-repudiation. Authenticity requires that participants involved in a transaction, e.g., a purchaser and supplier, must know each other's identity. Non-repudiation requires that the sender and receiver must not deny the acceptance of information being sent.

To the above properties, we add as a desirable, but not mandatory property, *resilience*. Conventionally the purpose of TM is to improve system resilience by ensuring that views of the system are not corrupted by partially completed or failed transactions. However, within the Web environment, transactions are particularly vulnerable to failure due to the unreliable nature of the Internet, the stronger requirements for autonomy of local systems and the consequentially increased likelihood of subtransaction failure through system failure or unavailability of the requested services, i.e., semantic failure. The resiliency property concerns the capability of a transaction to cope with system and semantic failures. Resilience is therefore an a priori property of a transaction, rather than an *a* posteriori measure of the correctness of its execution. Also, rather than being a Boolean property, as are the others, it has an associated strength. Resilience is increased, by associating alternative transactions with the subtransactions, thus creating alternative subtransaction sequences that result in successful completion.

5. Conclusions

This paper has reviewed characteristics of Web-multidatabase transactions and the applicability of classical TM. We have also reviewed current Web TM technologies, protocols and correctness criteria. Our conclusions are as follows.

More generic TM solutions can potentially be achieved by implementing Web TM as middleware. Though current solutions are predominantly based upon 2PC or its variants, we see these as being over restrictive. NT models provide the capability to handle the complexity of Web-multidatabase transactions, but neither the open or closed variants provide a completely generic solution. In general the unregulated nature of the Web environment suggests hybrid solutions that can be tailored to specific application requirements. Some of this flexibility can be provided by flexible transaction approaches that utilise compensating and alternative transaction strategies. Accordingly, we believe that the conventional ACID test is inappropriate for Web transactions, given that atomicity and independence are not realistic objectives. Instead, more relaxed criteria are required. Our proposal is to test transaction correctness based upon semantic atomicity, consistency and durability. In addition, strongly resilient transactions are very desirable as they support alternative subtransaction sequences in the presence of semantic failures of component systems or subtractions. We use the acronym, SACReD (Semantic Atomicity, Consistency, Resilience and Durability) to denote these criteria.

We are currently implementing and evaluating a flexible Web Transaction Model (WebTraM) based upon these conclusions, as prototype CORBA-compliant middleware. WebTraM implements an open NT model, with nested open and closed nested transactions. Compensating and alternative subtransactions are used to provide flexibility and resilience. Our aim is to manage SACReD Web-multidatabase transactions.

Our final observation is that, given the unregulated and ad hoc nature of the Web and its development, and the primitive level of Web support for transactions, a fully generic TM system is over-ambitious. Also, the starting point for the work reviewed in this paper has been to adapt existing TM technology, but in general that assumes a level of control over the transactions which may be contradictory to the ethos of the Web, and is certainly not currently supported. It may be that concepts of classical TM are inappropriate, and some more radical approach is needed.

References

[Atz⁺99] P. Atzeni, S. Ceri, S. Paraboschi, R. Torlone „*Database Systems: Concepts, Languages, and Architectures*", McGraw Hill, 1999, Pages 378-381, ISBN 007 7095 006.

[BE96]   O.A. Bukhres, K. Elmagarmid „*Object-Oriented Multidatabase Systems: A Solution for Advanced Applications*" Prentice Hall, 1996.

[Ber96]   Philip A. Berstein „*Middleware: A Model for Distributed System Services*" Communications of the ACM, Vol. 39, No. 2, February 1996, Pages 86-98

[Ber92]   Tim Berners-Lee „HTTP Protocol Specification" CERN, 1992
          http://www.w3.org/Protocols/HTTP/HTTP2.html

[BGS92]   Y. Breitbart, H. Garcia-Molina, A. Silberschatz „*Overview of Multidatabase Transaction Management*" Technical Report TR-92-21, Department of Computer Science, The University of Texas at Austin, May 1992.

[BHG87]   Berstein, P.A., Hadzilacos, N., Goodman, N. „*Concurrency Control and Recovery in Database Systems*" Addison-Wesley, USA, 1987.

[Bil98]   D. Billard „*Transactional Services for the Internet*" Proc. of International Workshop on Web and Database (WebDB'98), Valencia, Spain, March 27-28 1998.

[BK91]   Naser S. Barghouti, Gail E. Kaiser „*Concurrency Control in Advanced Database Applications*" ACM Computing Surveys, Vol. 23, No. 3, September 1991, Pages 269-317.

[CBS96]   T. M. Connolly, C. E. Begg, A. D. Strachan „*DATABASE SYSTEMS: A Practical Approach to Design, Implementation and Management*" Addison-Weseley, pp. 582, 1996.

[CEH97]   S. Conrad, B. Eaglestone, W. Hasselbring, et al. "*Research Issues in Federated Database Systems: Report of EFDBS'97 Workshop*" SIGMOD Vol. 26, No. 4, December 1997, Pages 54-56.

[CP87]   S. Ceri, G. Pelagatti „*Distributed Databases: Principles & Systems*"
          McGraw-Hill International Editions, 1987. Page 337, ISBN 0-07-Y66215.
[CR94]   Panos K. Chrysanthis, Krithi Ramamritham „*Synthesis of Extended
          Transaction Models using ACTA*" ACM Transactions on Database
          Systems, Vol. 19, No. 3, September 1994, Pages 450-491
[EB97]   Sylvanus A. Ehikioya, Ken Barker „*A Formal Specification Strategy for
          Electronic Commerce*" Proc. of the International Database Engineering and
          Application Symposium (IDEAS), Montreal, Canada, August, 1997.
[EKL97]   K. Evans, J. Klein, J. Lyon „*Transaction Internet Protocol —
          Requirements and Supplemental Information*" Internet-Draft, October
          1997.
          http://www.ietf.org/ids.by.wg/tip.html
[EKR97]   G. Ehmayer, G. Kappel, S. Reich „*Connecting Databases to the Web: A
          Taxonomy of Gateways*" 8th International Conference on Database and
          Expert Systems Applications (DEXA'97), Toulouse, France, Sept. 1997.
[GS87]   H.Garcia-Molina, K.Salem „*Sagas* " Proc. of ACM-SIGMOD International
          Conf. on Management of Data, San Francisco, USA, 1987, Pages 249-259.
[HC95]   Yousef J. Al-Houmaily, Panos K. Chrysanthis " Two-Phase Commit in
          Gigabit-Networked Distributed Databases" Proc. of 8th International
          Conference on Parallel & distributed Computing Systems, September 1995.
[Ing+95] D.B. Ingham, M.C. Little, S.J. Caughey, S.K. Shrivastava, „*W3Objects:
          Bringing Object-Oriented Technology to the Web*" The Web Journal, 1(1),
          Pages 89-105, Proc. of the 4th International World Wide Web Conference,
          Boston, USA, December 1995.
[JK97]   Sushil Jajodia, Larry Kerschberg „*Advanced Transaction Models and
          Architectures*" Kluwer Academic Publishers, 1997, ISBN 0-7923-9880-7
[KRR99]   G. Kappel, S. Rausch-Schott, W. Retschitzegger "*Transaction Support for
          DataWeb Applications - A Requirement's Perspective*" Proc. of Fifth
          American Conference on Information Systems (AMCIS'99), Milwaukee,
          Winconsin (USA), August 1999.
[LEK98]   J. Lyon, K. Evans, J. Klein, „*Transaction Internet Protocol: Version 3.0*"
          Internet-Draft, April 1998 (http://www.ietf.org/ids.by.wg/tip.html)
[LKS91]   E. Levy, H.F. Korth, A. Silberschatz „*An Optimistic Commit Protocol for
          Distributed Transaction Management*" Proc. of ACM SIGMOD, Denver,
          Colorado, May 1991.
[LS+97]   M.C. Little, S.K. Shrivastava, S.J. Caughey, D.B. Ingham „*Constructing
          Reliable Web Applications using Atomic Actions*" Proc. of 6th International
          WWW Conference, Santa Clara, California, USA, April, 1997.
[LS98]   M.C. Little, S.K. Shrivastava „*Java Transactions for the Internet*" Proc. of
          4th USENIX Conference on Object-Oriented Technologies and Systems
          (COOTS'98), April 1998.
[MGN97]   M. Mock, M. Gergeleit, E. Nett „*Cooperative Concurrency Control on the
          Web*" Proc. of 5th IEEE Workshop on Future Trends of Distributed
          Computing System, Tunis, October 1997.
[MLO86]   C. Mohan, B. Lindsay, R. Obermarck "*Transaction Management in the R*
          Distributed Database Management System*" ACM Transactions on
          Database Systems, 11(4), 1986, Pages 378-396

[MR97]   Peter Muth, Thomas C. Rakow „*VODAK Open Nested Transactions —
           Visualizing Database Internals*" Proc. of the ACM SIGMOD, International
           Conf. on Management of Data, Washington DC, May 1993.

[NM97]   Edgar Nett, Michael Mock, „*A Recovery Model for Extended Real-Time
           Transactions*" Proc. of 2nd International IEEE Workshop on High
           Assurance Systems Engineering (HASE'97), Washington DC, August
           1997.

[OH98]   R. Orfali, D. Harkey "*Client/Server Programming with JAVA and CORBA*"
           2nd Edition, John Wiley & Sons, Inc. 1998, Pages 373-388.

[OMG97]   OMG „*CORBAservices: Common Object Service Specification*" November
           1997 (http://www.omg.org/corba/csindx.htm)

[OV91]   Tamer Ozsu, Patrick Valduriez „*Principles of Distributed Database
           Systems*" Prentice-Hall Inc., 1991, ISBN 0-13-715681-2

[PS98]   Frantisek Plasil, Michael Stal "*An Architectural View of Distributed
           Objects and Components in CORBA, Java RMI, and COM/DCOM*"
           Software Concepts and Tools, Vol. 9, No.1, Springer 1998

[TK98]   Owen Tallman, J. Bradford Kain "*COM versus CORBA: A Decision
           Framework*" Distributed Computing, September - December 1998.
           http://www.quoininc.com/quoininc/COM_CORBA.html

[Tuxedo96] BEA Corp. „BEA TUXEDO" November 1996
           http://www.beasys.com/products/tuxedo/tuxwp_pm/tuxwp_pm1.htm

[WS92]   G. Weikum, H.Schek, „*Concepts and Applications of Multilevel
           Transactions and Open Nested Transactions*" In A. K. Elmagarmid
           (Editor), Database Models for Advanced Applications, Morgan Kaufmann
           Publishers, 1992.

[YK98]   Jingshuang Yang, Gail E. Kaiser, „*JPernLite: An Extensible Transaction
           Server for the World Wide Web*" to appear in: IEEE Transactions on
           Knowledge and Data Engineering, 1999.

[Zha+94]   A. Zhang, M. Nodine, B. Bhargava, O. Bukhras „*Ensuring Relaxed
           Atomicity for Flexible Transactions in Multidatabase Systems*" In Proc. of
           the ACM SIGMOD International Conference on Management of Data,
           May 1994. Pages 67-78.

A Publish/Subscribe Framework:
Push Technology in E-Commerce

[1]Edward C. Cheng and [2]George Loizou

[1] OCT Research Laboratory, Three Waters Park, MS 215, San Mateo, CA 94403, USA
cheng@db.stanford.edu
[2]Department of Computer Science, University of London, Birkbeck College, Malet Street,
London WC1E 7HX, UK
george@dcs.bbk.ac.uk

Abstract. Publish/Subscribe (P/S) technology conceptually divides resource managers (RM's) and applications within a transaction tree into two categories: resource producers and resource consumers. Publishers enqueue information and the P/S system pushes it to the subscribers. Applying the P/S paradigm to Internet-based E-Commerce (sometimes also known as *Webcasting)*, the RM's that produce and consume information can be real people. In this case, customers subscribe voluntarily or unknowingly to provide merchants their own information. Based on these customer profiles which may include information about their household or buying patterns, companies make decisions to push products and marketing messages to the relevant prospects electronically. Up until now, the Internet P/S mechanism was managed in a rather ad-hoc manner. Although in most cases the customer profiles are stored in RDBMS's, other objects such as products, promotion plans, web pages, news items, marketing messages, and service contracts are not modelled formally. As a result, it requires excessive human intervention to match the subscriber-base; it thus fails to support very high volume and flexible push of relevant and just-in-time information.

In this paper, an object-oriented organizational model, called OMM, is presented as an underlying model to support two aspects of P/S in E-Commerce. Firstly, it allows companies to flexibly model both the consumers and the materials to be consumed. Secondly, it allows users to specify business policies in SQL-like queries to match the consumers with the materials. Every time a new material is published, OMM automatically pushes it to the right audiences. The paper describes the OMM reference model and shows how it can be applied flexibly to capture the different classes of resources involved in an E-Commerce application, and to maintain the complex and dynamic matching relationships between consumers and resource materials. The paper also discusses our experience of applying the research prototype, OMM/PS, to support the E-Commerce strategy of a commercial insurance firm.

B. Lings and K. Jeffery (Eds.): BNCOD 17, LNCS 1832, pp. 153-170, 2000.
© Springer-Verlag Berlin Heidelberg 2000

1 Introduction

E-Commerce applications aim to conduct business over the electronic network. Although electronic business transactions, evolved from EDI protocols, will continue to play a major role in E-Commerce, the rapid growth of the Internet (in 1998, 2+ million new users were added to the Internet every quarter [4]) has pushed companies to expand the scope of E-Commerce applications to cover the full range of business activities which include marketing, negotiation, fulfilment and follow-up, all on the Web. Publish/Subscribe (P/S), a form of push technology, plays a significant role in E-Commerce by ensuring high volume, high performance and reliable processing of data as well as transactions over a number of RM's [1,2,3]. P/S typically divides *agents* into two categories: publishers and subscribers. Publishers produce resources and the P/S system pushes them to the subscribers who consume the resources. A subscriber may in turn generate resources and become a publisher. With P/S, subscribers do not need to know *what, when* and *where* the information is; the P/S system is responsible for finding the subscribers every time when a new material is published. In the Internet-based E-Commerce environment, publishers are the agents representing the merchants while subscribers are the customers and business prospects. Applying the P/S paradigm to the Internet-based E-Commerce environment has helped electronic marketing and customer services to propagate large amounts of information to their consumer base. Some even suggest that, with the maturing of push technology, the age of finding products through Web browsing will soon be over [5].

Unfortunately, P/S implementations have historically focused on technologies around data delivery options, delivery mechanism, reliable queues, and transactional behaviour [1,2,3]. Although many companies have attempted to automate P/S on the Internet by in-house development, there is no formal model proposed in this area. For most businesses, the large amounts of information regarding the subscribers are stored in RDBMS's or corporate directories, but the connections between the publishers and the subscribers are handled in a rather ad-hoc manner. Furthermore, the produced materials such as products, promotion plans, Web pages, news items, marketing messages, and service contracts are not modelled into the P/S system formally. As a result, it requires excessive human intervention to sort and match the materials with the subscriber base; it thus fails to support very high volume push of relevant and just-in-time information.

This paper presents an organizational model, namely OMM (Organization Modelling and Management), to support the two aspects of P/S. Firstly, it provides an object-oriented reference model to flexibly model both the publisher and the subscriber. To model the publisher means to include all kinds of materials that are produced by the publisher. To model the subscriber means to capture the customer profiles. Secondly, it allows users to define business policies in SQL-like queries to match the consumers and the produced materials.

The next section covers the related research work in P/S and organization modelling. Section 3 describes the OMM conceptual and reference models for enterprise modelling. OMM does not assume a particular process or application architecture. With this generic approach, OMM is able to map its object types to other organizational data schemes and to present an integrated multi-dimensional view of different organizational resources. Section 4 presents the P/S concept in E-Commerce and discusses a Java-based prototype, OMM/PS, which is used to implement a P/S system for a Web-based commercial insurance firm, called InsurePoint. Section 5 discusses the OMM/PS system architecture. The paper concludes in Section 6 with a summary and our future research direction.

2 Related Work

Push technology has been around in various forms for many years. Early work on using computer networks for pushing data was carried out in the 1980's [1]. The Boston Community Information System at MIT [6] and the Datacycle database system [7] are examples that incorporate some form of push technology. Their focus is mainly on broadcasting large amounts of data with very high throughput, but none of these systems focuses on doing business on the Web, and none addresses the issue of P/S matching.

The P/S work initiated by Tibco and Oracle Corporation focuses exclusively on supporting low level transactions [3]. Although the Advanced Queueing (AQ) in Oracle 8 allows users to build P/S systems to support Internet-based push technology, it lacks the relationship model in order to automate the matching of publisher and subscriber. As a result, it fails to support high-volume and just-in-time push of relevant information.

Other researchers have proposed organization models and methodologies mainly to support workflow systems. Representative works include M*-OBJECT [13], ORM [14], SAM* [15], and ObjectFlow [16,17]. They all start from the process view and tightly couple the organization model with the role model, and some even with the process model. Among them, ORM [14] is the closest to supporting P/S modelling. ORM is a standalone client-server database application to support organization modelling in WorkParty, a workflow system developed by SIEMENS[18]. ORM has an application programming interface (API) and a graphical user interface to allow users to define and populate the organizational database. Although ORM separates the organization model from the process model, it does not separate the organization model from the role model; the two are still integrated. Also, the organization definition and the role definition of ORM are still static like all other previous works, and it thus suffers from the lack of a dynamic relationship model. The OVAL work at MIT supports easy modelling of organizations but it only has a static relationship model to define links between objects [32,33].

Still other past efforts address the organizational resource modelling issue through directory services. Directory services (DS) and other naming services aim to support distributed object lookup with a naming convention [19]. Each object in the system is assigned a static and universally unique identifier (UUID). This approach yields an efficient solution for simple point-to-point interaction in collaborative software; it resolves static addresses for electronic mail, video conferencing, group scheduling and the like. Nevertheless, DS lacks an organization model and support for dynamic relationships between resources. Consequently, it fails to support advanced applications such as in E-Commerce P/S applications where deferred binding till runtime is necessary to find out all the potential audiences of new publications.

Some past significant directory technologies have been developed with the intent to provide global organization infrastructure. The X.500 DS [19] supports remote directory access, centralized and distributed topologies, and centralized or distributed update methods, as well as peer-entity authentication, digital signatures, and certificates [31]. The X.500 DS has a multiple class inheritance model and is able to describe the organizational hierarchy and capture subscriber information. As a directory service, X.500 and the associated protocols focus on retrieving objects with a UUID; it does not support dynamic relationships and lacks method extension. OMM can coexist with an X.500 directory, it can also be mapped to the LDAP (Lightweight Directory Access Protocol) directory and retrieve information through the LDAP interface so that users can access and update the publisher and subscriber information in the directory through OMM.

Overall, the existing approaches to P/S and the modelling of various P/S objects and the associated connections suffer from the following common weaknesses:

- Focus exclusively on supporting push mechanisms and transactions. We need to apply the P/S paradigm to support Internet-based E-Commerce applications which require pushing of large amounts of *just-in-time* information to only *relevant* audiences.

- Lack a conceptual organization reference model. We need a generic solution so that we can apply the model to different electronic business environments.

- Support only some predefined resource types. Network DS focus on machine nodes, users and applications; messaging DS on user addresses; and BPR organization sub-components on users, groups and roles. To model the consumer base as well as the different types of materials to be pushed in E-Commerce, the P/S system must be extensible and flexible in order to define the characteristics of various resource types which include customers, employees, marketing materials, products, promotion packages, news briefs, and others.

- Assume only static and hardwired relationships between resources. In reality, consumers and their demands are rapidly changing, in the sense that their interests in receiving certain types of information also change.

- Lack a flexible matching model to automate the push of information. Most in-house implementations of P/S today embed the matching mechanism in the programming logic. As a result, adding new types of resources into the automated P/S system is rather difficult.

3 The OMM Organization Model

A generic organization model is a reference model, which can be applied to describe the different aspects of an organization, such as employees, products, marketing materials, business partners and customers. A specific organization model is the output of applying the generic model to a particular aspect of an enterprise. As mentioned earlier, existing organizational modelling systems tightly integrate the role model and organization model together. More accurately, most systems do not even have an organization model; they simply use the database's user model to keep track of the users and nothing else, and the role model is just a labelling - an attribute - of the user model. Such integration makes it difficult to create dynamic roles that go beyond the organization model. For instance, an organization may already have a role, called *CEO*, but in a business-to-business e-commerce environment where there are thousands of companies online, it might be desirable to create and maintain a role, called *startup_CEO*, whose definition is based on the *Age* and *Size* of the company and the *Title* of the person. It would be hard for an organization designer to foresee all possible roles needed at the organization design phase. Furthermore, if the role were defined as an attribute inside an organization, it would be challenging to maintain the dynamic nature of the role when the organizational information changes. Finally, it would be difficult for the system designer to define roles that go across multiple organizations if a role is defined as part of an organization.

OMM addresses this issue by separating the role model from the organization model of the BPM (Business Process Management), and puts a formal concept on reasoning about organizations and relationships within and amongst them [18,23,24]. Figure 1 shows how the different models interface with one another. With the OMM approach, organizations are modelled separately from the business processes and applications. Role definitions are done through the organizational modelling and management interface. Abstracting the organization component from workflow allows us to get rid of the constraints from the workflow system and be flexible in modelling the enterprise. In addition, the organization component becomes a stand-alone application, which is now able to support more than just workflow but also other aspects of E-Commerce such as P/S in this case.

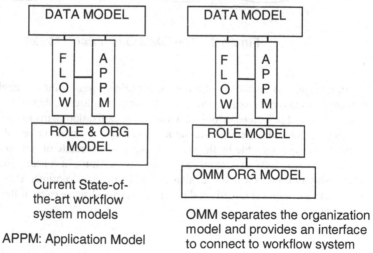

Figure 1. OMM Separates the Role and Organization Models

The OMM employs a generic reference model which can be applied flexibly to define different resource types and their inter-relationships. Resource types are user-defined; they may include customers, employees, products, services, marketing materials, documents, new briefs, URL's and others. Modelling of an enterprise involves defining these types of resources and the dynamic relationships amongst these resource objects. A P/S system is interested in pushing either a piece of newly published material to a subset of customers, or a subset of readily available materials to a new or changed customer. For example, an insurance company will be interested to publish and push the news item regarding travel safety in Uganda to all commercial clients that have branch offices in East Africa. Similarly, a client who has updated his profile through the web to indicate that the company has grown beyond 10 employees should receive the information about a new worker's compensation insurance policy.

There are three fundamental entities in the OMM model, namely the *organizations, members,* and *virtual links.*

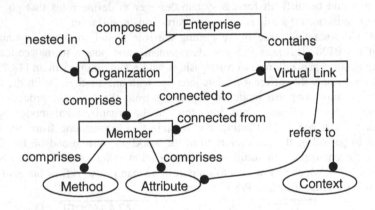

Figure 2. The OMM Organization Model

An enterprise is composed of a number of OMM organizations. Each *organization* represents a class of resources such as customers, employees, departments, products or news articles. Each *member* object within an organization maps to an actual entity of the corporation. Members of the same class share a common set of attributes and methods that is extensible by the user. A member can relate or link to other members through *virtual links.* Contrary to static connections, a virtual link only has a relationship definition which is evaluated and resolved at runtime. Figure 2 uses an E-R diagram to show the OMM model. Hereafter we discuss each of the OMM objects in greater detail.

3.1 Organizations

An enterprise is composed of a number of OMM organization objects. OMM organizations are created to map to the different dimensions and components of a company. Each organization has a unique identifier across the global enterprise. Using the OMM organizations, resources can be partitioned both *vertically* and *horizontally*; vertically into different dimensions or resource types, such as people, products, services and so on. Horizontal partitioning can be applied to break components of the same type into smaller units, such as partitioning people into engineers, sales and marketing, and temporary workers.

For instance, an OMM organization may be defined to represent the people of the company, another to represent the different products, yet another to represent the marketing publications, and so on. This creates a view of vertical partitioning of the corporation. Each partition keeps the organization information of a particular dimension. In addition, we can further divide an organization within the same dimension horizontally. For instance, people belonging to the engineering department may be included in one organization class, while people in the marketing department are placed in another. In other words, vertical partitioning helps to define the different types of resources within the enterprise, while horizontal partitioning allows users to logically divide resources of the same dimension into smaller sub-components. Figure 3 depicts the horizontal and vertical partitioning of OMM organizations.

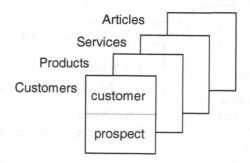

Figure 3. Horizontal and Vertical Partitioning of OMM Organizations

Partitioning helps to conceptually categorize resources into multiple OMM organizations. Since different departments or divisions now own their individual organizational definition, a much greater level of autonomy in defining and managing organizational information is granted to them. They can update, delete, or append to their own organizational definition without impacting others. For major restructuring, users may alter the organization schema of the resources which they own exclusively. In addition, the granularity of partitioning is controlled entirely by the user. Users have the flexibility to decide how fine they want to divide the resources. When the business conditions change, they may choose to merge together or to further divide their resource categories. They may add or delete a kind of published material which has quite a different set of attributes when compared to other materials.

The organization partitioning methodology also makes implementation simple. The different partitions of OMM organizations correspond naturally to database tables. It is typical to use some tables within a database environment to capture the information of an organizational partition. The OMM methodology does not dictate the underlying data model, although our current implementation uses the JDBC interface to talk to an RDBMS. When a relational database implementation is used, users define the attributes of the members as column names in a relational table. In an object-oriented database environment, the member attribute definition maps directly to a class definition. This constitutes a class of members for each OMM organization.

3.2 Members and the Information Model

OMM uses an object-oriented model to capture its member information. An enterprise has a main member class which is the super-class containing a list of system-defined attributes and methods. All user-defined member classes are subclasses of the main member class and inherit the properties of the super-class. Figure 4 shows the class hierarchy.

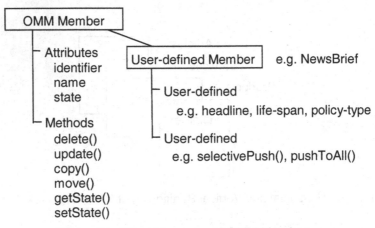

Figure 4. Class Hierarchy of OMM Member

The identifier attribute is unique for each member across the entire enterprise. Each member object has a name that is given by the user and is unique only within an OMM organization. Each member object in OMM goes through a life-cycle which is represented by the state transition diagram shown in figure 5.

When a resource is created, it enters the *active* state. Thereafter the state changes are triggered by the user through a member method, setState(). A published object may cycle between the *active* and *inactive* states, simulating the reality of some information being on-hold, irrelevant, or expired. When a resource is *removed*, its information may still be retained in the repository and be queried until it enters the *forgotten* state which corresponds to the situation where the resource information is archived away. Similarly, a consumer also cycles through these states. In addition to using the attribute values of each object to do the match, the P/S system also uses the states of both the publisher and subscriber as a filter to reduce the number of recipients.

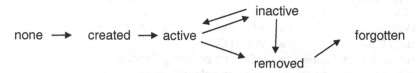

Figure 5. State Transitions of an OMM Member

From the class definition point of view, the OMM model is similar to the *Object Class* in the directory model of X.500 [19]. OMM members are different from the members of X.500 in that they support class inheritance, method extension, and object life-cycle. The latter captures the dynamic behaviour of a resource within an actual corporation. It also allows the P/S system to properly reduce the amount of traffic by eliminating inactive resources from the pool of communication links. Furthermore, the OMM model is unique in that objects may relate dynamically to one another through *virtual links*.

3.3 Virtual Links and the Relationship Model

As collaborative efforts exist between company resources, it is necessary to model relationships between them [25,26]. OMM uses *virtual links* to define dynamic relationships between member objects. Virtual links are business rules constructed on the basis of member attributes and contextual variables. The OMM engine evaluates the business rules to identify roles and relationships that resources have in the company. This evaluation is done by mapping the business rule expression into an SQL query, which is then executed by the underlying DBMS. In OMM, a relationship is established from one resource to another, and as such it can be represented as a directed edge. If a bi-directional relationship (such as a supervisor-subordinate relationship) is desired, it can be modelled as two relationships; one as a *reverse* relationship of the other. In this respect, resource objects are like nodes in a directed graph while virtual links are the arcs thereof. A virtual link is defined by the following BNF syntax [27]:

```
<Virtual Link>        ::=   <Owner>, <Relationship Type> , <Expression>,
                            <Organization Scope>
<Owner>               ::=   null I <Member ID>
```

```
<Member ID>           ::=   <Character String Constant>
<Relationship Type>   ::=   <Relationship Name> [REVERSE <Relationship
                            Name>] [TRANSITIVE]
<Relationship Name>   ::=   <Character String Constant>
<Expression>          ::=   <Expression> <Log Op> <Expression> |
                            <Attribute Name> <Op> <Value> |
                            (<Expression>)
<Attribute Name>      ::=   <Character String Constant>
< Op>                 ::=   == | != | >= | > | < | <=
<Value>               ::=   <Constant> | <Attribute Name>
<Log Op>              ::=   AND | OR
<Organization Name>   ::=   <Character String Constant>
<Organization Scope>  ::=   <Organization Name>⁺
```

The connection between resources is dynamic and virtual because any relationship is defined via a computable expression over the attributes rather than a pair of static resource IDs. There may be a predefined owner of a relationship, or the owner can be assigned at runtime. When a virtual link is resolved on an owner, a member object, the relationship expression is evaluated over all the members in the organization scope, and there may be any number of resources satisfying the relevant criteria, thus indicating a relationship with the *owner* in question. An example of a relationship can be:

```
Owner:                  null
Relationship Name:      match_region_news
Expression:             ($X.region = $owner.region) OR
                        ($X.interestedRegion = $owner.region)
Organization Scope:     customer
```

When a news item is created, the user specifies the values of its attributes. In this example, the news item has an attribute, called *region*, which represents the region of the world that this news is concerned; the customer class has two attributes, namely *region* which indicates the location of the customer, and *interestedRegion*, which the customer declares in his profile that s/he is interested in those regions for future expansion. When the user publishes the news item, OMM resolves the virtual link, *match_region_news*, over that news item. The news item becomes the *owner* of this resolution instance. The *region* attribute value of the news item is retrieved from the OMM database. For this example, let us assume the value is 'East Africa'. The virtual link expression now becomes:

($X.region = 'East Africa') OR ($X.interestedRegion = 'East Africa')

The P/S system now calls OMM to resolve this expression over the customer class. All customers whose profiles indicate their *region* or *interestedRegion* to be 'East Africa' are the candidates to receive the news item, and the P/S system will push the actual article or a URL link of the article to them through Internet Email. We will cover the detailed *Push* mechanism in Section 4.

Note that a link may or may not be *transitive* in nature. When a transitive relationship r_1 is defined, and if member m_1 relates to member m_2 in r_1, and m_2 relates to member m_3 in r_1, it follows that m_1 also relates to m_3 in r_1. For example, a customer updates his profile and triggers P/S to evaluate a relationship *policy_document* which is defined as:

Expression:	($X.policy = $owner.holdingPolicy) OR
	($X.parentPolicy = $owner.policy)
Organization Scope:	document

In the first instance of evaluation, the updated customer is the *owner*. All those documents with *policy* type matching the *holdingPolicy* of the owner will be returned. If the transitive relationship is to be evaluated, each document selected will become the owner of a second round evaluation of the relationship. All documents which identify the *owner* document as their *parentPolicy* will be returned. The evaluation tree will go on until no document is returned. Obviously there is a cost associated with resolving transitive relationships; they should therefore be used with care.

Figure 6 shows a relationship graph within an organization; note that here the *parentPolicy* and the *childPolicy* are represented by reverse links to each other:

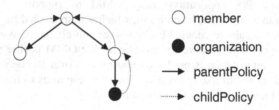

○	member
●	organization
→	parentPolicy
┈►	childPolicy

Figure 6. OMM Relationship Graph

Although the example only covers relationships within an organization, virtual links can actually be defined from a single object to multiple organizations. In this case, the organization scope will list all OMM organizations involved. For instance, a relationship graph may be desirable to represent the connections from customers to news items, products and promotions. Here, the owner is a particular *customer* while the organization scope includes *news, products* and *promotions*.

A virtual link may also be defined between a member and an organization. When an OMM organization object is part of a relationship, all member objects within that organization are involved in it. For instance, if *message A* is a merge-and-acquisition announcement to all the customers, then all people in the customer class will receive the pushed information.

4 Publish/Subscribe With OMM

P/S is a form of *push technology* [1,3] that concerns mainly the flow of information from a set of resource producers to a set of resource consumers. P/S allows consumers to pre-declare their interests and situation. When some relevant information is published, the P/S system automatically pushes the resource to the subscribed members. In addition, a P/S system may also monitor the subscribers so that when their subscriptions change, readily published information may be pushed to them. As such, P/S not only concerns the push of large amounts of data over the network, but specifically deals with the issue of matching publisher or the published resources with the subscriber.

OMM supports P/S by firstly allowing flexible modelling of both publishers and subscribers within an object-oriented organization model. Note that in the E-Commerce environment, there could be many types of publishers and many types of subscribers, and OMM is capable to include them all. Furthermore, OMM uses a policy-based relationship model to support the P/S system to define matching criteria between the publishers and subscribers. Every time when a resource is published, the P/S system will query OMM to identify the matching subscribers and push the resource to them.

As part of our research effort to support P/S in E-Commerce, we have built a research prototype P/S application using OMM to support an Internet-based commercial insurance company, InsurePoint, which was sponsored by Atlantic Mutual Insurance Co. with the aim to conduct E-Commerce entirely on the Web. The purpose of the OMM/PS prototype is to verify our claims that OMM is able to automate P/S when a variety of information is published and pushed over the network to selective customers. We also would like to observe customer responses to the P/S solution, as well as issues that may arise in such an environment.

4.1 An OMM/PS Prototype

InsurePoint has about 150 customers all classified as hi-tech, start-up firms (nationwide, under 25 employees). InsurePoint sells to its clients various insurance policies including general liability, workers' compensation, and others. It has always maintained the most current customer profiles. Indeed, customers can simply logon to their personal page on InsurePoint's Web site and update their own profile. In the past, they relied on the account managers to periodically query the database to identify further business opportunities with these existing clients. InsurePoint management would like to further nurture customer relations and to capture more speedily business opportunities using P/S technology. As a starting point, firstly they want to publish periodic news briefs which would help their clients better manage their risks in doing business; this would help build customer loyalty. Secondly, they would like to automatically push relevant new product information to clients who have just updated

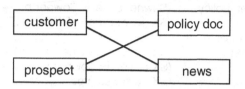

Figure 7. OMM/PS Classes For InsurePoint

their profiles. Notification should also be sent to the corresponding account managers so that they can further follow up with the customers.

With OMM/PS, we modelled the classes *customer, prospect* (people who asked for a quote over the Web), *insurance policy document* (nested documents to introduce certain types of insurance policies), and *news*. Virtual links are defined to capture the relationships between these classes. Figure 7 shows how these classes are related to one another.

About a dozen attributes are defined for each class. For simplicity, we list below only those attributes that are used to define the virtual links:

customer:	asset, propertyCoverage, projectedSales, liabilityCoveredSales, region, regionCoverage, businessType
prospect:	region, businessType
policy doc:	policyType, liabilityCoveredSales, region
news:	region, businessType

Subscribers in this case can either be customers or prospects. Customer profiles are captured when the customer purchases a policy from InsurePoint. Prospect profiles are obtained when potential clients asked for quotations of insurance policies by filling out a form over the Web. Also customers using their user name and password can update their profiles to provide their latest situation anytime on the Web.

Whenever a customer changes his profile, the P/S system evaluates the following virtual links over the policy document class to decide if certain documents should be pushed to the client. There are certain criteria which InsurePoint has identified to be conditions of push. We list them below along with the policy that helps to discover such conditions:

1.   When customer's projected sales increase beyond the recommended liability coverage.

new_liability	($owner.projectedSales > $owner.liabilityCoveredSales) AND ($X.policyType = 'GENERAL LIABILITY')

2.   When customer's asset policy grows to beyond the current asset coverage.
   new_asset_policy   ($owner.asset > $owner.propertytCoverage) AND
                        ($X.policyType = 'PROPERTY')
3.   When customer expands to a new region.
   New_region   ($X.region = $owner.region) AND
                        ($X.region != $owner.regionCoverage) AND
                        ($X.businessType = $owner.businessType)

In all three cases, X is in the policy document class while owner is a customer object. When customers update their profiles, each of these business rules will be evaluated by OMM/PS, and documents found to satisfy the rules will be sent to the customers electronically. Users can also add other business rules to include new conditions for pushing information when customers update their profiles.

In addition to triggering push by customer update, InsurePoint can also initiate pushing of information by publishing a news item. When a news brief is published, the author will profile the news item through a Web interface. The *region* attribute indicates if the item is location-sensitive; the *businessType* attribute indicates if the contents concern a specific industry such as Consulting, Electronics, Manufacturing, Pharmaceuticals and others. Once the item is published, OMM/PS evaluates the following business rule to decide who among the customers and prospects should receive this news brief:

   matching_news   ($X.region = $owner.region) OR
                     ($X.businessType = $owner.businessType)

5 The OMM System Architecture

In almost all commercial environments, there already exist some organizational databases such as the customer profiles, the corporate directory and some marketing document databases. OMM provides a mapping mechanism to ease the job of referencing existing databases. With the OMM object mapping mechanism, existing databases are analyzed and mapped to the OMM organization design. Based on this mapping, the *agent programs* which make up a part of the OMM server architecture can populate the OMM data store by accessing the existing databases. In some cases, due to the continual usage of legacy HR applications over the existing organizational databases, it is necessary to periodically refresh some part of the OMM data store by rerunning the agent programs. The actual mapping of the various database schemes to the object-oriented OMM scheme is outside the scope of this paper [27].

At runtime, the P/S system accesses the OMM organizational information and performs P/S matching by calling the OMM API. The OMM server evaluates the business rule representing the matching policy on the current organization database and returns the result to the P/S system. Customers may also access OMM and update their profile through a Java Applet by calling the OMM API.

Figure 8 shows the OMM run-time system architecture with the RM and existing organizational databases.

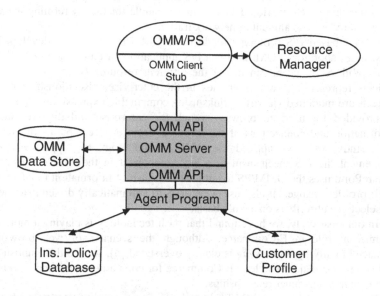

Figure 8. OMM Run-time System Architecture

6 Conclusion

In this paper, a dynamic organizational information system, the OMM methodology and organization model, along with its system architecture are presented as a comprehensive tool to model business rules to support a dynamic push technology in E-Commerce. The application of the OMM methodology in P/S to support an E-Commerce based commercial insurance company is discussed. Compared to previous attempts of P/S [1,2,3], we have proposed a formal model to automate the matching of publishers and subscribers, thus enabling a rapidly changing E-Commerce environment to support high-volume push of just-in-time and relevant information. With reference to previous efforts of organization modelling [17,19,20,24,32], OMM has a strong object model and separates the organization model from the process model. However, OMM also abstracts the organization model from role definition, thus giving flexibility in complex organization modelling. It is novel in having a dynamic inter-relationship notion that is expressed by using computable expressions over member attributes, system-defined variables and contextual variables. This paper shows that the relationship model is essential in automating subscription matching for pushing information in business-to-business E-Commerce. By using virtual links, OMM can model dynamic business rules so that matching policies between various objects can be defined and maintained. Finally, the explicit life-cycle of the OMM members reflects the dynamic state changes of resources in the real world. This provides a handle for further refining the subscriber base and reduce the amount of network traffic.

A Java-based P/S prototype (code name OMM/PS) has been developed at OCT Research Laboratory. OMM/PS is a P/S application based on the OMM S-25 system [36]. With S-25, users can model the different resource types and create resource objects representing various entities in the enterprise. Relationships between the objects are modelled via virtual links using computable expressions. A web interface is provided for users to browse through the enterprise and discover the detailed information and connections of the resources from different points of view. In our case study, we have applied the OMM methodology to support InsurePoint to implement the P/S mechanism as a key component in their E-Commerce strategy. InsurePoint uses the OMM/PS to automate its push of information to customers when their profiles change. It also uses OMM/PS to automatically disseminate news briefs to selective subscribers on a daily basis.

In our case study, we have found that push technology is playing a more and more significant role in E-Commerce. Although the scenario of web browsing being replaced totally by *webcasting* is clearly overstated [5], we see that publish/subscribe is becoming a major vehicle in E-Commerce for companies to expand market size and enhance their customer relationships.

Further research with OMM/PS includes giving a weight factor to attributes so that the system can have more intelligence to filter the audience. We are also working on using push mechanisms different from e-mail and attachments. One specific example is to change the contents of a customer's personal Web page when the profile is updated.

Acknowledgments

Most of the research on OMM has been initiated at the OCT Research Laboratory. The authors would like to express their thanks to the many designers and developers who have contributed to the concept and implementation of the OMM system. Brutus Lo has been most instrumental in providing guidance of applying the OMM/PS technology to the commercial insurance industry. Thanks also go to Dieter Gawlick for his input on workflow and the requirements of publish/subscribe which have greatly impacted our thoughts on the topic. ECC thanks his wife for her continuous support and encouragement throughout the entire project.

References

[1]   Franklin, M., Zdonik, S. „Data In Your Face": Push Technology in Perspective. *Proceedings of SIGMOD '98*, Seattle, WA, 1998.

[2]   Hal Berghel. The New Push for Push Technology. *NetWorkers*, 2(3):28-36, 1998.

[3]   Transactional Publish/Subscribe: The Proactive Multicast of Database Changes. *Proceedings of SIGMOD '98*, Seattle, WA. 1998.

[4]   Internet Trak, 2nd Quarter, 1998. *Ziff-Davis Publishing*, July, 1998. http://www.zd.com/marketresearch/IT2Q.htm.

[5]   Push! Kiss your Browser Goodbye. *Wired Magazine*, March 1997.

[6]   Gifford, D. Polychannel Systems for Mass Digital Communication. *CACM*, 33(2): 141-151, 1990.

[7]   Herman, G., et al. The Datacycle Architecture for Very High Throughput Database Systems. *Proceedings of SIGMOD '87*, San Francisco, CA, 1987.

[8]   Cheng, E., et. al. An Open and Extensible Event-based Transaction Manager. *Proceedings of USENIX Conference*, 1991.

[9]   Cheng, E. Re-engineering and Automating Enterprise-wide Business Processes. *Proceedings of International Working Conference on Information Industry*, Bangkok, Thailand, April, 1995.

[10]   Cheng, E. An Object-Oriented Organizational Model to Support Dynamic Role-based Access Control in E-Commerce Applications. *Proceedings of HICSS'99*, Maui, Hawaii, January, 1999.

[11]   Howard, M. Work Flow: the Coordination of Business Processes. *Gartner Group Presentation Highlights*, August, 1991.

[12]   Hsu, C., Rattner, L. Information Modeling for Computerized Manufacturing. *IEEE Transactions on Systems, Man, and Cybernetics*, 20(4):758-776, 1990.

[13]   Di Leva, A., Giolito, P., Vernadat, F. The M*-OBJECT Organisation Model for Enterprise Modelling of Integrated Engineering Environments. *Concurrent Engineering - Research and Applications*, 5(2):183-194, 1997.

[14]   Rupietta, W. Organization Models for Cooperative Office Applications. *Database and Expert Systems Applications. Proceedings of the 5th International Conference, DEXA '94*, Athens, Greece, 1994.

[15]   Su, S. Modeling Integrated Manufacturing Data with SAM-*. *Computer*, 19(1):34-49, 1986.

[16]   Hsu, M. An Execution Model for an Activity Management System. *Digital Technical Report*, April, 1991.

[17]   Hsu, M., Kleissner, C. Objectflow - Towards a Process Management Infrastructure. *Distributed and Parallel Databases*, 4(2):169-194, 1996.

[18]   Bussler, C. Analysis of the Organization Modeling Capability of Workflow Management Systems. *Proceedings of the PRIISM '96 Conference*, Maui, Hawaii, January, 1996.

[19]   *CCITT Recommendation X.500 to X.521: Data Communication Networks, Directory*. Blue Book. Also ISO/IEC Standards ISO 9594-1 to ISO 9594-7, 1988.

[20]   Berio, G., et. al. The M*-OBJECT Methodology for Information System Design in CIM Environments. *IEEE Transactions on Systems, Man, and Cybernetics,* 25(1):68-85, 1995.

[21]   Vanderaalst, W., Vanhee, K. Business Process Redesign - a Petri-net Based Approach. *Computers in Industry,* 29(1-2):15-26, 1996.

[22]   Murata, T. Petri Nets: Properties, Analysis and Applications. *Proceedings of the IEEE,* 77(4):541-580, 1989.

[23]   Mertins, K., Heisig, P., Krause, O. Integrating Business-process Re-engineering with Human-Resource Development for Continuous Improvement. *International Journal of Technology Management,* 14(1):39-49, 1997.

[24]   Bussler, C. Enterprise Process Modeling and Enactment in GERAM. *Proceedings of the 3ʳᵈ International Conference on Automation, Robotics and Computer Vision (ICARCV '94),* Singapore, November, 1994.

[25]   Willcocks, L., Smith, G. IT-enabled BPR - Organizational and Human-resource Dimensions. *Journal of Strategic Information Systems,* 4(3):279-301, 1995.

[26]   Roos, H., Bruss, L. Human and Organization Issues. *The Workflow Paradigm,* pp. 35-49, Future Strategies Publishing, 1994.

[27]   Cheng, E. The OMM Model. *Technical Report* of the OCT Research Lab and College of Notre Dame. Belmont, CA, November, 1997.

[28]   Medina-Mora, et. al. The Action Workflow Approach to Workflow Management Technology. *Proceedings of the Communications of the ACM CSCW,* November, 1992.

[29]   Vidgen, R., Rose, J., Woodharper, T. BPR - The Need for a Methodology to Revision the Organization. *IFIP Transactions A - Computer Science and Technology,* 54:603-612, 1994.

[30]   Gottlob, G., Schref, M., Röck. B. Extending Object-Oriented Systems with Roles. *ACM Transactions on Information Systems,* 14(3):268-296, 1996.

[31]   Blum, D., Litwack, D. *The E-Mail Frontier: Emerging Markets and Evolving Technologies.* Addison-Wesley Publishing Co, pp. 295-319, 1994.

[32]   Malone, T.W., Lai, K.-Y., Fry, C. Experiments with Oval: A Radically Tailorable Tool for Cooperative Work. *ACM Transactions on Information Systems,* 13(2):177-205, 1995.

[33]   Malone, T.W., et. al. Tools for Inventing Organizations: Toward a Handbook of Organizational Processes. *Proceedings of the 2ⁿᵈ IEEE Workshop on Enabling Technologies Infrastructure for Collaborative Enterprises,* Morgantown, WV, April, 1993.

[34]   *Oval Version 1.1 User's Guide.* Center for Coordination Science, MIT, Cambridge, 1992.

[35]   Swenson, K. et. al. A Business Process Environment Supporting Collaborative Planning. *Journal of Collaborative Computing,* 1(1):15-34, 1994.

[36]   Cheng, E. A Rule-based Organization Modelling System to Support Dynamic Role Resolution in Workflow. Parallel and Distributed Computing Systems. *Proceedings of the ISCA 11ᵗʰ International Conference,* Chicago, Illinois, September, 1998.

Characterizing Data Provenance

Peter Buneman

University of Pennsylvania

peter@central.cis.upenn.edu

Abstract. When you see some data on the Web, do you ever wonder how it got there? The chances are that it is in no sense original, but was copied from some other source, which in turn was copied from some other source, and so on. If you are a scientist using a scientific database or some other kind of scholar using a digital library, you will probably be keenly interested in this information because it is crucial to your assessment of the accuracy and timeliness of the data. Data provenance is the understanding of the history of a piece of data: its origins and the process by which it travelled from database to database. Existing database tools give us little or no help in recording provenance; indeed database schemas make it difficult to record this kind of information. I shall report on some recent work that characterizes data provenance. It is based on a model for data, both structured and semistructured, which accounts for both the structure and location of data. Using this model, we can draw a distinction between "why provenance" and "where provenance". The former expresses all the data in the source databases that contributed to the existence of the data of interest; the latter specifies the locations from which it was drawn. In particular, we can take a query in a generic semistructured query language and use it to provide a formal derivation of both forms of provenance and to derive a number of useful properties of these forms. The work generalizes existing work on relational databases that is limited to why provenance. This is a report of joint work with Sanjeev Khanna and WangChiew Tan.

B. Lings and K. Jeffery (Eds.): BNCOD 17, LNCS 1832, p.171, 2000.
© Springer-Verlag Berlin Heidelberg 2000

A Grammar Based Model for XML Schema Integration

Ralf Behrens

Institut für Informationssysteme
Osterweide 8,D-23562 Lübeck
Medizinische Universität zu Lübeck
Germany
behrens@ifis.mu-luebeck.de

Abstract. XML is just becoming a standard for document processing and interchange on the Internet. In this context, XML's DTD structuring mechanism is especially important. This paper addresses, among others, the problem of integration of several DTDs by introducing a grammar based model for XML based on so called *xtrees* and *xschemes*. Although it can be shown that we can always find a DTD describing the intersection of the languages defined by two arbitrarily given DTDs, the same is not true for the union. This result shows that pure DTDs are not sufficient for schema integration. The paper presents a solution to this problem by introducing and investigating a generalized model based on so called *s-xschemes*. Using these *s-xschemes* we can obtain additional information about XML documents belonging to certain classes, thus enabling computation and transformation of information more specifically.

1 Introduction

With the extend of the World Wide Web the publication of electronically available data drastically increases. Although most data is published in HTML, this language is not well suited to export semantically rich information. With XML a standard arises that is mainly focused on data structuring and exchange [2]. Since XML was originally developed for document mark-up, its use has to be reconsidered in the database field.

What we need for XML are several universal database operations such as data extraction, integration, transformation and storing [28]. In this paper, we address, among others, the problem of integration of different XML schemata, i.e. the problem of integration of different DTDs. For this purpose, it is necessary to find out what kind of integration problems can be solved by XML and by corresponding DTDs. As [21] points out, a formal model for XML is needed to analyze the potential of XML.

As a matter of fact, we can show by a grammar based formalism, namely the notion of *xtrees* and *xschemes*, that even very simple integration problems cannot be solved using pure DTDs. E. g. we can always find a DTD describing the intersection of the languages defined by two arbitrarily given DTDs, while the same is not true for the union. The union operator is very important for integration purposes. For example, in case of a merger of two different companies, a DTD would be needed to describe the union of all XML documents of the two companies.

Therefore, in order to solve these problems extensions to DTDs are needed. We present an abstract solution by defining the notion of *s-xschemes* and show how these *s-xschemes* solve the problem of unions just mentioned. Moreover, we show how *s-xschemes* can be used for other problems, for example describing a recursion with a restricted depth. An example is the problem of allowing subsections in a document only up to a certain depth. This problem is not solvable by pure XML if all subsections are supposed to have the same tag and if we assume that no extra tags are to be present in the document only for the purpose of depth restriction.

In addition to the problems just mentioned, the proposed formalism can be used to describe information on different levels of abstraction. Thereby we can transform documents more specifically using additional structure information. Moreover, important decidability questions are solved and proven.

B. Lings and K. Jeffery (Eds.): BNCOD 17, LNCS 1832, pp. 172□190, 2000.
□ Springer-Verlag Berlin Heidelberg 2000

Related Work

In the literature several approaches concerning modeling of structured documents can be found. [3, 4] migrate structured documents to a logical level using context-free grammars enriched by semantic actions. It is shown that this approach runs into important undecidabilities.

In [17] so called "object grammars" are proposed, focusing primarily on declarative transformation of textual data in the Web context.

A formalism for the definition of wrappers to migrate derivation trees of regular grammars into a relational database is presented by [15]. Additionally, exceptions for invalid documents are handled. In contrast to our work, documents are not considered at different levels of abstraction.

Document modeling and querying is done by a restricted form of attributed grammars in [26]. In [25] automata for this model are defined. It is proven that these automata have exactly the expressiveness of monadic second order logic. However, the results are not carried over to XML.

Unranked trees are inspected in [12]. Based on this [24] describes queries and transformation of documents by pointed tree representations. From a users point of view, it is not quite clear whether the shown operators are sufficient in general.

Our *s-xschemes* are similar to the specialized DTDs of [27, 5]. In contrast to their approach we use these extensions not only to characterize views and query results, but also to define XML schemas for documents. Our *s-xschemes* are especially important for more strict schema definition and grammar based metadata extraction.

Our work is structured as follows: First of all we give a brief overview over XML (Section 2). Section 3 presents a model for XML concentrating on structural expressiveness. The model is based on the notions of *xtrees* and *xschemes*. Important properties as the problems and deficiencies mentioned above are proven formally. Section 4 defines an extension of the model by introducing *s-xschemes*. Section 5 applies the regular tree automata of [12] to our model, allowing to show that the extension is really an improvement over basic XML. In Section 6 we present a concrete syntax and cases where our approach can greatly enhance transformation and metadata extraction. We close with a discussion and an outlook on further work.

2   Basics of XML

XML is a new standard for type description and document creation, proposed by the W3C group [30]. Currently this description language is becoming more and more popular in the World Wide Web, since XML enables the authors to describe grammars which can specify their own special document type.

XML is a strict fragment of SGML. It is more powerful than HTML in three major respects [10]:

- Users can define new tags for nearly any purposes.
- Document structures can be nested at any depth.
- Every XML document contains an optional description of its grammar. Such a grammar can be used by applications for structural validations.

Data in XML is grouped into elements delimited by tags. Fig.1 shows an example of a simple XML document.

XML Data is self describing and bears obvious similarities to semistructured data [1, 13, 22]. However, as already mentioned XML is designed to be a mark-up language only. Therefore it does not have a associated data model. Nevertheless XML has several similarities with traditional data models.

Attributes: XML elements may contain attributes. These attributes characterize elements. In Fig.1 the attribute "status" of a "journal" decides, whether it is "published" or "unpublished".

References: Elements can be given explicit object identifiers (oids) and can refer to oids of other elements using reserved XML attributes. For example in Fig.1 the "publisher" named "Springer" has an identifier (id) which is referred to by a particular "journal" named "Lecture Notes". The

```
<literature>
  <novel id="a1" publisher="p2">
     <title> Ordinary Worlds </title>
     <author> Can Miller </author>
  </novel>
  <journal id="a2" publisher="p1"
      status="published">
     <title> Lecture Notes </title>
     <volume> 23 </volume>
  </journal>
  <publisher id="p1">
     <name> Springer </name>
  </publisher>
  <publisher id="p2">
     <name> Warner </name>
  </publisher>
</literature>
```

Fig. 1. An example of XML Data

definition of XML leaves it up to the application how to interpret references. It only requires that all referred oids are defined.

Links: XML documents can have links to elements inside the same or other XML documents. Links can cross server boundaries, like HTML anchors do.

Order: By definition, an XML document with its elements is ordered. This is an important feature for query languages, since they usually deal with unordered data [16].

The grammar part of an XML document is called Document Type Definition (DTD). An XML-DTD specifies how elements can be nested by means of regular grammars. Fig.2 shows a DTD that captures the former XML document.

```
<!ELEMENT literature    (novel|journal|
                         publisher)*>
<!ELEMENT novel         (title, author)>
<!ATTLIST novel         id ID
                        publisher IDREF>
<!ELEMENT journal       (title, volume)>
<!ATTLIST journal       id ID
                        publisher IDREF
                        status="published|
                        unpublished">
<!ELEMENT publisher     (name)>
<!ATTLIST publisher     id ID>
<!ELEMENT title         (#PCDATA)>
<!ELEMENT author        (#PCDATA)>
<!ELEMENT name          (#PCDATA)>
<!ELEMENT volume        (#PCDATA)>
```

Fig. 2. An example of an XML-DTD

As already seen in the examples given, the choice of modeling objects by elements or attributes is somehow arbitrary. In many cases the meaning of element content and attributes blurs. For that reason, we neglect the distinction between these two facilities in our model, although there are important differences like the fact that elements are ordered while attributes are not. We believe that our model can be extended to capture attributes as well.

XML uses some more instruments like "entities" or "namespaces", which can principally be seen as syntactic sugar. Therefore, they are not relevant for our theoretical investigations.

3   Structural Abstraction of XML

Although the necessity of modeling XML is known, only some special details are formally specified. We need such a model e. g. to analyze decidability questions and for formulating a query calculus. Clearly positive answers of decidability questions need further examinations of their complexity.

We believe that modeling XML in a monolithic way would lead to a collosal object which would not be handable anymore. Therefore we introduce our model stepwise for different levels of abstraction. We will briefly explain the notations used in this work. We assume the reader is familiar with basic concepts of formal language and parsing theory [19]. We denote a finite alphabet by Σ, the empty word by ε. For a regular expression r_Σ over Σ we denote by $L(r_\Sigma)$ the language which is determined by r_Σ.

Modeling documents is done by labeled ordered trees. If n is a node in a tree t, then $name(n)$ is the label of the node, $name(n) \in \Sigma$. For a sequence $n_1, \ldots, n_k$ of nodes, $name(n_1, \ldots, n_k)$ provides the sequence of the names. The subtree rooted n is $tree(n)$ and the root of t is denoted by $root(t)$. The function $children(n)$ results in the set of all children of n in t and $leaves(t)$ results in the set of the leaves of the tree. The set of all nodes in the tree is $nodes(t)$. The expression $t[n/t']$ is a tree which is obtained by replacing the subtree $tree(n)$ by t' in t.

As mentioned we will merely look at the structure of XML objects. Terminal strings are not taken into account. Since string elements can be transformed to attribute values, they are of no relevance for structural examinations, too. An XML instance can be seen as an ordered tree with a labeling of its nodes. Every node represents an XML element labeled by the element name. The child nodes' name sequence represents the content of a concrete XML element.

Definition 1 (xtree). *An xtree over a finite alphabet Σ (element names) is a finite tree. Every node is labeled by an element name of Σ, while the sequence of the child nodes is ordered.*

Every XML instance has a nested structure, therefore it can unambiguously be assigned to an *xtree* (Fig.3).

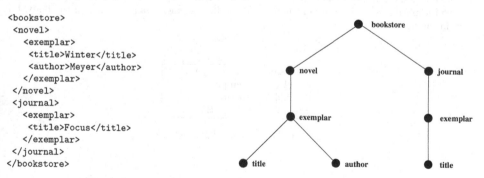

```
<bookstore>
 <novel>
   <exemplar>
    <title>Winter</title>
    <author>Meyer</author>
   </exemplar>
 </novel>
 <journal>
   <exemplar>
    <title>Focus</title>
   </exemplar>
 </journal>
</bookstore>
```

Fig. 3. An example of an XML instance and its corresponding *xtree*

Apart from *xtrees* representing concrete instances, schematic information is required for classifying sets of *xtrees*. This is done by so called *xrules* and *xschemes*. While *xrules* are used to define possible sequences of child nodes, sets of *xrules* (*xschemes*) classify complete tree structures.

Definition 2 (xrule). *An* xrule *over Σ is a tuple $\langle e : type(e) \rangle$, where $e \in \Sigma$ and $type(e)$ is a regular expression over Σ. The element name e is the* head *of the xrule, while $type(e)$ is its* body.

An *xrule* is the counterpart of an element type declaration in an XML-DTD. Seen for itself, the body $((type(e)))$ of an *xrule* describes the language $L(type(e))$.

Remark. Using regular expressions, the XML content model *EMPTY* corresponds to the body of an *xrule* with the empty word ε and *ANY* to the body $(e_1 + \ldots + e_n)^*$ with $\Sigma = \{e_1 \ldots e_n\}$.

Example 1. An "exemplar" is described by "title" and "author" or only by "title" (see the *xtree* in Fig.3):

$$\boxed{\text{exemplar} : \text{title}, \text{author?}}$$

An *xrule* is assumed to be unambiguous. Unfortunately the XML notion of unambiguity differs from that of formal language theory [9], since it is more strict. The XML unambiguity is denoted by [11] as "1-unambiguity" and declares that each word can be unambiguously parsed with regard to a regular expression by a one-element look-ahead. This ensures that each word can be parsed in linear time and space. For example the following *xrule* is unambiguous in the sense of [9], but it is not 1-unambiguous.

$$\boxed{\text{exemplar} : (\text{title}, \text{author}) + (\text{title}, \text{date})}$$

An XML instance consists of nested objects (elements). The structure of these objects is described by an XML-DTD. This is done by specifying the possible sequence of sub-object types (content type) for each object type (element name). A DTD is modeled by an *xtree scheme* (*xscheme*). An *xscheme* is a combination of *xrules*, together with a marked starting element.

Definition 3 (xscheme). *An* xscheme *d is a 3-tuple $\langle \Sigma, s, \mathcal{R} \rangle$, where*

- Σ *is a finite alphabet.*
- $s \in \Sigma$ *is the starting element.*
- $\mathcal{R}$ *is a set of xrules over Σ of the form $\langle e : type(e) \rangle$.*

From now on we represent an *xscheme* by a list of its *xrules*. The starting element is the head of the first *xrule* and the alphabet Σ is the set of all occurring element names. To simplify matters, we will implicitly assume *xrules* of the form $\langle e : \varepsilon \rangle$ if an element name e exists in the body, but not in the head of an *xrule*.

$$\boxed{\begin{array}{ll} \text{bookstore} : & (\text{novel} + \text{journal})^* \\ \text{novel} & : \text{exemplar}^* \\ \text{journal} & : \text{exemplar}^* \\ \text{exemplar} & : \text{title}, \text{author?} \end{array}}$$

Fig. 4. An example of an *xscheme*

Up to now *xrules* and *xschemes* only describe textual languages. The relation to *xtrees* is done by the notion of "validity". Like in DTDs, an *xtree* is *valid* in an *xscheme* if it corresponds to the particular *xrules*.

Definition 4 (Validity of xtrees). *An* xtree *t is* valid *in an* xscheme *$d = \langle \Sigma, s, \mathcal{R} \rangle$ (in terms $\models_t d$), iff*

$-$ $name(root(t))=s.$
$-$ for every node n in t with child nodes $n_1, \ldots, n_k$ the word $name(n_1) \ldots name(n_k)$ is in $L(type(name(n)))$, where $\langle name(n) : type(name(n)) \rangle \in \mathcal{R}$.

An *xscheme* d describes a (possibly infinite) set of *xtrees*. $G(d)$ denotes the set of all *xtrees* which are valid in d, i. e. $t \in G(d) \Leftrightarrow \models_t d$. According to this definition the *xtree* of Fig.3 is valid in the *xscheme* of Fig.4.

Remark. In contrast to an XML document, an *xtree* is always *well formed* due to its hierarchical structure.

From now on we suppose that an *xscheme* $\langle \Sigma, s, \mathcal{R} \rangle$ is *minimal*, i. e. there are no ineffective *xrules* $(\neg \exists \langle e : type(e) \rangle \in \mathcal{R} : G(\langle \Sigma, s, \mathcal{R} \rangle) = G(\langle \Sigma, s, \mathcal{R} - \langle e : type(e) \rangle \rangle))$. In formal language theory, *xschemes* correspond to context-free grammars and *xtrees* correspond to derivation trees. However, there exists an important difference between grammars and *xschemes*. Words described by grammars can be represented as derivation trees and one word can have multiple derivation trees. However, an XML instance which is also a word of a grammar always has an unambiguous derivation tree (*xtree*).

Sometimes it is useful to use a textual representation *text(t)* of an *xtree* t. In this paper, we use a prefix notation with special delimiters $<, > \notin \Sigma$. E. g. the textual representation of the *xtree* t of the XML instance in Fig.3 is *text(t)*=bookstore<novel<exemplar< title author>>journal<exemplar <title>>>.

In contrast to the word derived by a grammar, an *xtree* is always equivalent to its textual representation, caused by the explicit tagging of the tree structure. For an *xscheme* d, the set $L(d) = \{text(t) | t \in G(d)\}$ is the textual language described by d and $G(d)$ is the corresponding tree language. Because of the regular expressions' unambiguity and the *xschemes* being minimal, the question of equivalence of *xschemes* $d_1 = \langle \Sigma_1, s_1, \mathcal{R}_1 \rangle$ and $d_2 = \langle \Sigma_2, s_2, \mathcal{R}_2 \rangle$ can be restricted to the test whether the sets $\mathcal{R}_1, \mathcal{R}_2$ and the start elements s_1, s_2 at are equal at a time.

The notion of "correctness" denotes that all *xtrees* of a set are expressible by one *xscheme*.

Definition 5 (Correctness). *Let M be a set of xtrees. An xscheme d is* correct *with respect to M iff $\forall t \in M : \models_t d$.*

If a set of *xtrees* is correct with respect to an *xscheme* the question comes up how close it is described by this *xscheme*. Therefore we invent the notion of "precision" with different versions:

Definition 6 (Precision). *Let M be a set of xtrees. A correct xscheme d is*

1. precise *for M, if $G(d) = M$.*
2. more exact *than an xscheme d', if $G(d) \subset G(d')$.*
3. approximated, *if no other correct xscheme d' exists, with $G(d') \subset G(d)$.*

An *xscheme* is intuitively more exact than another if the sets of *xtrees* are in subset relation. This corresponds to the question if one context-free language contains another. However, it is decidable whether an *xscheme* is more exact than another, because this question can be reduced to the containment of the bodies in the corresponding *xrules*. Later, we will show that in case that an approximated *xscheme* exists, it is uniquely determined.

The following examples show that the notions *precise* and *approximated* are not the same.

Example 2. We restrict the set of *xtrees* described by the *xscheme* of Fig.4 in a way that only *xtrees* are allowed containing "title" and "author" for "novel", and "title" for "journal". This set is not representable by an *xscheme*. Following our definitions, the *xscheme* is the approximation. It is however not precise. Yet a more exact *xscheme* cannot be found because the dependent use of "title" and "author" is not expressible by an *xscheme*.

As one can easily see, if a precise *xscheme* exists, it is approximated. If no precise *xscheme* exists, an approximated *xscheme* of a set of *xtrees* may not exist as well, as the following example shows:

Example 3. Consider a set consisting of *xtrees* for "bookstores", where the number of "exemplars" for a "novel" is prime. For this set, we can neither find a precise nor an approximated *xscheme*.

...
(i) novel : exemplar, exemplar + (exemplar, exemplar, exemplar, exemplar*)
...
(ii) novel : exemplar, exemplar + (exemplar, exemplar, exemplar) +
          (exemplar, exemplar, exemplar, exemplar, exemplar, exemplar*)

Fig. 5. *xschemes* with different precision

The *xscheme* (ii) in Fig.5 is more exact than (i), since it only allows a subset of *xtrees*. However, we cannot find a precise *xscheme*.

Such a restriction of *xschemes* by finite enumeration is only possible within *xrules*. Trying to restrict the *xscheme* in Fig.4, in a way that the overall number of "exemplars" for "novels" and "journals" is prime, is beyond the power of *xschemes*. It is not feasible to specify such an ancestor sensitivity (see below).

Now an important problem can be treated by these definitions. Given a set of *xtrees*, it is interesting if a common *xscheme* exists, whether this is precise or which is the approximation.

Definition 7. *A set M of xtrees over a finite alphabet Σ_{all} can have the following independent properties:*

1. *If the roots of all xtrees are labeled with the same element name, then M is* consistent.
   $(\forall t, t' \in M : name(root(t)) = name(root(t')))$
2. *Let $L_{all}(e)$ be a language for every $e \in \Sigma_{all}$ which contains all words $name(n_1 \ldots n_k)$, where a node n exists with $name(n) = e$ and child nodes $n_1, \ldots, n_k$. If $L_{all}(e)$ is regular ($\forall e \in \Sigma_{all}$), then M is* regular.
   $(\forall e \in \Sigma_{all} : \{e_1 \ldots e_n | \exists t \in M, n \in t : name(n) = e \wedge name(children(n)) = e_1 \ldots e_n\}$ is regular)
3. *If every xtree which is built by replacing a subtree by another subtree of some xtree (where the roots are labeled equally) is in M, then M is called* local.
   $(\forall t, t' \in M, n \in nodes(t), n' \in nodes(t') : name(n) = name(n') \rightarrow t'[n/tree(n')] \in M)$

If a set is not local, the element names in an *xtree* depend on the element names of their ancestor nodes. This dependency is also called "ancestor sensitivity". The notions in Definition 7 are explained by an example:

Example 4. Consider the three sets of *xtrees* in Fig.6.

- (iii) is neither consistent as all roots are labeled differently, nor it is local, due to the absence of the *xtrees* in (i) and (ii). We have an ancestor sensitivity, e. g. a single child node "title" only occurs below a "journal", which itself is below "bookstore".
- (iii) is regular, since for all nodes the sequence of names of the child nodes is expressible by a regular expression. In this case this is quite clear, because the number of *xtrees* is finite.
- (i) and (ii) for themselves are local.
- The union of (i) and (iii) is not local, since there are still ancestor sensitivities.
- The union of (i), (ii) and (iii) is local, since subtree replacement remains inside the set. It is also regular but it is still not consistent.

The conditions of regularity and locality of a set of *xtrees* are independent, shown by the following example:

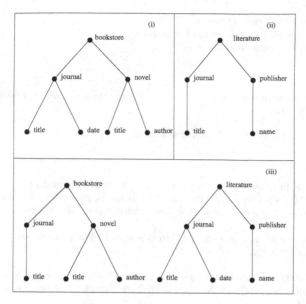

Fig. 6. An example of *xtree* sets

Example 5. We restrict the *xscheme* of Fig.4 such that in each *xtree* the number of "exemplar" child nodes under the same node is prime. This set of *xtrees* is apparently not expressible by a precise *xscheme*. It is not regular, but local. In contrast a set consisting of the *xtree* of Fig.3 only is not local, but regular.

Theorem 1. *For a set M of xtrees there exists a correct xscheme iff M is consistent.*

Proof:

Because Σ_{all} is finite, only a finite number of *xrules* exists. Therefore the *xscheme* $d = \langle \Sigma_{all}, s, \mathcal{R} \rangle$, with $\mathcal{R} = \{\langle e : (e_1 + \ldots + e_n)^* \rangle | e \in \Sigma_{all} = \{e_1, \ldots, e_n\}\}$ and $s = root(t)(\forall t \in M)$ is always correct.   □

Theorem 2. *For a set M of xtrees there exists a precise xscheme iff it is consistent, regular and local.*

Proof:

The precise *xscheme* of a consistent, regular and local set M is the *xscheme* d with $L(type(e)) = L_{all}(e)(\forall e \in \Sigma_{all})$.
⇒:
If d is the precise *xscheme* of M, M is

- consistent, because d has only one start element.
- regular, because, according to the definition, the bodies of the rules of an *xscheme* describe regular languages.
- local, because the ancestor sensitivities cannot be expressed by an *xscheme*.

⇐:
If M is consistent, regular and local, d is a precise *xscheme*, because

- there exists a unique start element.
- the *xrules* correspond exactly to the languages $L_{all}(e)$.
- no further dependencies of nodes exist.

□

If a set M of *xtrees* has no precise *xscheme*, it is important to find an *xscheme* being as close as possible to this set.

Theorem 3. *For a set M of xtrees an approximated xscheme exists iff it is consistent and regular.*

Proof:

Once more the approximated *xscheme* for a set M which is consistent and regular, is the *xscheme* d with $L(type(e)) = L_{all}(e)(\forall e \in \Sigma_{all})$. It is not possible to find a more exact *xrule* because the languages $L_{all}(e)$ are regular. Ancestor sensitivities cannot be expressed by *xschemes*. □

In Theorem 4 we assume that a set M of *xtrees* is described by an arbitrary formalism satisfying certain decidability criteria:

Theorem 4. *If consistency, regularity and locality are decidable for a set M of xtrees and if regular expressions for all sets $L_{all}(e)$, $e \in \Sigma_{all}$ can be effectively constructed for a regular set M of xtrees, the following holds:*

(a) It is decidable whether an xscheme is the approximated one for M.
(b) It is decidable whether an xscheme is the precise one for M.

Proof:

(a) By Theorem 3 we can decide whether an approximated *xscheme* exists for M. If one exists, the proof of Theorem 3 shows that we can effectively construct it. A comparison with the given *xscheme* gives the decision.
(b) Same as (a), use Theorem 2 instead.

□

We will now consider the closure properties of *xschemes*. A language class is called closed according to an operation, if the use of this operation does not leave the class. In the sequel we examine whether *xschemes* are closed under Boolean operations.

Theorem 5 (Closure of xschemes). *xschemes are closed under intersection and difference, they are not closed under union and complementation.*

Proof:

- *Intersection*:
  First of all the intersection of the involved regular expression is closed. For a node with a sequence of its child nodes there must be an *xtree* in both sets described by the *xschemes*. As this holds transitively, there cannot be any ancestor sensitivities.
- *Difference*:
  The difference of two *xschemes* is closed, as the regular expressions are closed under difference. Like in the intersection, there cannot appear any ancestor sensitivities.

- *Union*:

Consider the *xschemes* with their *xtrees* in Fig.7. If we build the union of the *xtrees* of these two *xschemes* (*i*) and (*ii*), the approximated *xscheme* would be (*iii*). A more exact *xscheme* cannot be found, thus the union is not closed. Therefore the shown *xtree* is valid in (*iii*), but it is not valid in (*i*) or (*ii*).

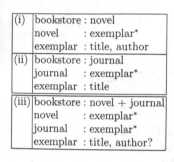

(i)	bookstore : novel
	novel : exemplar*
	exemplar : title, author
(ii)	bookstore : journal
	journal : exemplar*
	exemplar : title
(iii)	bookstore : novel + journal
	novel : exemplar*
	journal : exemplar*
	exemplar : title, author?

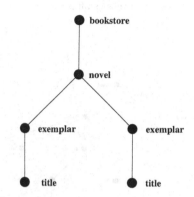

Fig. 7. Inconsistent union of two *xschemes*

- *Complementation*:

The complementation of *xschemes* is not closed in general, as otherwise the union would be expressible by intersection and complementation.

□

An immediate consequence of Theorem 5 is that a set cannot have different approximated *xschemes*. A set of *xtrees* either has an approximated *xscheme*, or for every correct *xscheme* a more exact *xscheme* can be found (see Fig.5). For this reason, one can talk about *the* approximated *xscheme*.

Theorem 5 shows an important drawback of *xschemes*: In general, two *xschemes* coming from different sources do not have a common *xscheme*. Carried over to XML, this means that two different DTDs do not need to have a common DTD. Therefore, different XML data sources cannot be integrated by means of a DTD. In the following section we show how *xschemes* can be extended to overcome these limitations.

4   Describing Information using different Levels of Abstraction

As already mentioned above, an *xscheme* (i. e. a DTD) can be seen as the schema of a document. Nevertheless an *xscheme* is much more flexible in the way it imposes structure to an object. On the one hand it can structure data as strict as e. g. the relational model. On the other hand one element can contain any other element. Altogether an *xscheme* defines a structure that is less restrictive and gives more facilities for variations of data, than a conventional scheme does [28].

This flexibility can be exploited for the description of real world data. Treating data on different levels of abstraction enables us to exactly consider the structural information given. With an *xscheme* a set of *xtrees* can be specified by describing the possible child nodes of every node using regular expressions. However, we miss a possibility to restrict the structure depending on previous nodes. The requirement of locality drastically reduces the expressiveness. Therefore we need a mechanism which memorizes the past of a node, like the stack in a push down automata. With such a mechanism, we could e. g. express ancestor sensitivities.

Example 6. The set in Example 2 cannot be described by an *xscheme*. Even the set consisting of the *xtree* in Fig.3 is not describable by an *xscheme*. Both sets are not local by Definition 7.

Example 7. We want to develop an *xscheme* for specialized XHTML[1] -pages belonging to staff members of some institute. Simplified, these pages begin with a picture, followed by a list of (two) research topics and a list of (one) publication, and finally an optional address. An example *xtree* with regard to those staff XHTML-pages is seen in Fig.8.

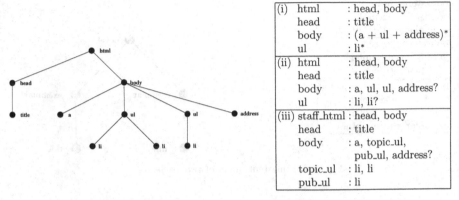

(i)	html	: head, body
	head	: title
	body	: (a + ul + address)*
	ul	: li*
(ii)	html	: head, body
	head	: title
	body	: a, ul, ul, address?
	ul	: li, li?
(iii)	staff_html	: head, body
	head	: title
	body	: a, topic_ul,
		pub_ul, address?
	topic_ul	: li, li
	pub_ul	: li

Fig. 8. An *xtree* for a staff member page

While (i) is a simplified XHTML-*xscheme*, (ii) is a specialized XHTML-*xscheme* for staff members and (iii) is a staff-*xscheme* including non XHTML-tags.

The general XHTML-Syntax (i) cannot be restricted by an *xscheme*, such that it describes XHTML-pages for staff members. E. g. documents with one research topic and two publications would be possible in (ii). Otherwise the staff page (iii), which is structurally correct, does not conform to XHTML.

Example 8. In XHTML lists can contain lists. It shall be defined that the nesting of these list elements is valid up to a particular depth. Analogous to the former case this nesting can only be done by introducing additional elements or by loss of the constraint on the depth of recursion.

We will now invent a convenient mechanism to solve the described problems. We use a homomorphic function $h()$ which is used on words as well as on (sets of) *xtrees*.

Definition 8 (s-xscheme). *A specialized xscheme (s-xscheme)* $d_S = \langle \Sigma, \Sigma', S, \mathcal{R}, h \rangle$ *is defined by finite alphabets* Σ, Σ', *a set of start elements* $S \subseteq \Sigma'$ *such that* $\forall s \in S : \langle \Sigma', s, \mathcal{R} \rangle$ *is an xscheme, and a mapping from elements to elements* $h : \Sigma' \mapsto \Sigma$.

Now we have to define the notion of *validity* for *s-xschemes*:

Definition 9 (Validity in s-xschemes). *Let* $d_S = \langle \Sigma, \Sigma', S, \mathcal{R}, h \rangle$ *be an s-xscheme. An xtree* t *over* Σ *is valid in* d_S *(in terms* $\models_t d_S$*), iff there is an* $s \in S$*, such that* $t \in h(G(d^s))$.

Here d^s means an *xscheme* with the start element s and the alphabet Σ'. Clearly the set of valid *xtrees* of an *s-xscheme* is the homomorphic mapping of the union of the sets described by the corresponding *xschemes*. With that, an *s-xscheme* is uniquely defined by a set of *xschemes* and a homomorphism over element names.

---

[1] XHTML is the XML definition of HTML [29]

Example 9. Consider the *xschemes* (*ii*) and (*iii*) for staff pages in Example 7. The specialized *xscheme* $d_S = \langle \Sigma, \Sigma', S, \mathcal{R}, h \rangle$ is defined as

Σ={html, head, body, title, a, ul, li, address}

Σ'={staff_html, head, body, title, a, topic_ul, pub_ul, li, address}

$$\mathcal{R} = \begin{array}{|ll|} \hline \text{staff\_html} & : \text{head, body} \\ \text{head} & : \text{title} \\ \text{body} & : \text{a, topic\_ul,} \\ & \quad \text{pub\_ul, address?} \\ \text{topic\_ul} & : \text{li li} \\ \text{pub\_ul} & : \text{li} \\ \hline \end{array}$$

$$h(e) = \begin{cases} \text{html} & if \ e = \text{staff\_html} \\ \text{ul} & if \ e = \text{topic\_ul} \\ \text{ul} & if \ e = \text{pub\_ul} \\ e & otherwise \end{cases}$$

S={staff_html}

Example 10. Even the finite recursion of XHTML list elements can be described using *s-xschemes*. The specialized *xscheme* $d_S = \langle \Sigma, \Sigma', S, \mathcal{R}, h \rangle$ is defined as

$$\mathcal{R} = \begin{array}{|ll|} \hline \text{html} & : \text{head, body} \\ \text{head} & : \text{title} \\ \text{body} & : \text{a, ul , address?} \\ \text{ul} & : \text{ul1 ?} \\ \text{ul1} & : \text{ul2 ?} \\ \text{ul2} & : \text{ul3 ?} \\ \hline \end{array}$$

$$h(e) = \begin{cases} \text{ul} & if \ e = \text{ul1} \\ \text{ul} & if \ e = \text{ul2} \\ \text{ul} & if \ e = \text{ul3} \\ e & otherwise \end{cases}$$

S ={html}

and the resulting alphabets Σ and Σ'.

As we can see, this list can contain lists, up to a maximal depth of three by the use of identical list elements.

All other definitions for *xschemes* like correctness, precision and equivalence carry over to *s-xschemes*.

Theorem 6 (Word problem). *It is decidable whether an xtree is valid in an s-xscheme.*

Proof:

An *xtree* t is valid in an *s-xscheme* $d_S = \langle \Sigma, \Sigma', S, \mathcal{R}, h \rangle$, iff an $s \in S$ exists, such that $text(t) \in h(L(d^s))$ holds. Thus $L(d^s)$ is a context-free language and also $h(L(d^s))$ is context-free, caused by the homomorphic property of $h()$. It is well known that the union of context-free languages is closed. Thus our problem can be reduced to the word problem for context-free grammars. □

If an *xtree* over Σ is valid in an *s-xscheme* $d_S = \langle \Sigma, \Sigma', S, \mathcal{R}, h \rangle$, there exists at least one corresponding *xtree* over Σ' that is valid in an *xscheme* $\langle \Sigma', s, \mathcal{R} \rangle$, where $s \in S$.

Example 11. For the *s-xscheme* above the nodes of the *xtrees* over Σ (*i*) and Σ' (*ii*) correspond s follows:

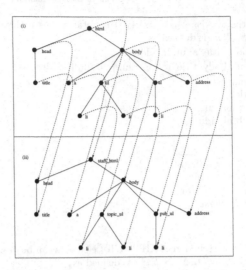

However, for *xtrees* over Σ several *xtrees* over Σ' may exist, as shown by the following example:

Example 12. We consider the *s-xscheme* $d_S = \langle \Sigma, \Sigma', S, \mathcal{R}, h \rangle$ with

$$
\mathcal{R} = \boxed{\begin{array}{ll}
\text{bookstore} : (\text{novel} + \text{journal})^* \\
\text{novel} & : \text{volume} \\
\text{journal} & : \text{volume}
\end{array}}
$$

$$
h(e) = \begin{cases}
\text{exemplar} & \textit{if } e = \text{novel} \\
\text{exemplar} & \textit{if } e = \text{journal} \\
e & \textit{otherwise}
\end{cases}
$$

and the resulting alphabets Σ and Σ'. The *xtrees* (ii) and (iii) are mapped onto the same *xtree* (i):

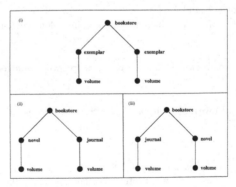

5   Characterization by an automaton

For the characterization of the properties concerning *s-xschemes* we will show the correspondence to tree automata models [18, 14] like in formal languages. The automata are namely the regular tree automata of [12]. Since this work has not been published we will recapitulate the basic concepts here, enriching them by examples and carrying the results over to our *s-xschemes*.

The main difficulty in formalizing an automata model for *xtrees* comes by the fact that the number of children is unranked. For this reason transition functions for an unlimited amount of child nodes must be defined. This can be done by assigning a state to every leave in an *xtree*. A node receives a state depending on the states of its child nodes. If the sequence of these states is in a regular language, a transition is done. With this approach an infinite transition function can be defined in a finite way.

Definition 10 (NATA). *A non deterministic ascending tree automaton $\mathcal{M}$ (NATA) is a 4-tuple $\langle Q, \Sigma, \delta, F \rangle$, where*

1. *Q is a finite set of states.*
2. *Σ is an alphabet over element names.*
3. *$\delta \subseteq \Sigma \times Q^* \times Q$ is a relation (called transition relation), such that for every $q \in Q$ and $e \in \Sigma$ the language $\{q_1 q_2 \ldots q_n | n \geq 0, \delta(e, q_1 q_2 \ldots q_n, q)\}$ is regular.*
4. *$F \subseteq Q$ is a set of accepting states.*

We will denote the language $\{q_1 q_2 \ldots q_n | n \geq 0, \delta(e, q_1 q_2 \ldots q_n, q)\}$ by $L(e, q)$. As the automaton is able to define different states for one element name, ancestor sensitivities can be expressed. The automaton can be restricted to a deterministic ascending tree automaton (*DATA*) by the additional condition $\delta(e, q_1 q_2 \ldots q_n, q) \wedge \delta(e, q_1 q_2 \ldots q_n, q') \to q = q'$. The equivalence between these two automaton models is shown in [12]. Unlike the non deterministic variant of a tree automaton, given an element name, the deterministic one can only switch into one state. Thus we also call the transition relation a "state transition function" here. Computations of an automaton are defined inductively by the structure of an *xtree*:

Definition 11 (Computation). *The computation $M(t)$ of an automaton $\mathcal{M}$ over an xtree t is defined as*

1. *$M(t) = \{q | \varepsilon \in L(e, q)\}$, where t has only one node marked by e.*
2. *$M(t) = \{q | \exists q_1 \in M(t_1), \ldots, q_n \in M(t_n) \wedge q_1 \ldots q_n \in L(e, q)\}$, if the root of t is labeled by e and t contains the subtrees $t_1, \ldots, t_n$.*

The states in $\{q | \varepsilon \in L(e, q)\}$ are also called "starting states". An *xtree* is recognized by an automaton, iff the computation yields an accepting state:

Definition 12 (Accepting an xtree). *An xtree t is accepted by an automaton $\mathcal{M}$ iff $M(t) \cap F \neq \emptyset$.*

The set of all *xtrees* accepted by an automaton $\mathcal{M}$ is denoted by $G(\mathcal{M})$. A set M of *xtrees* is recognizable iff an automaton $\mathcal{M}$ exists, where $G(\mathcal{M}) = M$.

Example 13. Consider the *xscheme* in Fig.4 and the *xtree* of Fig.3. The *DATA* $\mathcal{M} = \langle Q, \Sigma, \delta, F \rangle$ is defined as follows:

δ contains the tuples

   (*title*,ε,q_1), (*author*,ε,q_2), (*exemplar*,r_1,q_3), (*novel*,r_2,q_4), (*journal*,r_3,q_5), (*bookstore*,r_4,q_6),

where

   r_1 is in $L((q_1, q_2) + q_1)$, r_2, r_3 are in $L(q_3^*)$, r_4 is in $L(q_4, q_5)$.

The accepting states is $F = \{q_6\}$ and the sets Q and Σ are straightforward. The transition of the automaton can be seen in Fig.9.

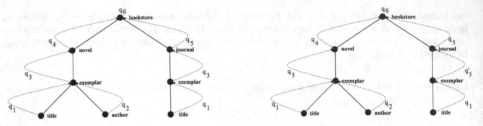

Fig. 9. Tree automaton transitions for an *xscheme* resp. *s-xscheme*

Now we restrict the set of *xtrees*, such that an "exemplar" below a "novel" always has a "title" and an "author", while an "exemplar" below a "journal" only has a "title", like in Example 2.

With these restrictions an "exemplar" can have two different states (q_3, q'_3), depending on its occurrence in an *xtree*. The transition function changes as follows:

δ consists of the tuples
    (exemplar,r_1,q_3),
    (exemplar,r'_1,q'_3),
    (novel,r_2,q_4),
    (journal,r_3,q_5),

and *bookstore*, *title* and *author* like in the former case. For the regular expressions holds

r_1 is in $L(q_1, q_2)$,
r'_1 is in $L(q_1)$,
r_2 is in $L(q_3{}^*)$,
r_3 is in $L(q'_3{}^*)$,
r_4 is in $L(q_4, q_5)$.

The transitions of the automaton working on the *xtree* now are shown in the second tree of Fig.9.

In the sequel we need a property of the defined tree automata; we can always find an automaton with no two element names receiving the same state:

Lemma 1. *For every DATA $\mathcal{M} = \langle Q, \Sigma, \delta, F \rangle$ an equivalent DATA $\mathcal{M}' = \langle Q', \Sigma, \delta', F' \rangle$ exists, such that*

$$\left.\begin{array}{l} (e, q_1 \ldots q_n, q) \in \delta', \\ (e', q'_1 \ldots q'_m, q') \in \delta', \\ (e \neq e') \end{array}\right\} \Rightarrow q \neq q'$$

Proof:

We define

$Q' = Q \times \Sigma$
$F' = \{(q, e) \in Q | q \in F\}$
$\delta' = \{(e, (q_1 e_1) \ldots (q_n e_n), (q, e)) | e_1, \ldots, e_n \in \Sigma, (e, q_1 \ldots q_n, q) \in \delta\}$

Obviously, $M' = \langle Q', \Sigma, \delta', F' \rangle$ satisfies the requirements stated in the lemma.   □

By the equivalence of deterministic and non deterministic tree automata, we can show that tree automata describe the same tree languages as s-$xschemes$.

Theorem 7 (s-xscheme and NATA/DATA). *For a set M of xtrees there exists a precise s-xscheme d_S iff there is a DATA resp. NATA $\mathcal{M}$, which recognizes M.*

Proof:

$\Rightarrow$:
We suppose that M is generated by an s-$xscheme$ $d_S = \langle \Sigma, \Sigma', S, \mathcal{R}, h \rangle$. Let $\mathcal{M} = \langle Q, \Sigma, \delta, F \rangle$ be an $NATA$, where $Q = \Sigma'$ and $F = S$. The relation $\delta : \Sigma \times Q^* \times Q$ is defined as $\delta(e, q_1 q_2 \ldots q_n, q)$ for a $\langle q : r \rangle \in \mathcal{R}, n \geq 0, q_1 q_2 \ldots q_n \in L(r)$ with $e = h(q)$.

$\Leftarrow$:
Let the set M be accepted by a $DATA$ $\mathcal{M} = \langle Q, \Sigma, \delta, F \rangle$. Let $d_S = \langle \Sigma, \Sigma', S, \mathcal{R}, h \rangle$ be an s-$xscheme$, where $\Sigma' = Q$ and $S = F$. By Lemma 1 we can assume that no two element names receive the same state, the mapping h is uniquely defined by $h(q) = e \Leftrightarrow \exists q_1, q_2, \ldots, q_n \in Q : (e, q_1 \ldots q_n, q) \in \delta$. For every $q \in Q$ and $e \in \Sigma$ let $r_{q,e}$ be a regular expression over Q, such that $L(r_{q,e}) = L(e, q)$. The set of $xrules$ $\mathcal{R}$ is defined as $\bigcup_{q \in Q, e \in \Sigma} \{\langle q : r_{q,e} \rangle | \exists q_1, q_2, \ldots, q_n \in Q : (e, q_1 q_2 \ldots q_n, q) \in \delta\}$. Thus $G(d_S) = G(\mathcal{M})$.   □

We can now show that s-$xschemes$ form a Boolean algebra.

Theorem 8 (Closure of s-xschemes). *The s-xschemes are closed under intersection, union, difference and complementation.*

Proof:

We will show the closure under union and complementation of s-$xschemes$. The closure under intersection and difference follows directly by this fact.

- *Union:*
  Let G_1 and G_2 be two tree languages recognized by some $DATA$ $\mathcal{M}_1 = \langle Q_1, \Sigma, \delta_1, F_1 \rangle$ resp. $\mathcal{M}_2 = \langle Q_2, \Sigma, \delta_2, F_2 \rangle$. Since we can rename the states of a tree automaton, it can be assumed w. l. o. g. that $Q_1 \cap Q_2 = \emptyset$. We consider the automaton $M = \langle Q, \Sigma, \delta, F \rangle$, for which $Q = Q_1 \cup Q_2$, $\delta = \delta_1 \cup \delta_2$ and $F = F_1 \cup F_2$ holds. The equivalence of $G(\mathcal{M})$ and $G(\mathcal{M}_1) \cup G(\mathcal{M}_2)$ is straightforward.
- *Complementation:*
  Let G be a tree language recognized by an automaton $\mathcal{M}$. We build an automaton with the complementary set of accepting states $F^c = Q - F$. Thus $\mathcal{M}^c = \langle Q, \Sigma, \delta, F^c \rangle$ recognizes the complement of G.

□

Theorem 9 (Emptiness of s-xschemes). *It is decidable whether an s-xscheme describes an empty set of xtrees.*

Proof:

We consider the $DATA$ for an $xscheme$. We have to check the transition graph for a way from a starting state to an accepting state. This can be done by marking all states including the starting states, that are reachable by any $e \in \Sigma$. This is repeated as long, as either an accepting tate is marked or no other state can be reached. This is always possible since there is only a finite number of states.   □

Remark. As an *xscheme* can also be seen as an *s-xscheme*, the same holds there.

Theorem 10 (Containment). *It is decidable whether an s-xscheme is more exact than another.*

Proof:

Let d_S and d'_S be two *s-xschemes*. Since *s-xschemes* build a Boolean algebra, we can describe $G(d_S) - G(d'_S)$ by an *s-xscheme*. The question whether containment can be reduced to the question if $G(d_S) - G(d'_S) = \emptyset$ holds.   □

6   Concrete System and Applications

The theoretical foundations developed in the former sections will now be put into a concrete syntax. This homomorphic relation is expressed by a MAPPING statement, tying each element name to its possible enriched archetypes. Notice that this statement is not part of the standard DTD definition, as proposed by the W3C. Consider the *s-xscheme* of Example 9 describing XHTML pages for the institute staff. The concrete syntax for is shown in Fig.10:

```
<!ELEMENT staff_html    head, body>
<!ELEMENT head          title>
<!ELEMENT body          a, topic_ul, pub_ul, address?>
<!ELEMENT topic_ul      li, li>
<!ELEMENT pub_ul        li>
<!MAPPING ul            topic_ul, pub_ul>
<!MAPPING html          staff_html>
```

Fig. 10. A specialized DTD for staff XHTML pages

Once an XML document conforming to the schema above is parsed, we can perform transformations that take advantage of the additional information delivered by enriched element names.

```
<xsl:stylesheet>
 <xsl:template match="staff_html/body">
  <OUTPUT>
    <H1> Research Topic List of : <xsl:apply-templates select="//address"/> </H1>
    <UL> <xsl:apply-templates select="//topic_ul/li"/> </UL>
  </OUTPUT>
 </xsl:template>
 <xsl:template match="address">
  ''<xsl:apply-templates/>''
 </xsl:template>
 <xsl:template match="li">
  <LI> <xsl:apply-templates/> </LI>
 </xsl:template>
</xsl:stylesheet>
```

Fig. 11. An XSL transformation program for staff XHTML pages

In Fig.11 we give an XSL program [31, 32] which is applied to an XML document's archetype. This transformation takes documents according to staff_html pages, and collects all research topics, grouping them in a special list tagged by ul. This would not be be possible without the additional information delivered by an *s-xscheme*, since every unordered list would be a topic list candidate.

```
<html>
  <head> <title> R. Behrens </title> </head>
  <body>
    <a href="Picture.gif"></a>            <OUTPUT>
    <ul>                                    <H1> ''Research Topic List of R. Behrens,
      <li> XML </li>                              IfIs '' </H1>
      <li> Web </li>                        <UL>
    </ul>                                     <LI>  ''XML'' </LI>
    <ul>                                      <LI>  ''Web'' </LI>
      <li> Grammar Model for XML </li>      </UL>
    </ul>                                 </OUTPUT>
    <address> R. Behrens, IfIs </address>
  </body>
</html>
```

Fig. 12. Input and output of an XSL program with enriched elements

7 Discussion

The main contribution of this paper was to develop a grammar based model for XML [30] allowing to show that XML has important drawbacks as far as integration of several schemas is concerned. The model consists of so called *xtrees* modeling concrete XML documents and of *xschemes* modeling DTDs. We showed that *xschemes* are not closed under union which means that in general there is no DTD describing the union of the languages defined by two DTDs.

In order to overcome this and other drawbacks, we developed an extension of *xschemes* called *s-xschemes*. Besides being closed under union and other operations, *s-xschemes* allow to model information with different granularity. This can greatly improve the transformation of documents and the extractions of meta information. Since we use *s-xschemes* to restrict the schema of XML documents, it is important to develop an efficient parsing algorithm for this kind of language. We presented our approach for this in [7]. The language constructs we developed are implemented by a parsing system. This will be integrated into our digital media archive for teaching MONTANA [23, 8, 6].

In the future, it will be of interest to generalize the type of an *xrule* from regular structures to more general ones. In addition, modeling of structure by attribute grammars [20] can be used to express attributes and computations.

Acknowledgement The author would like to thank Gerhard Buntrock, Carsten Lecon and Volker Linnemann for fruitful discussions on preliminary versions of this paper.

References

1. S. Abiteboul. Querying semi-structured data. In *International Conference on Database Theory (ICDT)*, pages 1–18, Delphi, 1997.
2. S. Abiteboul. On views and XML. In *ACM Symposium on Principles of Database Systems (PODS)*, pages 1–9, 1999. Invited talk.
3. S. Abiteboul, S. Cluet, V. Christophides, T. Milo, G. Moerkotte, and J. Siméon. Querying documents in object databases. *Journal on Digital Libraries*, 1(1):5–19, 1997.

4. S. Abiteboul, S. Cluet, and T. Milo. A logical view of structured files. *VLDB Journal*, 7(2):96–114, 1998.

5. C. Beeri and T. Milo. Schemas for integration and translation of structured and semi-structured data. In *International Conference on Database Theory (ICDT)*, pages 296–313, 1999.

6. R. Behrens. MONTANA: Towards a web-based infrastructure to improve lecture and research in a university environment. In *2nd International Workshop on Advance Issues of E-Commerce and Web-based Information Systems*, San Jose, 2000. to appear.

7. R. Behrens. On the complexity of standard and specialized DTD parsing. In *12. GI-Workshop "Grundlagen von Datenbanken"*, 2000. to appear.

8. R. Behrens, C. Lecon, V. Linnemann, and O. Schmitt. MONTANA: A digital media archive for teaching (in german). Technical report, Institut für Informationssysteme, Med. Univ. Lübeck, September 1998.

9. R. Book, S. Even, S. Greibach, and G. Ott. Ambiguity in graphs and expressions. *IEEE Transactions on Computers*, 20:149–153, 1971.

10. J. Bosak. XML, Java and the future of the Web. Technical report, SUN, 1997.

11. A. Brüggemann-Klein and D. Wood. One-unambiguous regular languages. *Information and Computation*, 140(2):229–253, 1998.

12. A. Brüggemann-Klein and D. Wood. Regular tree languages over non-ranked alphabets. Working paper, 1998.

13. S. Cluet. Modeling and querying semi-structured data. In *International Summer School on Information Extraction (SCIE)*, volume 1299 of *Lecture Notes in Computer Science*, pages 192–213. Springer-Verlag, 1997.

14. H. Comon, M. Dauchet, R. Gilleron, F. Jacquemard, D. Lugiez, S. Tison, and M. Timmasi. *Tree Automata - Techniques and Applications*. unpublished book, 1997.

15. V. Crescenzi and G. Mecca. Grammars have exceptions. *Information Systems*, 23(8):539–569, 1998.

16. A. Deutsch, M. Fernandez, D. Florecsu, A. Levy, and D. Suciu. XML-QL: A query language for XML. In *QL98 - The Query Languages Workshop*. W3C, 1998.

17. L. Faulstich, M. Spiliopoulou, and V. Linnemann. WIND - a warehouse for internet data. In *British National Conference on Databases (BNCOD)*, pages 169–183, 1997.

18. F. Gécseg and M. Steinby. *Handbook of Formal Languages - Beyond Words*, volume 3, pages 1–61. Springer-Verlag, 1996. In G. Rozenberg and A. Salomaa, editors.

19. J. Hopcroft and J. Ullman. *Introduction To Automata Theory, Languages and Computation*. Addison-Wesley, 1979.

20. D. Knuth. Semantics of context-free languages. *Mathematical Systems Theory*, pages 127–145, 1968.

21. D. Maier. Database desiderata for an XML query language. In *QL98 - The Query Languages Workshop*. W3C, 1998.

22. T. Milo and D. Suciu. Type inference for queries on semistructured data. In *ACM Symposium on Principles of Database Systems (PODS)*, pages 215–236, 1999.

23. Homepage of the digital media archive MONTANA. http://passat.mesh.de:4040.

24. M. Murata. Data model for document transformation and assembly. In *Proceedings of the Workshop on Principles of Digital Document Processing*. Springer-Verlag, 1998.

25. F. Neven and T. Schwentick. Query automata. In *ACM Symposium on Principles of Database Systems (PODS)*, pages 205–214, 1999.

26. F. Neven and J. Van den Bussche. Expressiveness of structured document query languages based on attribute grammars. In *ACM Symposium on Principles of Database Systems (PODS)*, pages 11–17, 1998.

27. Y. Papakonstantinou and P. Velikhov. Enhancing semistructured data mediators with document type definitions. In *International Conference on Data Engineering (ICDE)*, pages 136–145, 1999.

28. D. Suciu. Semistructured data and XML. In *Proceedings of the 5th International Conference on Foundations of Data Organization and Algorithms (FODO)*, 1998.

29. The Extensible HyperText Markup Language (XHTML). W3C Recommendation, http://www.w3.org/TR/xhtml1/, 2000.

30. eXtensible Markup Language (XML) 1.0. W3C Recommendation, http://www.w3.org/TR/REC-xml/, 1998.

31. eXtensible Stylesheet Language (XSL) specification. W3C Working draft , http://www.w3.org/TR/WD-xsl/, 1998.

32. XSL transformations 1.0. W3C Working draft , http://www.w3.org/TR/WD-xslt/, 1999.

CORBA and XML: Design Choices for Database Federations

Graham J.L. Kemp[1], Chris J. Robertson[1,2], Peter M.D. Gray[1]
, and Nicos Angelopoulos[1,2]

[1] Department of Computing Science, University of Aberdeen,
King's College, Aberdeen, Scotland, AB9 2UE
[2] Department of Molecular and Cell Biology, University of Aberdeen,
Polwarth Building, Foresterhill, Aberdeen, Scotland, AB25 2ZD

Abstract. The newly established standards of CORBA and XML make
it much easier to interoperate between different database software running on different platforms. We are using these in a mediator-based architecture that supports integrated access to biological databases. We
discuss, in turn, design issues that arise from using each of the standards. In CORBA an important design issue is the use of *coarse grain*
access, which supports a query language over an extensible integrated
data model, as compared with *fine grain* access, which is tailored for
specific queries. We discuss experience in using CORBA in these two
ways. On the other hand we describe scenarios where returning results
are communicated in XML format. We present a classification based on
design choices.

1 Introduction

The Common Object Request Broker Architecture (CORBA) and the Extensible
Markup Language (XML) are currently promoted as providing standardisation
in distributed computing applications. However, these technologies do not in
themselves provide application designers with a single solution to their design
problems. Rather, they serve as infrastructure standards that can be employed
in many alternative ways in building a system.

In this paper we describe a federated database architecture that we are building to support integrated access to biological databases. We concentrate on
the design of the interoperability layer and present a number of approaches based on the technologies of CORBA for implementing a client-server database
architecture, and XML for formatting the results of database queries.

A major problem in integrating multiple internet data resources is that they
do not all make their data intelligible to remote programs. Some resources depend entirely on communicating directly with a person observing a screen. This
prevents one from using intelligent *mediator* programs (as proposed by Weider-
hold [13]) to intercept the communication and automate the data fusion and
integration. Better resources present data in well defined text formats that can
be used by programs as well as humans. Still better data resources will provide

B. Lings and K. Jeffery (Eds.): BNCOD 17, LNCS 1832, pp. 191–208, 2000.

access through database management software, thus enabling remote programs to generate their own queries and process the answers. This requires the structured framework of a schema for integration with data from other resources. It is this latter kind of access that we are seeking to provide through our work with the P/FDM object database system.[1]

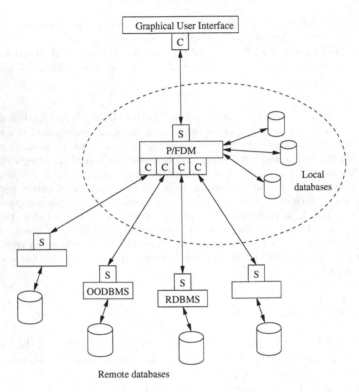

Fig. 1. CORBA and database access. Clients [C] send queries to CORBA servers [S] and sets of results are returned.

Our general architecture is shown in Figure 1 which shows how each remote data source can act as a server surrounded by a CORBA wrapper, while the integrated output from the mediator can itself be accessed through another CORBA wrapper.

In this paper we discuss some limitations of the access styles provided by many current biological data resources, and contrast this with the query capabilities of an object database. We describe alternative ways in which CORBA can be used to provide access to biological databases and show how coarse grain CORBA interfaces can provide efficient access to databases, illustrating this with

---

[1] http://www.csd.abdn.ac.uk/~pfdm/

an example using our antibody structure database. Finally, we discuss the role that XML can play in making the results easier to process or browse.

2 Degrees of Accessibility

2.1 Browsing and Viewing

Many internet resources are intended for interactive inspection and interpretation by users observing a screen. Images, such as a metabolic pathway diagram or a graphical representation of an enzyme with its active site highlighted, or free text descriptions, such as journal abstracts or entries in biological data resources such as PROSITE (a database of protein families and domains [4]), contain information which is readily digested by users viewing these. However, the information contained within these is not easily available to programs. Image processing and natural language processing technologies still have a long way to advance before they can be used by remote programs to interpret the content of such data resources, let alone relate these observations to data from other sources and form scientific hypotheses.

Many web-based data resources only provide this kind of access. The World-Wide Web has evolved to suit human users, who tend to search for particular pages of interest, controlling navigation interactively. The search techniques used are generally those developed by the information retrieval community for free-format text. Since the program does not understand the text, it uses probabilistic matching, for example by scoring keywords, and expects to retrieve some *false matches*. Database queries, by contrast, are expected to return sets which *exactly* fit the given criteria, and may involve numerical comparisons. The data model they use effectively describes the meaning of data in the form of carefully checked formatted records, and does not have to deal with free-format natural language sentence structures. This is what allows queries to be more precise.

2.2 Formatted Text Files

Formatted data files, such as SWISS-PROT entries and Protein Data Bank entries, can be used more easily by programs. Many such collections are now accessible via the World-Wide Web. Using command line web interfaces like Lynx, it is possible for programs (e.g. UNIX scripts or application programs written in C or Java) to fetch a web page automatically and then process it like any other external file. However, this requires the user to have programming skills, knowledge of the data file formats, and time to write a new program whenever they wish to access different data values or different data banks or to use these for a different purpose.

The SRS[2] system [6] goes some way towards providing indexes and a query interface for flat file data banks on the same server, but the querying capabilities are not as expressive or flexible as database query languages. For example, all result fields requested must be from the same data bank.

---

[2] http://srs.ebi.ac.uk/

2.3 Database Management Systems

Database management systems (DBMS) provide *ad hoc* querying capabilities, enabling complex data retrieval requests to be expressed in a high level query language. These requests can include sophisticated data selection criteria and may traverse the data in ways not envisaged by those who created the database. The DBMS will provide optimisation capabilities that can use all of the information in the query in designing an efficient execution strategy.

Some may argue that a collection of indexed web pages constitutes a primitive database. However, the search capabilities provided are far below what one would expect from a database management system. When web pages are indexed for searching, this usually takes the form of a keyword index which enables searches for links to pages containing a specified word or phrase. Hypertext links between web pages do provide a kind of index for interactive browsing, but these links cannot be queried easily by automatic programs. If one does implement an automatic searching program which can follow links to retrieve related pages, then it is still necessary for the related pages to be retrieved one-at-a-time and for these to be processed on the client machine; each would have to be scanned sequentially to see if it matches the search criteria. It is more efficient to send selection conditions across to a remote part of a distributed database and to send back just the items required than it is to transport the data as whole web pages, only to reject much of it on arrival. This principle is at the heart of the design of the coarse grain CORBA interface described in Section 3.3.

3   CORBA Interfaces to Biological Databases

CORBA is an architecture standard proposed by the Object Management Group[3] and widely supported by manufacturers. It provides a way to present an interface on the local machine to remote objects and their associated methods. CORBA is currently attracting widespread interest in the bioinformatics community as a technology which can assist in integrating distributed heterogeneous resources, e.g. the EMBL data model for genome data[4] is designed around the use of CORBA interfaces. We believe that CORBA can assist with the low level integration of distributed software components and with wrapping legacy systems. However, a straightforward mapping between CORBA objects, defined using the interface definition language (IDL), and database objects can lead to inefficient systems and lose the benefits of data independence which database management systems, by definition, provide. In this section we describe the use and misuse of CORBA with database systems with examples from our antibody database [9].

3.1 Fine Grain and Coarse Grain Database Access with CORBA

Cormac McKenna [11] describes two alternative ways to use CORBA with an object-oriented database system (OODBS). That paper describes his experience

---

[3] http://www.omg.org/
[4] http://corba.ebi.ac.uk/EMBL/embl.html

using the ODB-II OODBS and the DAIS CORBA-compliant object request broker (ORB). In the first approach each object class and each OODBS instance is represented as an ORB object. An example of this kind of interface is given in Section 3.2 and Figure 3. This approach requires the programmer to specify the execution plan in terms of the limited set of access functions provided in the IDL. Each step needed to achieve a task has to be programmed explicitly. This is laborious for the programmer and the resulting code is potentially very inefficient since an application task may require many small requests to be sent from the client to the database server and many small packets of data being sent from the client to the server (fine grain access) with data selection being done on the client. McKenna comments that "the main difficulty with this approach is developing the infrastructure required to access objects from the database using queries" and that "queries cannot be passed very naturally to IDL methods".

In the second approach a single ORB object is used as the interface to the entire database, providing a server that can execute queries expressed in a high level query language. Here, the IDL resolves down to a single object rather than multiple objects which enables large queries containing several selections to be sent to the server for bulk execution (coarse grain access), taking advantage of optimisation strategies and indexes available on the server. McKenna's paper shows how queries expressed in ODQL (ODB-II's query language) can be embedded in C applications. Section 3.3 describes a coarse grain interface to a P/FDM server.

CORBA does not in itself provide a general purpose way to query data held at distributed sites. However, it does provide an architecture within which one can build the infrastructure and services to support the distribution of data. The language and platform independence which it promotes gives it an edge over sockets as a technology for enabling interprocess communication across platforms from different vendors (e.g. UNIX and Windows-NT) by providing programmers with a higher level of abstraction that hides details of the transport layer. With Object Request Brokers becoming more freely available, we should see more client-server database applications migrating to CORBA. However, we believe that it is important that database services accessible through an Object Request Broker should at least allow coarse grain access via a high level query language.

3.2 An Example of Fine Grain Access Using CORBA

Suppose we want to find out whether the values of the phi and psi angles of the residues at Kabat position "27C" in antibody light chains from high resolution antibody structures correlate with the chain class. In this section and the next, we will consider two alternative approaches to this task.

Figure 2 shows how an interface to part of the antibody database can be defined in CORBA's IDL. Figure 3 shows part of a possible client program. Note particularly the cost of using a CORBA call, such as get_residues, to bring across a whole array of results, each of which has to be set up as a CORBA stub for a Residue object, capable of calling across the net to get its data values! Worse still, many of these objects will turn out not to be required. The advantages of returning a batch of results as tuples, possibly wrapped in XML tags, is clear in this case.

The approach taken in this example is rather extreme, and has been chosen to show IDL code that closely resembles a database schema. Of course, additional access methods could be provided in the interface. However, the client programmer would still be responsible for designing the execution plan and the server programmer would have to write additional implementation code to support any additional methods.

```
module Antibody {

        interface Residue {
                unsigned long           pos();
                string                  name();
                string                  kabat_position();
                double                  phi();
                double                  psi();
        };

        interface Chain {
                string                  chain_id();
                unsigned long           num_residues();
                string                  chain_class();
                sequence<Residue>       get_residues();
        };

        interface Structure {
                string                  protein_code();
                string                  protein_name();
                string                  source();
                string                  authors();
                double                  resolution();
                string                  ig_name();
                sequence<Chain>         get_chains();
        };

        interface StructureDatabase {
                sequence<Structure>     get_structures()
        };

};
```

Fig. 2. IDL code for a fine grain CORBA interface.

```
// CLIENT CODE
//
// ("Pseudo-Java")

import Antibody.*;
import org.omg.CORBA.*;


// Variable declarations

org.omg.CORBA.Object    obj;

StructureDatabase       dbRef;
Structure[]             structureRefs;
Chain[]                 chainRefs;
Residue[]               residueRefs;
int                     i, j, k;

// Connect to the database using CORBA
ORB orb = ORB.init( this, null );
// ... etc. ...
dbRef = StructureDatabaseHelper.narrow( obj );

structureRefs = dbRef.get_structures();
for (i=0; i < structureRefs.length; i++) {
    if (structureRefs[i].resolution() < 2.5) {
        chainRefs = structureRefs[i].get_chains();
        for (j=0; jchainRefs.length; j++) {
            if (chainRefs[j].chain_id() == "L") {
                residueRefs = chainRefs[j].get_residues();
                for (k=0; k < residueRefs.length; k++) {
                    if (residueRefs[k].kabat_position() == "27C") {
                        System.out.println(
                                structureRefs[i].protein_code()
                        +"  "+chainRefs[j].chain_class()
                        +"  "+residueRefs[k].name()
                        +"  "+residueRefs[k].phi()
                        +"  "+residueRefs[k].psi());
                    }
                }
            }
        }
    }
}
```

Fig. 3. "Pseudo-Java" code to compare the phi/psi angles of the residues at Kabat position "27C" in light chains of high resolution antibody structures.

3.3 An Example of Coarse Grain Access Using CORBA

We have implemented a coarse grain CORBA interface to P/FDM in Java using the ORBacus[5] object request broker. Part of the IDL code for this interface is shown in Figure 4.

```
module PFDM  {

        // Exceptions here ...

        // Type definitions

        typedef sequence<string> clauseArray;    // Holds schema clauses

        interface pfdm {

                void            openModule( in string module_name )
                                raises (ModuleUnknownException,
                                        OpenModuleFailedException,
                                        UnableToOpenDBException);

                clauseArray     getSchemaClauses()
                                raises (ModuleUnknownException);

                void            sendQuery( in string daplex_query )
                                raises (IncorrectSyntaxException,
                                        UnableToOpenDBException);

                string          getTuple()
                                raises (NoResultsException);

                boolean         hasMoreTuples();

        };

};
```

Fig. 4. IDL code for a coarse grain CORBA interface.

The IDL shows that a single object is used to represent the entire database. This object provides the methods openModule, getSchemaClauses, sendQuery, getTuple and hasMoreTuples.

openModule Data in P/FDM are partitioned into modules, with each module containing data on a related set of entity classes. Significantly for integrating heterogeneous databases, different modules can have different physical

---
[5] http://www.ooc.com/ob/

representations. Our antibody database consists of two modules; one containing structural data and the other containing sequence data from the Kabat data bank. Once connected to a P/FDM database, the user can choose which database modules should be opened. Several modules may be open at the same time.

getSchemaClauses This method returns the database schema as an array of Daplex data definition clauses. These can be used by client applications to generate a graphical representation of the schema at run-time. This method will not be needed if the client application is a customised user interface which has knowledge of the database module's schema encoded within it, or if the user interface is simply an entry box for users to type their queries and the users are already familiar with the schema.

sendQuery This method takes a Daplex query string as its argument. The query is passed to the database and is executed.

getTuple This method returns a string containing one row of results for the query. The client process can retrieve all of the results by calling this method repeatedly, giving flow control. An alternative approach would be implement method returning *all* results for the query as a sequence of strings.

hasMoreTuples This is a predicate which returns true if there are further result tuples to be retrieved.

The task described in the Section 3.2 can be achieved much more simply using the following high level Daplex query (Daplex is the query language for P/FDM and plays the role of SQL for an object database):

```
for each r in residue such that kabat_position(r) = "27C"
  for each c in residue_chain(r) such that chain_id(c) = "L"
    for each s in chain_structure(c) such that resolution(s) < 2.5
print(protein_code(s), chain_class(c), name(r), phi(r), psi(r));
```

The query can either be typed directly or, more likely, composed incrementally using a graphical user interface. Several interfaces are possible as shown in Figure 5. In the simplest case, a canned query can be parametrised, and the parameters entered into an HTML form. This uses the well known CGI-bin mechanism to call out to C and hence to CORBA. A richer graphic interface can be provided by using a Java applet, provided the CORBA implementation is known and trusted by the browser that is hosting the applet. The most general solution we have built is a Visual Navigator [7] which is a Java application that displays the integration schema as a diagram, so that the user can then interact with it in order to build up successively more complex queries. This is done by displaying query results as mouse-active tables; simply highlighting data values of interest results in their incorporation in refined selection conditions. The query can then be extended by the user to search for further details on the data of interest, which can then in turn be refined.

When complete, the query string can be passed to the P/FDM server using the sendQuery method. The database management system has an optimiser

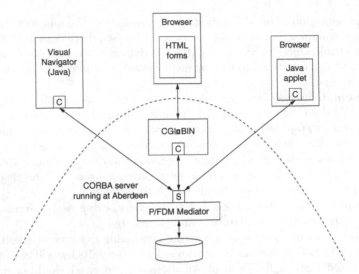

Fig. 5. Three different interfaces being used with a single shared CORBA server. They range from simple web forms to a complex Java application.

which can analyse the query as a whole and design an efficient execution plan using knowledge of the database's internal structure and indexes. Thus, selection is done efficiently on the server; not on the client, as in Section 3.2. In Section 3.2, the client does most of the work, many small access requests are sent from the client to the server, and lots of data are passed back from the server. While more access methods could be added to the interface in Section 3.2 so that larger chunks of the problem could be passed to the server, providing specific methods to cover all possible access requests would require an unending programming effort, and efficiency would still rely on the client programmer making best use of the available methods.

4   Role of CORBA in Providing Integrated Access to Biological Databases

Figure 1 shows an architecture in which graphical user interface connects to the P/FDM system via the coarse grain CORBA server interface described in Section 3.3. The P/FDM system will coordinate query processing, generating code to access both the local and remote databases. CORBA client code can be used to enable P/FDM to connect to the remote database server. To allow best use to be made of these remote resources, these should also provide coarse grain interfaces enabling large queries to be passed for processing.

Why have P/FDM at the centre of Figure 1? Others may prefer to have a different software component performing the task of splitting queries, designing execution plans and sending sub-queries to remote databases. To support such architectures, the coarse grain query interface to P/FDM described in this article is available for others to use in their programs.[6] However, there are several reasons why P/FDM is well suited for this role. First, it is based on the Functional Data Model (FDM) [12] which was itself designed for use in the MULTIBASE project [10], an earlier project in integrating distributed heterogeneous database systems. A strong semantic data model like the FDM provides data independence [8]. Thus the Daplex query makes no assumptions about the storage model that is used in each remote database (O-O, relational, hash table, flat file etc.) and we have experimented with several alternative physical storage formats [9] P/FDM has an expressive query language, called Daplex, which we have found to be better able to combine calculation with data retrieval than the query languages provided by other remote database management systems for which we have tried generating queries automatically. The P/FDM system is itself implemented largely in Prolog (with some calls to C routines) and we have chosen this because it is very efficient for transforming queries into an internal term structure representation, matching and manipulating patterns within user queries and then translating queries into the languages (such as SQL and OQL) used by other remote databases.

As usual, the mediator is capable of generating queries to send to separate databases and joining the results. This fits with the philosophy of sending the selection conditions to the data rather than sending all the data to the selection process, as noted earlier. However, some data are cached to avoid repeating the same query.

5   XML for Query Results

The data returned through a coarse grain interface is in the form of tuples containing structured values taken from remote objects. Recently we have experimented with formatting these structured values in XML. XML offers a simple and flexible mark-up language syntax for documents containing data values along with their description. This is of interest in the design of a database federation based on coarse grain database interfaces. Thus, instead of returning results wrapped up in CORBA objects, as in the fine grain case, we return them as tagged tuples in streams. These streams are essentially lines of text that have to be parsed by client processes. The presence of XML mark-up tags within the result strings can make the task of parsing the results much easier. For example, we can use downloadable XML parsers to spot patterns in the results and to display the results in a mouse-active form.

5.1   Tags Based on the Result Format

The simplest style of mark-up for query results is one in which tags are used to reflect the tabular structure of the results (Figure 6). A P/FDM query typically

---

[6] Contact the authors for further details.

for each s in structure
print(protein_code(s), resolution(s))

```
<RESULTS>                      <RESULTS>
1BBD 2.8                         <ROW> 1BBD 2.8 </ROW>
1BBJ 3.1                         <ROW> 1BBJ 3.1 </ROW>
1CBV 2.6                         <ROW> 1CBV 2.6 </ROW>
</RESULTS>                       </RESULTS>
     (a)                              (b)
```

```
<RESULTS>
<ROW><FIELD> 1BBD </FIELD><FIELD> 2.8 </FIELD></ROW>
<ROW><FIELD> 1BBJ </FIELD><FIELD> 3.1 </FIELD></ROW>
<ROW><FIELD> 1CBV </FIELD><FIELD> 2.6 </FIELD></ROW>
</RESULTS>
                    (c)
```

```
<RESULTS query="for each s in structure
                print(protein_code(s),resolution(s))">
<ROW><FIELD type="string"> 1BBD </FIELD>
    <FIELD type="float"> 2.8 </FIELD></ROW>
<ROW><FIELD type="string"> 1BBJ </FIELD>
    <FIELD type="float"> 3.1 </FIELD></ROW>
<ROW><FIELD type="string"> 1CBV </FIELD>
    <FIELD type="float"> 2.6 </FIELD></ROW>
</RESULTS>
                    (d)
```

Fig. 6. XML for query results, based on the result format. The results of the query shown at the top have been formatted with tags that delimit the set of results (a,b,c,d), result rows (b,c,d) and result values (c,d). Information about the original query and data types can also be returned (d).

produces many rows of results, where each row comprises a list of values for the expressions given as arguments to the print statement. When parsing the results of a query we need to be able to identify where the results start and end, so the results can be delimited by tags such as <RESULTS> and </RESULTS>. Next, we want to identify the start and end of each row, and then the individual fields within a result row. Which of the formats shown in Figure 6 is most appropriate depends on whether the parser knows about the expected structure of the row or whether it needs extra tags in order to distinguish between strings, integers and floating point values.

```
<RESULTS>
<ROW><FUNCTION name="protein_code"  type="string"> 1BBD </FUNCTION>
     <FUNCTION name="resolution" type="float"> 2.8 </FUNCTION></ROW>
<ROW><FUNCTION name="protein_code"  type="string"> 1BBJ </FUNCTION>
     <FUNCTION name="resolution" type="float"> 3.1 </FUNCTION></ROW>
<ROW><FUNCTION name="protein_code"  type="string"> 1CBV </FUNCTION>
     <FUNCTION name="resolution" type="float"> 2.6 </FUNCTION></ROW>
     </RESULTS>
```

(a)

```
<RESULTS>
<ROW><FUNCTION name="protein_code"  argtype="structure"
         arg="structure(1)" resulttype="string"> 1BBD </FUNCTION>
     <FUNCTION name="resolution" argtype="structure"
         arg="structure(1)" resulttype="float"> 2.8 </FUNCTION></ROW>
<ROW><FUNCTION name="protein_code"  argtype="structure"
         arg="structure(2)" resulttype="string"> 1BBJ </FUNCTION>
     <FUNCTION name="resolution" argtype="structure"
         arg="structure(2)" resulttype="float"> 3.1 </FUNCTION></ROW>
<ROW><FUNCTION name="protein_code"  argtype="structure"
         arg="structure(3)" resulttype="string"> 1CBV </FUNCTION>
     <FUNCTION name="resolution" argtype="structure"
         arg="structure(3)" resulttype="float"> 2.6 </FUNCTION></ROW>
</RESULTS>
```

(b)

Fig. 7. XML for query results, based on the data model. The results of the query in Figure 6 have been formatted with FUNCTION tags separating function values.

5.2 Tags Based on the Data Model

As an alternative to focusing on the result structure, we can instead concentrate on the concepts that are central to data model (Figure 7). In the functional data model these are *entities* and *functions*.

We can extend this to include information about function arguments, their types and the function's result type.

5.3 Tags Based on the Schema

Another approach is to use tags that are based on the entity class names and function names that are declared in the schema (Figure 8). Taking this to an extreme, the XML tags could be organised to match the structure of the full query graph.

A drawback with this approach is that the tags used will vary from query to query and from database to database. This means that application programs will have to be able to parse a wide variety of named tags, and process the data values within these appropriately. It also means that the XML Document Type

```
<RESULTS>
<ROW><STRUCTURE>
        <PROTEIN_CODE> 1BBD </PROTEIN_CODE>
        <RESOLUTION> 2.8 </RESOLUTION></STRUCTURE></ROW>
<ROW><STRUCTURE>
        <PROTEIN_CODE> 1BBJ </PROTEIN_CODE>
        <RESOLUTION> 3.1 </RESOLUTION></STRUCTURE></ROW>
<ROW><STRUCTURE>
        <PROTEIN_CODE> 1CBV </PROTEIN_CODE>
        <RESOLUTION> 2.6 </RESOLUTION></STRUCTURE></ROW>
</RESULTS>
```
(a)

```
<RESULTS>
<ROW><STRUCTURE id="structure(1)">
        <PROTEIN_CODE> 1BBD </PROTEIN_CODE>
        <RESOLUTION> 2.8</RESOLUTION>
    </STRUCTURE></ROW>
<ROW><STRUCTURE id="structure(2)">
        <PROTEIN_CODE> 1BBJ </PROTEIN_CODE>
        <RESOLUTION> 3.1 </RESOLUTION>
    </STRUCTURE></ROW>
<ROW><STRUCTURE id="structure(3)">
        <PROTEIN_CODE> 1CBV </PROTEIN_CODE>
        <RESOLUTION> 2.6 </RESOLUTION>
    </STRUCTURE> </ROW>
</RESULTS>
```
(b)

```
<RESULTS>
<ROW><STRUCTURE id="structure(1)">
        <PROTEIN_CODE> 1BBD </PROTEIN_CODE></STRUCTURE>
    <STRUCTURE id="structure(1)">
        <RESOLUTION> 2.8 </RESOLUTION></STRUCTURE></ROW>
<ROW><STRUCTURE id="structure(2)">
        <PROTEIN_CODE> 1BBJ </PROTEIN_CODE></STRUCTURE>
    <STRUCTURE id="structure(2)">
        <RESOLUTION> 3.1 </RESOLUTION></STRUCTURE></ROW>
<ROW><STRUCTURE id="structure(3)">
        <PROTEIN_CODE> 1CBV </PROTEIN_CODE></STRUCTURE>
    <STRUCTURE id="structure(3)">
        <RESOLUTION> 2.6 </RESOLUTION></STRUCTURE></ROW>
</RESULTS>
```
(c)

Fig. 8. XML for query results, based on the schema. The results of the query in Figure 6 have been formatted with tags derived from entity class names and function names that are declared in the database schema.

Definition (DTD) will be much more complex. In contrast, the representations described in the previous subsections have the advantage of uniformity and can be used more easily by generic applications.

5.4 Combinations of Tags

It is possible to use combinations of tag styles to describe a query's results. For example, we can mark up results with tags describing the result structure inside which are tags based on the schema. Such an approach can make the same database output useful to application programs that need to know only about the tabular structure of the results in order to display these in a simple table or spreadsheet, and also to applications that generate more sophisticated displays based on the semantic information encoded in schema-based tags.

6 Discussion and Related Work

The way in which we have used CORBA contrasts with the approach taken by Barillot *et al.* [2]. In their work, they are using the Oracle 7.3 relational database management system to store genome map data, and have implemented a CORBA server in Java that uses JDBC to access the Oracle system. Significantly, the CORBA interface does not provide coarse grain query access for remote users. Instead, remote users must use the specific methods defined in the IDL to access individual attributes or execute canned queries. If one wanted to achieve *ad hoc* query access then it would be necessary to implement a query processor on the client that breaks queries into individual access requests that call out to methods provided by the CORBA interface, i.e. fine grain access. Since these requests would have to be made from a language such as Java or C++ which has a CORBA binding it would also be necessary to first compile the generated calls before these could be executed. To get efficient, flexible access to the genome map database, remote users would need access either to a coarse grain CORBA interface, or direct access to the JDBC driver.

The use of XML described in this paper is different to that in work by Abiteboul (e.g. [1]) where the aim is to query data collections held as semi-structured data in an XML format. We are only using XML as a format for delivering results from a database server. We are not currently querying data in XML files, although we envisage generating queries (e.g. in XQL [7]) to access remote XQL data sets in the database federation as XQL query engines become more widely used.

Some biological database do have query-level interfaces that can be accessed via HTML forms. The appearance of such systems is encouraging since these provide a way for whole queries to be sent to remote databases for efficient processing. These web-based query interfaces make use of CGI programs to access databases, and these CGI programs return the query results as HTML pages. Modifying these programs to generate XML data descriptions in addition to HTML formatting tags is a natural extension that we can expect to see as the use of

XML becomes more widespread and browsers and client applications capable of exploiting XML tags are developed.

6.1 Object Identifiers in CORBA and XML

A crucial difference between the use of CORBA and XML to return objects as results turns on the need for further processing of these objects. If the objects are to be processed just for their data content, like records, then XML is much more efficient, since it transfers results in batches and does not have to create object stubs. If instead the intention is to apply methods defined on the remote object class, then CORBA is better because the object stub is in the right form for method application. A compromise is possible where XML is used to return the unique object identifier (within its class) for the object instance (e.g. structure(3) as in Figure 8). This allows one to formulate and send a query to the remote object concerned, where a Daplex function can carry out the method call. A similar principle is used by the Visual Navigator [7] discussed earlier. However, a more natural way to do this in XML would be to represent the object identifier as a hypertext link. If the server was capable of generating and returning the objects as XML mini-pages in response to such requests then it could be a good functional alternative to CORBA.

7 Conclusions

CORBA's interface definition language (IDL) is seen by some as an adequate way to represent data to be shared in a distributed environment. So why should anyone need a data model? One needs to be aware of what objects are in the CORBA world. As seen in Figure 2, to the onlooker IDL can look remarkably like a schema definition language used with an ODMG-compliant object database [5]. However, more detailed examination shows that it plays a very different role. IDL is used to declare types which can be used in programs written in different languages and at different sites, and data values conforming to the IDL declarations can be passed between these programs. Rather than describing long term persistent data, it is better to think of IDL as a way of declaring structs of the kind seen in C, or equivalent type definitions in an OOPL. In doing this, CORBA IDL provides for language and platform independence but, significantly, it does not provide for data independence in the way that a data model does. Thus, while CORBA IDL provides a good interface for programs, it provides nothing special for databases and must not be seen as a substitute for a proper data model.

Programs can't click. Web interfaces are designed to respond to mouse-click events, which trigger appropriate parametrised routines depending on screen location. However, a remote program cannot usefully emulate mouse-clicks. Instead, it is much more convenient to emulate a human typing to a command line interface, since it only has to generate a text string according to a given syntax. Humans may be bored by command lines but computers love them! They are concise, easy to copy and send on to another machine, and their syntax can be carefully checked. CORBA interfaces are easily adapted to use them.

The relationship between CORBA and distributed databases is described by Brodie and Stonebraker [3]. They advocate that these should be viewed as complementary technologies, and that there are advantages in using software architectures which combine these. In Section 8.1.5 of their book they suggest variants of a combined architecture, ranging from a "minimal database architecture" in which distributed DBMSs support just the data management functions declared in the IDL, to a "maximal database architecture" in which an entire distributed database solution is constructed and then a bridge is built to make this accessible from a CORBA environment. We believe that a "maximal database architecture" with a semantic data model at its heart is the best way forward when data integration, rather than distributed computation, is the main goal.

8 Acknowledgements

We would like to thank Andreas Larsson and Lars Sundberg for assistance with testing the CORBA interface. This work is supported by a grant from the BBSRC/EPSRC Joint Programme in Bioinformatics (Grant Ref. 1/BIF06716).

References

1. S. Abiteboul. On Views and XML. In *Proceedings of the Eighteenth ACM SIGACT-SIGMOD-SIGART Symposium on Principles of Database Systems, May 31 - June 2, 1999, Philadelphia, Pennsylvania*, pages 1–9. ACM Press, 1999.
2. E. Barillot, U. Leser, P. Lijnzaad, C. Cussat-Blanc, K. Jungfer, F. Guyon, G. Vaysseix, C. Helgesen, and P. Rodriguez-Tomé. A Proposal for a standard CORBA interface for genome maps. *Bioinformatics*, 15(2):157–169, 1999.
3. M.L. Brodie and M Stonebraker. *Migrating Legacy Systems: Gateways, Interfaces and the Incremental Approach*. Morgan Kaufmann Publishers, Inc., San Francisco, 1995.
4. P. Bucher and A. Bairoch. A generalized profile syntax for biomolecular sequence motifs and its function in automatic sequence interpretation. In R. Altman, D. Brutlag, P. Karp, R. Lathrop, and D. Searls, editors, *ISMB-94: Proceedings 2nd International Conference on Intelligent Systems for Molecular Biology*, pages 53–61, 1994.
5. R.G.G. Cattell, editor. *The Object Database Standard: ODMG 2.0*. Morgan Kaufmann Publishers, 1997.
6. T. Etzold and P. Argos. SRS an indexing and retrieval tool for flat file data libraries. *CABIOS*, 9:49–57, 1993.
7. I. Gil, P.M.D. Gray, and G.J.L Kemp. A Visual Interface and Navigator for the P/FDM Object Database. In N.W. Paton and T Griffiths, editors, *Proceedings of User Interfaces to Data Intensive Systems (UIDIS'99)*, pages 54–63. IEEE Computer Society Press, 1999.
8. P.M.D. Gray and G.J.L. Kemp. Object-Oriented Systems and Data Independence. In D. Patel, Y. Sun, and S. Patel, editors, *Proc. 1994 International Conference on Object Oriented Information Systems*, pages 3–24. Springer-Verlag, 1994.

9. G.J.L. Kemp, Z. Jiao, P.M.D. Gray, and J.E. Fothergill. Combining Computation with Database Access in Biomolecular Computing. In W. Litwin and T. Risch, editors, *Applications of Databases: Proceedings of the First International Conference*, pages 317–335. Springer-Verlag, 1994.
10. T. Landers and R. L. Rosenberg. An Overview of MULTIBASE. In H.-J. Schneider, editor, *Distributed Data Bases*. North-Holland Publishing Company, 1982.
11. C. McKenna. Integrating the Object Database System ODB-II with Object Request Brokers. *ICL Technical Journal*, 1996.
12. D.W. Shipman. The Functional Data Model and the Data Language DAPLEX. *ACM Transactions on Database Systems*, 6(1):140–173, 1981.
13. G. Wiederhold. Mediators in the Architecture of Future Information Systems. *IEEE Computer*, 25(3):38–49, 1992.

Rewriting XQL Queries on XML Repositories

Peter T. Wood

Department of Computer Science, King's College London,
Strand, London WC2R 2LS, UK.
ptw@dcs.kcl.ac.uk

Abstract. XQL is one of the query languages proposed for querying
XML documents on the world wide web. In this paper, we consider the
logical rewriting of XQL query expressions in order to improve the efficiency of query evaluation when XML document type definitions (DTDs)
are present. We first define three classes of constraint which can be derived from a given DTD. With a suitable representation of an XML
repository R as a relational database D, it turns out that these DTD
constraints correspond to tuple- and equality-generating dependencies
which must hold on D.
Next, we identify a subset of XQL queries on R which is equivalent to a
class of conjunctive queries on D. Given a conjunctive query C equivalent to an XQL query Q, we then apply techniques from relational dependency theory to reduce the number of conjuncts in C, yielding query
C'. Conjunctive query C' can then be mapped back to an XQL query
Q' in which redundant filter subexpressions and unnecessary selections
have been removed.
Whether Q' can be evaluated more efficiently than Q depends on whether
or not appropriate indices exist in R. However, the techniques presented
in this paper can provide a query optimizer with a set of equivalent XQL
expressions from which to select the best. The representation of queries
in relational form and of constraints as dependencies should also permit
the application of these results to other XML query languages.

Keywords: Web databases, XML, constraints, query optimisation.

1 Introduction

The expectation surrounding the use of XML (eXtensible Modelling Language)
as a universal syntax for data representation and exchange on the world wide
web continues to grow. This is apparent when looking at the amount of effort
being committed to XML by numerous companies as well as the World Wide
Web Consortium (W3C). What is clear is that significant amounts of data will
be stored in XML repositories in the near future, necessitating the use of query
languages to extract the data of interest to users and programs.

A number of query languages for XML have already been proposed [10,11,
18], while query languages for semi-structured data can be (and sometimes have

B. Lings and K. Jeffery (Eds.): BNCOD 17, LNCS 1832, pp. 209–226, 2000.

been) modified to allow querying of XML [4,16]. In this paper, we focus on the query language XQL [18]. One reason for this is simply that it provides a concise syntax for the class of queries we wish to study. Our results could equally well be applied to fragments of other XML query languages. Another reason is that the XQL subset we study is also used in the W3C proposals XPointer [22] and XSLT [23].

We assume that we have a repository R of XML documents which we wish to query using XQL. In this paper, we restrict our discussion to a subset of XQL expressions, namely those involving a *path* of XML element names, possibly including *filter expressions* [18].

Example 1. Assume that XML repository R stores documents describing the contents of bookstores. Let Q_1 be the following XQL path expression:

/bookstore/book/author

The answer of Q_1 on R, denoted $Q_1(R)$, is the set S of author elements, such that for each element $a \in S$ there is a document d in R in which a is a child of a book element in d which is a child of the root bookstore element of d.

In contrast, using a filter expression (enclosed in square brackets), the XQL expression Q_2

/bookstore/book[price]

returns the set of book elements which are children of the root bookstore element and have a price element as a child.   □

We are interested in the logical rewriting of XQL expressions into equivalent forms which may be able to be evaluated more efficiently [21]. Our purpose in this paper is to study such rewritings when all the documents in a repository are valid with respect to the same *document type definition* (DTD). As pointed out by Maier [15], it is important that when DTDs are available for documents, they should be exploited by the query language processor at compile time.

Example 2. Let R be the XML repository from Example 1. Consider the XQL expression Q_3

/bookstore/*/author

which uses the wild-card * to denote any element name. $Q_3(R)$ is the set T of author elements, such that for each element $a \in T$ there is a document d in R in which a is a grandchild of the root bookstore element of d.

Recall XQL expression Q_1 from Example 1 and its answer set S on repository R. In general, of course, sets S and T are not equal; in other words, expressions Q_1 and Q_3 are not equivalent. However, if every document d in R is valid with respect to a document type definition (DTD) $\mathcal{D}$ which requires that every author element is a child of a book element, then Q_1 and Q_3 are indeed equivalent.   □

Example 3. Now consider the XQL expression Q_4:

/bookstore/book

on repository R. $Q_4(R)$ is the set of book elements in documents in R which are children of the root bookstore element.

Recall XQL expression Q_2 from Example 1. If every document in R is valid with respect to a DTD $\mathcal{D}$ which requires that every book element has a price element as a child, then Q_4 and Q_2 are equivalent with respect to repositories satisfying $\mathcal{D}$. □

In [20], we introduced the concepts of *parent* and *child constraints*, showing how they might be used to optimise conjunctive queries on sets of XML documents. In this paper, we apply these constraints, as well as newly defined *singleton constraints*, to XQL expressions. We do this by providing a relational semantics for XQL expressions in terms of Datalog programs in Section 4, as well as an algorithm for query rewriting based on the *chase* procedure in Section 6. In addition, we show that all three types of constraint can be derived from a given DTD in polynomial time.

An instance of a parent constraint was mentioned in Example 2, namely, that every author element is a child of a book element. If this constraint holds, then Q_1 is equivalent to Q_3. So parent constraints can be used to replace selections with wild-cards in XQL path expressions. Whether or not such a rewriting will speed up query evaluation depends on the implementation. Our contribution is simply to show that the two expressions are equivalent and hence that the rewriting can be applied in either direction.

On the other hand, child constraints can be used to remove redundant (parts of) filter expressions in XQL expressions. An example is given by the child constraint mentioned in Example 3, namely, that every book element has a price element as a child. If this constraint holds, we can remove the redundant filter expression from Q_2 in Example 1, yielding Q_4.

In the next section, we outline research related to that reported here. Section 3 covers background material on documents, DTDs and XQL. It also introduces a subset of XQL, called sXQL, to which we apply our rewriting algorithm. The relational semantics of sXQL is defined in Section 4, while the derivation of parent, child and singleton constraints from a DTD is described in Section 5. It turns out that the above DTD constraints correspond to *tuple-generating* and *equality-generating dependencies* on relational databases. The rewriting algorithm, which is based on applying the *chase* technique using these dependencies, is described in Section 6. Conclusions and areas for further research are given in Section 7.

2   Related Work

Most of the work on optimisation of queries on web data and semi-structured data complements rather than competes with that reported here. The relevant papers can be divided into those which study the physical, rather than logical, optimisation of queries, those which study optimisation using constraints other than DTDs, and those which study optimisation using DTDs.

Papers dealing with physical optimisation issues for web or semi-structured data include those by Goldman and Widom [13] and McHugh and Widom [16], which discuss the physical, cost-based optimisation of queries on the Lore database system, and that by Abiteboul et al. [1], which describes the optimisation of OQL-doc queries on SGML documents stored in an O_2 database.

A number of papers study the use of constraints other than DTDs for optimising queries on web or semi-structured data. In [7,12], graph schemas are used to optimise queries on semi-structured data. However, graph schemas cannot express many of the constraints provided by DTDs, including constraints involving alternation and ordering.

Path constraints on semi-structured data, which can be used to optimise web queries, are studied in [3,8], mostly with respect to their associated implication problems. As an example, a path constraint may state that the set of nodes found by traversing one path is the same as, or a subset of, the set of nodes found via another path. In the context of web documents, these constraints place restrictions on element *contents* rather than on element *structure*, and so are complementary to the constraints implicit in DTDs.

Buneman, Fan and Weinstein [9] study how the interaction of type constraints with path constraints affects the decidability of the implication problem for path constraints. The type constraints they consider are more general than those which can be expressed using DTDs.

Papers which use DTDs for optimisation include [6,14,17,20]. The paper by Liefke is concerned with using information in DTDs to optimise queries about the *order* of elements in XML documents rather than their nesting structure [14]. Once again, this is complementary to our work.

Böhm et al. [6] define constraints which they call *exclusivity* and *obligation*. These are the transitively closed versions of the *parent* and *child* constraints, respectively, which we proposed independently in [20]. Indeed, *exclusivity* and *obligation* constraints could not be used to perform the optimisations described in the present paper or in [20], since they are tailored to optimising expressions in the PAT algebra [6].

Papakonstantinou and Vassalos have studied query rewriting in TSL, a language for querying semi-structured data [17]. The principal focus of their work is on rewriting a TSL query in terms of a set of views, although they include some rewritings based on structural constraints found in DTDs. They introduce labelled functional dependencies which correspond to our singleton constraints, and label inference which is related to, but different from, our child and parent constraints. They do not provide algorithms for deriving these constraints from a DTD.

3 DTDs, Documents, and XQL

In this section, we cover the necessary background on XML document type definitions (DTDs), XML documents and XQL queries.

3.1 XML DTDs and Documents

We begin by introducing the DTD which we will use as a running example in this paper.

Example 4. The following is an XML DTD $\mathcal{D}$ which defines the syntax of valid bookstore holdings[1]:

```
<!ELEMENT bookstore  ((book|magazine)+)>
<!ELEMENT book       (author*, title?, isbn, price)>
<!ELEMENT author     (first-name?, last-name)>
<!ELEMENT magazine   (title, volume?, issue?, date, price)>
<!ELEMENT date       (day?, month, year)>
```

Each element definition comprises two parts: the left side gives the name of the element, while the right side defines the *content model* for the element. The content model is defined using a regular expression built from other element names. The content models of element names not defined above are assumed to be PCDATA, that is, arbitrary text.

The five content models defined above are interpreted as follows. A bookstore comprises one or more books or magazines. Each book may have zero or more authors, may have a title, must have an isbn, and must have a price. An author must have a last-name, optionally preceded by a first-name. A magazine must have a title, may have a volume and issue, and must have both a date and a price. A date has an optional day, followed by a mandatory month and year. □

Example 5. Below we give an example of a document d which is valid with respect to the DTD $\mathcal{D}$ defined in Example 4.

```
<bookstore>
 <book>
  <author><last-name>Abiteboul</last-name></author>
  <author><last-name>Hull</last-name></author>
  <author><last-name>Vianu</last-name></author>
  <title>Foundations of Databases</title>
  <isbn>0-201-53771-0</isbn>
  <price>26.95</price>
 </book>
```

---

[1] We restrict the DTDs which we consider in this paper to those which define only the element structure of documents.

```
<magazine>
 <title>The Economist</title>
 <date><day>26</day><month>June</month><year>1999</year></date>
 <price>2.50</price>
</magazine>
<book>
 <isbn>0-934613-40-0</isbn>
 <price>34.95</price>
</book>
<magazine>
 <title>PC Magazine</title>
 <volume>8</volume><issue>6</issue>
 <date><month>June</month><year>1999</year></date>
 <price>2.99</price>
</magazine>
</bookstore>
```

Note that both **book** elements contain **isbn** and **price** elements as required. The first **book** also contains three **author** elements and a **title** element. Both **magazine** elements contain **title**, **date** and **price** elements as required. The second also contains **volume** and **issue** elements. Finally, both **date** elements contain the mandatory **month** and **year** elements, while the first also contains a **day** element.   □

Next, we turn our attention to how XQL can be used to extract data from documents such as that given above.

3.2   XQL Queries

In this section, we define the subset of XQL query expressions we will consider in this paper. We refer to the resulting language as *sXQL*. Before defining the syntax of sXQL, we give some examples of sXQL expressions, as well as the results of such expressions on the single document of Example 5.

An sXQL expression is always evaluated with respect to a *current context*, which is a set of elements. The *root context* is the set of root elements in the repository being queried. Given a context C and an sXQL expression E, $E(C)$ is the set of elements to which E_1 *evaluates* in context C. The simplest sXQL expression comprises an element name n. This selects those child elements of the current context which have element name n. Such sXQL expressions can be composed into *path expressions* which use the *path operator* ('/') to compose selections.

Example 6. Assume that the current context C is the set of all **book** and **magazine** elements in document d from Example 5. If E_1 is the sXQL expression

title

then $E_1(C)$ is

```
<title>Foundations of Databases</title>
<title>The Economist</title>
<title>PC Magazine</title>
```

If E_2 is the sXQL expression

`author/last-name`

then $E_2(C)$ is

```
<last-name>Abiteboul</last-name>
<last-name>Hull</last-name>
<last-name>Vianu</last-name>
```

namely, all `last-name` elements which are children of `author` elements which are children of an element in C.

Instead of mentioning element names explicitly, the wild-card '`*`' can be used to refer to any element name. So the expression E_3 which is

`author/*`

evaluates to the set of elements which are children of `author` elements. In the context C, it turns out that $E_3(C) = E_2(C)$. □

Filter expressions, which are enclosed in the brackets '[' and ']', are also allowed in sXQL expressions. Given the expression $E_1[E_2]$, the result $E_1[E_2](C)$ is equal to $E_1(C)$ if $E_1/E_2(C)$ is non-empty; otherwise, it is empty. Thus filter expressions are essentially Boolean subexpressions which must evaluate to true in order for the overall query to return a non-empty result.

Example 7. Assume now that the current context C is the `bookstore` element in document d from Example 5, that is, the set of `book` and `magazine` elements. The sXQL expression E_4

`book[author/first-name]`

in context C selects all `book` elements which are children of the `bookstore` element and which have at least one child `author` element a, such that a has a `first-name` element as a child.

Multiple filter expressions are also allowed as in E_5

`author[first-name][last-name]`

which returns `author` elements which have both a `first-name` element and a `last-name` element as children. □

As mentioned above, the root context is the set of all root elements in documents in the repository R. A full sXQL query expression Q is usually evaluated with respect to the root context, for simplicity indicated as $Q(R)$. In order for the result to be non-empty, the expression Q must start with a '/' to indicate evaluation with respect to the root context. By default, $Q(R)$, the answer of Q on R, is the collection of elements to which Q evaluates on R, in other words, those appearing last in the path expression. For simplicity, we will not deal with the explicit inclusion of elements in the answer, as indicated by use of the postfix operator '?' [18]. The applicability of our methods is unchanged whether or not we include this feature.

We now give a more formal definition of sXQL syntax and semantics. sXQL *path expressions* and *filter expressions* are defined inductively as follows:

1. An element name is a path expression.
2. If E_1 and E_2 are path expressions, then so is E_1/E_2.
3. If E is a path expression, then $[E]$ is a filter expression.
4. If E_1 and E_2 are filter expressions, then so is $E_1 E_2$.
5. If E_1 is a path expression and E_2 is a filter expression, then $E_1 E_2$ is a path expression.

Let E be an sXQL expression as defined above, and C be the current context of E. The semantics of E are defined as follows:

1. If E is element name n, then $E(C)$ is the set of elements with name n which are children of elements in C.
2. If $E = E_1/E_2$, then $E(C)$ is the set of elements given by $E_2(E_1(C))$.
3. If $E = [E_1]$, then $E(C)$ is true if $E_1(C) \neq \emptyset$ and false otherwise.
4. If $E = E_1 E_2$, where E_1 and E_2 are filter expressions, then $E(C)$ is true if both $E_1(C)$ and $E_2(C)$ are true; otherwise, it is false.
5. If $E = E_1 E_2$, where E_1 is a path expression and E_2 is a filter expression, then let $C' = E_1(C)$. Now $E(C)$ is C' if $E_2(C')$ is true, and is the empty set if $E_2(C')$ is false.

An sXQL *query expression* Q has the form $/E$, where E is a path expression. The answer of Q on R, written $Q(R)$, is given by $E(R)$.

In the next section, we introduce an alternative semantics for sXQL based on a relational representation of an XML repository. This will allow us to view DTD constraints as dependencies which hold on a relational database.

4   A Relational Semantics for sXQL

Recall that an XML repository R over DTD $\mathcal{D}$ is a set of documents, each of which is valid with respect to $\mathcal{D}$. We form an abstraction of an XML repository R, by representing it as a relational database D, comprising two relations $el(Document, Element, Name)$ and $par(Document, Parent, Child)$.

A tuple $(d, e, n) \in el$ denotes the fact that document d contains an element e with name n[2]. We assume that each document in the database has a unique identifier d, and that each element e is uniquely identifiable within document d, perhaps through the use of ID attribute values. Hence the *functional dependency* (FD) $Document, Element \rightarrow Name$ holds on relation el.

---

[2] It might have been neater to have each element name n appearing in $\mathcal{D}$ giving rise to a relation n in D, but this would have complicated the handling of wild-cards.

The relation $par(Document, Parent, Child)$ in D captures the nesting structure of elements in each document d: a tuple $(d, p, c) \in par$ denotes the fact that document d contains a pair of elements p and c such that p is the parent of c in the parse tree of d. Since each element in a document can have at most one parent element, the FD $Document, Child \rightarrow Parent$ holds on relation par.

Note that we have chosen not to represent the textual values of elements in D. This is because sXQL expressions simply return elements which we will model here by element IDs.

An sXQL query, as restricted in Section 3.2, is simply a conjunctive query on the relational database D. We choose to represent these conjunctive queries using Datalog syntax [2], except that we use lower-case letters to denote variables and upper-case letters to denote constants. In general, XQL queries do not correspond to conjunctive queries but instead to potentially recursive Datalog programs [21].

Given an sXQL query expression Q, let $T_1, \ldots, T_n$ be the sequence of element name occurrences which appears in Q. For example, if Q is A/B[C/D] [E] /F, then the sequence is A, B, C, D, E, F. It is useful to introduce a predecessor function p which is defined for each T_i, $2 \leq i \leq n$ in Q. Informally, this function specifies the required parent element name for any element name occurrence in Q. So for the above example, $p(F) = B$, $p(E) = B$, $p(D) = C$, $p(C) = B$, and $p(B) = A$.

Let Q be an sXQL query expression, $T_1, \ldots, T_n$ be the sequence of element name occurrences appearing in Q, and k, $1 \leq k \leq n$, be the largest index of an element name occurrence which does not appear in a filter expression. We construct a Datalog rule R corresponding to Q as follows:

1. The head of rule R is given by $q(e_0, e_k)$, where q is the answer predicate, e_0 is a variable representing elements in the current context, and e_k is a variable representing elements whose name is the k'th name occurrence in Q.

2. For each element name occurrence T_i, $1 \leq i \leq n$ in Q, add the subgoal $el(d, e_i, T_i)$ to R, where d is a variable denoting documents and e_i is a variable denoting elements. If the element name occurrence T_i is the wild-card, then the corresponding subgoal is $el(d, e_i, \_)$, where '$\_$' denotes a unique variable in R^3.

3. Add the subgoal $par(d, e_0, e_1)$. For each element name occurrence T_i, $2 \leq i \leq n$ in Q, add the subgoal $par(d, e_j, e_i)$ to R, where $p(T_i) = T_j$ is the predecessor of T_i as defined above, d is a variable denoting documents, and e_i and e_j are variables denoting elements.

Example 8. Consider the sXQL query expression Q given by

$$A/C[C/E] [F]/G.$$

Let us denote the constant corresponding to the element name occurrence A, say, by A, and the variable denoting an element occurrence with name A by e_A (since there is only one occurrence of each element name in Q). Step 1 above adds

---

[3] In fact, this subgoal for wild-cards is redundant because of inclusion dependencies which hold between relations in D.

the head $q(e_0, e_G)$ to the Datalog rule R. Step 2 adds the subgoals $el(d, e_A, A)$, $el(d, e_B, B)$, $el(d, e_C, C)$, $el(d, e_E, E)$, $el(d, e_F, F)$ and $el(d, e_G, G)$ to R. Step 3 adds the subgoals $par(d, e_0, e_A)$, $par(d, e_A, e_B)$, $par(d, e_B, e_C)$, $par(d, e_C, e_E)$, $par(d, e_B, e_F)$ and $par(d, e_B, e_G)$, yielding R as

$$q(e_0, e_G) : -\ el(d, e_A, A), el(d, e_B, B), el(d, e_C, C), el(d, e_E, E), el(d, e_F, F),$$
$$el(d, e_G, G), par(d, e_0, e_A), par(d, e_A, e_B), par(d, e_B, e_C),$$
$$par(d, e_C, e_E), par(d, e_B, e_F), par(d, e_B, e_G).$$

$\square$

The Datalog program returns a set of tuples, where each component is an element ID, rather than the set of (possibly nested) actual elements returned by sXQL. This difference is not relevant to the rewriting we will perform on Datalog programs and sXQL expressions later on. One can also imagine a post-processing phase after evaluation of the Datalog program which would assemble actual elements in the answer appropriately.

5 Deriving Constraints from DTDs

5.1 Child, Parent, and Singleton Constraints

In this section, we introduce three types of simple constraint which might be implied by a given DTD. We will use the DTD of Example 4 as a running example. We call the three types of constraint we consider *child*, *parent* and *singleton* constraints. Informally, a child constraint $A \Downarrow B$ states that every element with name A *must* have at *least* one child element with name B. A parent constraint $B \Uparrow A$ states that every element with name B *must* have a parent element with name A. A singleton constraint $A \downarrow B$ states that an element with name A *can* have at *most* one child element with name B.

As a shorthand, instead of writing child constraints $A \Downarrow B$ and $A \Downarrow C$, we can write $A \Downarrow \{B, C\}$. The same shorthand notation applies to singleton constraints. Similarly, instead of parent constraints $B \Uparrow A$ and $C \Uparrow A$, we can write $\{B, C\} \Uparrow A$.

Example 9. Consider the DTD $\mathcal{D}$ given in Example 4, in particular the definition of the content model for book elements. Because book elements *must* include isbn and price elements, the child constraint

$$book \Downarrow \{isbn, price\}$$

is implied by $\mathcal{D}$. Since book elements *may* include *at most one* title, isbn and price element, the singleton constraint

$$book \downarrow \{title, isbn, price\}$$

is implied by $\mathcal{D}$. Note that because there can be more than one author element, there is no singleton constraint $book \downarrow author$. Also, because the title element is optional, there is no child constraint $book \Downarrow title$.

Each of the elements `author` and `isbn` can appear only as a child of a `book` element, hence the parent constraint

$$\{author, isbn\} \Uparrow book$$

is implied by $\mathcal{D}$. Note that, for example, a `title` element can be a child of either a `book` element or a `magazine` element, hence no parent constraint with *title* on the left-hand side is implied by $\mathcal{D}$. $\qquad\qquad\qquad\qquad\qquad\qquad\qquad\qquad\qquad$ □

To be more precise in our definitions of the three types of constraint, let $\mathcal{D}$ be a DTD and A and B be element names defined in $\mathcal{D}$. The *child* constraint $A \Downarrow B$ is implied by $\mathcal{D}$ if for every document d valid for $\mathcal{D}$, whenever d contains an element u with name A, d contains an element v with name B such that v is a *child* of u in the parse tree of d. The *parent* constraint $B \Uparrow A$ is implied by $\mathcal{D}$ if for every document d valid for $\mathcal{D}$, whenever d contains an element v with name B, d contains an element u with name A such that u is the *parent* of v in the parse tree of d. The *singleton* constraint $A \downarrow B$ is implied by $\mathcal{D}$ if for every document d valid for $\mathcal{D}$, whenever d contains an element u with name A and an element v with name B such that v is a *child* of u in the parse tree of d, then d contains no other child element of u with name B.

Given an XML repository R and its relational representation D, both child and parent constraints on R can be represented as *tuple-generating dependencies* (tgds) [5] on D. Doing so will allow us to apply techniques from relational dependency theory to test equivalence of queries expressed in the relational form of sXQL. These queries can then be mapped back to sXQL expressions.

A *tuple-generating dependency* (tgd) [5] is a formula of the form $\forall \bar{x} \exists \bar{y} [\psi_1(\bar{x}) \rightarrow \psi_2(\bar{x}, \bar{y})]$, where $\bar{x}$ and $\bar{y}$ are vectors of variables and both ψ_1 and ψ_2 are conjunctions of atoms. As is common, we will write tgds without the quantifiers. We also allow constant symbols, representing element names, in our tgds. Constraint $A \Downarrow B$ is equivalent to the tgd:

$$el(d, a, A) \rightarrow el(d, b, B) \wedge par(d, a, b)$$

This tgd states that if document d contains an element a with name A, then d contains an element b with name B such that a is the parent of b in d. Note that variable b appears only on the right-hand side of the tgd and is therefore existentially quantified.

Constraint $B \Uparrow A$ is equivalent to the tgd:

$$el(d, b, B) \rightarrow el(d, a, A) \wedge par(d, a, b)$$

This tgd states that if document d contains an element b with name B, then d contains an element a with name A such that a is the parent of b in d.

Given an XML repository R and its relational representation D, singleton constraints can be represented as *equality-generating dependencies* (egds) [5] on D. The constraint $A \downarrow B$ is equivalent to the following egd:

$$el(d, a, A) \wedge par(d, a, b_1) \wedge el(d, b_1, B) \wedge par(d, a, b_2) \wedge el(d, b_2, B) \rightarrow b_1 = b_2$$

This egd states that if document d contains an element a with name A and a is the parent of b_1 with name B and b_2 with name B, then b_1 must equal b_2.

Example 10. Let us consider the representation of some of the constraints introduced in Example 9 as relational dependencies. The child constraint *book* $\Downarrow$ *price* can be represented as the tgd τ_1

$$el(d, b, book) \rightarrow el(d, p, price) \wedge par(d, b, p)$$

The singleton constraint *book* $\downarrow$ *price* can be represented as the egd

$$el(d, b, book) \wedge par(d, b, p_1) \wedge el(d, p_1, price) \wedge par(d, b, p_2) \wedge el(d, p_2, price) \rightarrow p_1 = p_2$$

The parent constraint *author* $\Uparrow$ *book* can be represented as the tgd τ_2

$$el(d, a, author) \rightarrow el(d, b, book) \wedge par(d, b, a)$$

□

5.2   The Complexity of Constraint Implication

Given a DTD $\mathcal{D}$, it is straightforward to determine the child constraints implied by $\mathcal{D}$.

Proposition 1. *Let $\mathcal{D}$ be a DTD containing a content model definition for element name A, given by*

`<!ELEMENT A (R)>`

where R is a regular expression over element names (the alphabet of R). DTD $\mathcal{D}$ implies the child constraint $A \Downarrow B$ if and only if B is in every string in $L(R)$.

Proof. If $\mathcal{D}$ implies $A \Downarrow B$, then, in any document valid with respect to $\mathcal{D}$, every element with name A must have an element with name B as a child. Since the strings in $L(R)$ denote all possible sequences of child elements for A, it must be the case that every string in $L(R)$ contains B.

If every string in $L(R)$ contains B, then in any parse tree for document d valid for $\mathcal{D}$ containing A, B must appear as a child of A. Hence, $A \Downarrow B$ is implied by $\mathcal{D}$.   □

Lemma 1. *Let $\mathcal{D}$ be a DTD containing the definition of a content model for element name A in terms of regular expression R, with B an element name appearing in R. Determining whether or not the child constraint $A \Downarrow B$ is implied by a DTD $\mathcal{D}$ can be done in time polynomial in the size of R.*

Proof. Given element name A, its content model is defined by a regular expression R over element names. Construct a nondeterministic finite state automaton (NFA) M which accepts the language denoted by R in the standard way[4]. This construction can be done in time polynomial in the size of R.

---

[4] In fact, XML content models are restricted to being deterministic.

DTD $\mathcal{D}$ implies the child constraint $A \Downarrow B$ if and only if B is on every path from the initial state of M to the final state of M. We can determine this in time linear in the size of M as follows. First delete every arc labelled B in M. Now $A \Downarrow B$ if and only if the final state of M is no longer reachable from the initial state of M. $\square$

Theorem 1. *The set C of child constraints implied by a DTD $\mathcal{D}$ can be determined in time polynomial in the size of $\mathcal{D}$, that is, the number of element names and grammar symbols appearing in $\mathcal{D}$.*

Proof. Recall that there is only one content model definition for each element name in $\mathcal{D}$. The result follows from Lemma 1 and the fact that the number of possible child constraints is bounded by the size of $\mathcal{D}$. $\square$

It is even easier to find the parent constraints implied by $\mathcal{D}$. DTD $\mathcal{D}$ implies the parent constraint $B \Uparrow A$ if and only if B appears only in the content model of A. Note that this applies independently of whether B is optional or repeated. All the parent constraints implied by $\mathcal{D}$ can be found in time which is linear in the size of $\mathcal{D}$ by simply counting the number of times an element name occurs on the right side of any rule in $\mathcal{D}$. This gives us the following result.

Theorem 2. *The set P of parent constraints implied by a DTD $\mathcal{D}$ can be determined in time linear in the size of $\mathcal{D}$.*

To determine whether or not the singleton constraint $A \downarrow B$ is implied by $\mathcal{D}$ we once again construct an NFA M corresponding to the content model of A. Then $\mathcal{D}$ implies $A \downarrow B$ if and only if no path in M from the initial to the final state has two arcs labelled with B.

Theorem 3. *The set S of singleton constraints implied by a DTD $\mathcal{D}$ can be determined in time polynomial in the size of $\mathcal{D}$.*

Proof. The number of possible singleton constraints is bounded by the size of $\mathcal{D}$. For each possible singleton constraint $A \downarrow B$, we construct an NFA M corresponding to the content model of A as defined in $\mathcal{D}$.

We now perform a modified depth-first search S_I of M, starting at the initial state. A parameter *found-label* of the depth-first search procedure indicates whether or not we have traversed an arc labelled B on the current path. Each state s can have at most two markings applied to it. Marking '0' indicates that s is on a path from the initial state which does not include an arc labelled B. Marking '1' indicates that s is on a path from the initial state which does include an arc labelled B. If s has no marking when it is visited, then s is marked with '0' if *found-label* is false or '1' if *found-label* is true. If s is already marked with '1' when it is visited, then it is not revisited. If s is marked with '0' when it is visited, then it is revisited only if *found-label* is true, in which case its marking is changed to '1'.

A second modified depth-first search S_F performs the same marking process, except that it starts from the final state of M and traverses arcs from head to tail rather than tail to head. Now state s has a marking of '1' if and only if there is a path with an arc labelled B from s to the final state.

Singleton constraint $A \downarrow B$ is implied by $\mathcal{D}$ if and only if no state is marked with '1' during both S_I and S_F. $\square$

6   Rewriting XQL Queries Using Constraints

Given a Datalog program P representing an sXQL query expression, we can proceed to remove redundant subgoals from P to give an equivalent program P' which can be mapped back to a simpler sXQL expression. The equivalence of P and P' is established by finding *containment mappings* [2] from P to P' and from P' to P. A containment mapping from P to P' must be the identity on distinguished variables (those appearing in the head of the rule comprising P) and constants, and must map each subgoal of P to a subgoal of P'. Since every subgoal in P' appears in P, there is always a containment mapping from P' to P. If there is a containment mapping from P to P', we write $P' \subseteq P$. It can be shown that if $P' \subseteq P$, then $P'(D) \subseteq P(D)$ for all databases D.

Programs which may not otherwise be equivalent may be equivalent on databases which satisfy certain dependencies. In our case, we know that database D satisfies the set $\mathbf{D}$ of dependencies which includes the FDs given in Section 4 and those corresponding to the set of DTD constraints. The *chase* process [5,19] can be used to apply a set $\mathbf{D}$ of dependencies to a program P to give a program $P' = chase_{\mathbf{D}}(P)$ which is equivalent to P on databases satisfying $\mathbf{D}$.

A tgd τ is applied to a program rule P as follows. If the left-hand side of τ can be unified with a subgoal of P, then the right-hand side of τ can be added to P as additional subgoals. In the case where the tgd has existentially quantified variables on the right-hand side (an *embedded* tgd), unique variables which did not previously exist in P must be introduced.

In general, the chase process will continue to apply dependencies to a program until none can be applied. This can lead to the generation of an infinite number of subgoals when the tgds are embedded. However, we argue below that a specialized version of the chase, which we call *Xchase*, is sufficient for our purposes and is guaranteed to terminate. We first present the rewriting algorithm.

Let Q be an sXQL query expression on XML repository R which satisfies DTD $\mathcal{D}$. Let D be the relational representation of R and $\mathbf{D}$ be the set of dependencies corresponding to the FDs from Section 4 and the sets of child, parent and singleton constraints derived from $\mathcal{D}$. The algorithm for rewriting Q is as follows:

1. Transform Q into a Datalog program P, as described in Section 4.
2. Consider each subgoal s of P in turn, until every subgoal has been considered.
   a) Let P' be P with subgoal s removed.
   b) Let $P'' = Xchase_{\mathbf{D}}(P')$.
   c) If $P'' \subseteq P$, then remove s from P.
3. Transform the (modified) program P back to an sXQL query expression Q'.

We note that the inverse transformation from a Datalog program P to an sXQL expression can always be performed, even after the removal of redundant subgoals from P.

We now consider in what way $Xchase$ differs from the usual chase process. We first note that no cycle of either parent constraints or child constraints can be derived from a DTD $\mathcal{D}$, since otherwise no document would be valid with respect to $\mathcal{D}$. Hence, the chase cannot generate a sequence of subgoals whose variables form a cycle. In fact, the only sequences of subgoals sharing variables which can be generated by the chase correspond to sequences of element names in which no name is repeated, as in the sequence of child constraints $A \Downarrow B$, $B \Downarrow C$ and $C \Downarrow D$ for example. Clearly each such sequence is finite. However, in the usual chase, the corresponding sequence of subgoals could be generated infinitely often. If we disallow any sequence which is a subsequence of one already generated, we may miss some redundancies. For example, in order determine that A[B/C][B/D] is equivalent to A on documents satisfying the constraints $A \Downarrow B$, $B \Downarrow C$ and $B \Downarrow D$, the tgd corresponding to $A \Downarrow B$ needs to be applied twice.

Let P be the original program generated from XQL expression Q, and P' be P with a subgoal removed. In $Xchase$ a tgd corresponding to a child constraint $A \Downarrow B$ is applied to P' as many times as A is the value for the predecessor function applied to an element name occurrence in Q. This ensures that there are sufficient subgoals in P' for a containment mapping from P if one exists. Because of the FD $Document, Child \rightarrow Parent$, the application of tgds corresponding to parent constraints never gives rise to an infinite number of subgoals. In fact, each such tgd need be applied at most once.

Example 11. Consider the sXQL expression Q

$$\texttt{bookstore/book[price]/author}$$

which combines the expressions Q_1 and Q_2 from Example 1. The Datalog program P corresponding to Q is

$$q(x, a) : - \; el(d, s, bookstore), el(d, b, book), el(d, p, price), el(d, a, author),$$
$$par(d, x, s), par(d, s, b), par(d, b, p), par(d, b, a).$$

Rather than deleting subgoals one by one, we will delete 3 subgoals from P to give P' and show that P' is equivalent to P. Program P' is

$$q(x, a) : - \; el(d, s, bookstore), el(d, a, author), par(d, x, s), par(d, s, b), par(d, b, a).$$

To show that $P' \equiv P$, we first chase P' with dependencies corresponding to the constraints derived from $\mathcal{D}$. Applying the tgd τ_2 (from Example 10)

$$el(d, a, author) \rightarrow el(d, b_1, book) \wedge par(d, b_1, a)$$

yields program

$$q(x, a) : - \; el(d, s, bookstore), el(d, b_1, book), el(d, a, author),$$
$$par(d, x, s), par(d, s, b), par(d, b, a), par(d, b_1, a).$$

The functional dependency $Document, Child \to Parent$ which holds on the par relation means that b_1 must equal b, which gives us program

$$q(x, a) : - \; el(d, s, bookstore), el(d, b, book), el(d, a, author),$$
$$par(d, x, s), par(d, s, b), par(d, b, a).$$

Applying the tgd τ_1 (from Example 10)

$$el(d, b, book) \to el(d, p_1, price) \wedge par(d, b, p_1)$$

yields program P''

$$q(x, a) : - \; el(d, s, bookstore), el(d, b, book), el(d, p_1, price), el(d, a, author),$$
$$par(d, x, s), par(d, s, b), par(d, b, p_1), par(d, b, a).$$

There is a containment mapping from P to P'' since non-distinguished variable p can be mapped to variable p_1. We conclude that program P' (which has 5 subgoals) is equivalent to program P (which has 8 subgoals). Transforming P' back to an sXQL expression yields

```
bookstore/*/author
```

which is the rewriting generated for the original expression Q.   □

Redundancies in sXQL expressions which are not due to DTD constraints can also be removed by our rewriting algorithm. For example, the expression

```
bookstore/book[author/first-name][author/last-name]
```

can first be rewritten as

```
bookstore/book[author/first-name][author]
```

using the constraint $author \Downarrow last\text{-}name$. This can then be rewritten as

```
bookstore/book[author/first-name]
```

without relying on any constraints.

7   Conclusion

We have introduced a subset of XQL query expressions and studied how these expressions might be rewritten into a form potentially more efficient for evaluation on repositories all of whose XML documents satisfy the same document type definition $\mathcal{D}$. In order to do this, we showed how to derive a number of constraints from $\mathcal{D}$ which turn out to correspond to well-known dependencies from relational database theory. This allowed us to transform the problem of rewriting XQL expressions into one of rewriting conjunctive queries using a modified chase process to ensure termination.

We could have applied our rewritings directly to sXQL expressions rather than transforming them first to Datalog programs. This would have been fairly straightforward when applying child and parent constraints, but somewhat more complicated when trying to detect other redundancies in an sXQL expression. Apart from the fact that it is interesting to see that, for example, tuple-generating dependencies can arise in real-world web-based applications, the transformation to a relational setting allows us to draw on previous results when extending the class of XQL queries and DTD constraints we study. For example, the results on equivalence of Datalog programs presented by Sagiv in [19] have proved useful when considering the rewriting of recursive XQL queries [21].

Many other constraints can be derived from DTDs. Some that we have already mentioned are the obligation and exclusivity constraints studied by Böhm *et al.* [6], which involve indirect containment of elements, and constraints dealing with the order of elements in documents used by Liefke [14]. Our final goal is the application of all these constraints to rewriting full XQL queries rather than the subset studied in this paper.

References

1. S. Abiteboul, S. Cluet, V. Christophides, T. Milo, G. Moerkotte, and J. Siméon. Querying documents in object databases. *Int. J. Digit. Libr.*, 1(1):5–19, April 1997.
2. S. Abiteboul, R. Hull, and V. Vianu. *Foundations of Databases*. Addison-Wesley, 1995.
3. S. Abiteboul and V. Vianu. Regular path queries with constraints. In *Proc. Sixteenth ACM Symp. on Principles of Databases Systems*, pages 122–133, 1997.
4. G. O. Arocena and A. O. Mendelzon. WebOQL: Restructuring documents, databases and webs. In *Proc. 14th Int. Conf. on Data Engineering*, pages 24–33, 1998.
5. C. Beeri and M. Y. Vardi. A proof procedure for data dependencies. *J. ACM*, 31(4):718–741, 1984.
6. K. Böhm, K. Aberer, M. T. Özsu, and K. Gayer. Query optimization for structured documents based on knowledge on the document type definition. In *Proc. Advances in Digital Libraries*. IEEE Press, 1998.
7. P. Buneman, S. Davidson, M. Fernandez, and D. Suciu. Adding structure to unstructured data. In *Proc. 6th Int. Conf. on Database Theory*, pages 336–350, 1997.
8. P. Buneman, W. Fan, and S. Weinstein. Path constraints on semistructured and structured data. In *Proc. Seventeenth ACM Symp. on Principles of Databases Systems*, pages 129–138. ACM Press, 1998.
9. P. Buneman, W. Fan, and S. Weinstein. Interaction between path and type constraints. In *Proc. Eighteenth ACM Symp. on Principles of Databases Systems*, pages 56–67. ACM Press, 1999.
10. S. Ceri, S. Comai, E. Damiani, P. Fraternali, S. Paraboschi, and L. Tanca. XML-GL: A graphical language for querying and reshaping documents. In *Proc. QL'98— The Query Languages Workshop*, 1998.
11. A. Deutsch, M. Fernandez, D. Florescu, A. Levy, and D. Suciu. XML-QL: A query language for XML, August 1998. Available at /tt http://www.w3.org/TR/NOTE-xml-ql.
12. M. Fernandez and D. Suciu. Optimizing regular path expressions using graph schemas. In *Proc. 14th Int. Conf. on Data Engineering*, pages 14–23, 1998.

13. R. Goldman and J. Widom. DataGuides: Enabling query formulation and optimization in semistructured databases. In *Proc. 23rd Int. Conf. on Very Large Data Bases*, pages 436–445, 1997.
14. H. Liefke. Horizontal query optimization on ordered semistructured data. In *Proc. WebDB'99: Int. Workshop on the Web and Databases*, 1999.
15. D. Maier. Database desiderata for an XML query language. In *Proc. QL'98—The Query Languages Workshop*, 1998.
16. J. McHugh and J. Widom. Query optimization for XML. In *Proc. 25th Int. Conf. on Very Large Data Bases*, pages 315–326, 1999.
17. Y. Papakonstantinou and V. Vassalos. Query rewriting for semistructured data. In *Proc. ACM SIGMOD Int. Conf. on Management of Data*, pages 455–466, 1999.
18. J. Robie, J. Lapp, and D. Schach. XML query language (XQL). In *Proc. QL'98— The Query Languages Workshop*, 1998.
19. Y. Sagiv. Optimizing Datalog programs. In J. Minker, editor, *Foundations of Deductive Databases and Logic Programming*, pages 659–698. Morgan Kaufmann, 1988.
20. P. T. Wood. Optimizing web queries using document type definitions. In *ACM CIKM'99 2nd International Workshop on Web Information and Data Management (WIDM'99)*, pages 28–32. ACM Press, 1999.
21. P. T. Wood. On the equivalence of XML patterns. Submitted for publication, 2000.
22. World Wide Web Consortium. XML pointer language (XPointer). http://www.w3.org/TR/WD-xptr, March 1998.
23. World Wide Web Consortium. XSL transformations (XSLT) specification. http://www.w3.org/TR/WD-xslt, April 1999. W3C Working Draft.

Author Index

Lecture Notes in Computer Science

For information about Vols. 1–1757
please contact your bookseller or Springer-Verlag

Vol. 1800: J. Rolim et al. (Eds.), Parallel and Distributed Processing. Proceedings, 2000. XXIII, 1311 pages. 2000.

Vol. 1801: J. Miller, A. Thompson, P. Thomson, T.C. Fogarty (Eds.), Evolvable Systems: From Biology to Hardware. Proceedings, 2000. X, 286 pages. 2000.

Vol. 1802: R. Poli, W. Banzhaf, W.B. Langdon, J. Miller, P. Nordin, T.C. Fogarty (Eds.), Genetic Programming. Proceedings, 2000. X, 361 pages. 2000.

Vol. 1803: S. Cagnoni et al. (Eds.), Real-World Applications and Evolutionary Computing. Proceedings, 2000. XII, 396 pages. 2000.

Vol. 1805: T. Terano, H. Liu, A.L.P. Chen (Eds.), Knowledge Discovery and Data Mining. Proceedings, 2000. XIV, 460 pages. 2000. (Subseries LNAI).

Vol. 1806: W. van der Aalst, J. Desel, A. Oberweis (Eds.), Business Process Management. VIII, 391 pages. 2000.

Vol. 1807: B. Preneel (Ed.), Advances in Cryptology – EUROCRYPT 2000. Proceedings, 2000. XVIII, 608 pages. 2000.

Vol. 1810: R.López de Mántaras, E. Plaza (Eds.), Machine Learning: ECML 2000. Proceedings, 2000. XII, 460 pages. 2000. (Subseries LNAI).

Vol. 1811: S.W. Lee, H.. Bülthoff, T. Poggio (Eds.), Biologically Motivated Computer Vision. Proceedings, 2000. XIV, 656 pages. 2000.

Vol. 1813: P.L. Lanzi, W. Stolzmann, S.W. Wilson (Eds.), Learning Classifier Systems. X, 349 pages. 2000. (Subseries LNAI).

Vol. 1815: G. Pujolle, H. Perros, S. Fdida, U. Körner, I. Stavrakakis (Eds.), Networking 2000 – Broadband Communications, High Performance Networking, and Performance of Communication Networks. Proceedings, 2000. XX, 981 pages. 2000.

Vol. 1816: T. Rus (Ed.), Algebraic Methodology and Software Technology. Proceedings, 2000. XI, 545 pages. 2000.

Vol. 1817: A. Bossi (Ed.), Logic-Based Program Synthesis and Transformation. Proceedings, 1999. VIII, 313 pages. 2000.

Vol. 1818: C.G. Omidyar (Ed.), Mobile and Wireless Communications Networks. Proceedings, 2000. VIII, 187 pages. 2000.

Vol. 1819: W. Jonker (Ed.), Databases in Telecommunications. Proceedings, 1999. X, 208 pages. 2000.

Vol. 1821: R. Loganantharaj, G. Palm, M. Ali (Eds.), Intelligent Problem Solving. Proceedings, 2000. XVII, 751 pages. 2000. (Subseries LNAI).

Vol. 1822: H.H. Hamilton, Advances in Artificial Intelligence. Proceedings, 2000. XII, 450 pages. 2000. (Subseries LNAI).

Vol. 1823: M. Bubak, H. Afsarmanesh, R. Williams, B. Hertzberger (Eds.), High Performance Computing and Networking. Proceedings, 2000. XVIII, 719 pages. 2000.

Vol. 1824: J. Palsberg (Ed.), Static Analysis. Proceedings, 2000. VIII, 433 pages. 2000.

Vol. 1825: M. Nielsen, D. Simpson (Eds.), Application and Theory of Petri Nets 2000. Proceedings, 2000. XI, 485 pages. 2000.

Vol. 1830: P. Kropf, G. Babin, J. Plaice, H. Unger (Eds.), Distributed Communities on the Web. Proceedings, 2000. X, 203 pages. 2000.

Vol. 1831: D. McAllester (Ed.), Automated Deduction – CADE-17. Proceedings, 2000. XIII, 519 pages. 2000. (Subseries LNAI).

Vol. 1832: B. Lings, K. Jeffery (Eds.), Advances in Databases. Proceedings, 2000. X, 227 pages. 2000.

Vol. 1834: J.-C. Heudin (Ed.), Virtual Worlds. Proceedings, 2000. XI, 314 pages. 2000. (Subseries LNAI).

Vol. 1835: D. N. Christodoulakis (Ed.), Natural Language Processing – NLP 2000. Proceedings, 2000. XII, 438 pages. 2000. (Subseries LNAI).

Vol. 1837: R. Backhouse, J. Nuno Oliveira (Eds.), Mathematics of Program Construction. Proceedings, 2000. IX, 257 pages. 2000.

Vol. 1838: W. Bosma (Ed.), Algorithmic Number Theory. Proceedings, 2000. IX, 615 pages. 2000.

Vol. 1839: G. Gauthier, C. Frasson, K. VanLehn (Eds.), Intelligent Tutoring Systems. Proceedings, 2000. XIX, 675 pages. 2000.

Vol. 1840: F. Bomarius, M. Oivo (Eds.), Product Focused Software Process Improvement. Proceedings, 2000. XI, 426 pages. 2000.

Vol. 1841: E. Dawson, A. Clark, C. Boyd (Eds.), Information Security and Privacy. Proceedings, 2000. XII, 488 pages. 2000.

Vol. 1842: D. Vernon (Ed.), Computer Vision – ECCV 2000. Part I. Proceedings, 2000. XVIII, 953 pages. 2000.

Vol. 1843: D. Vernon (Ed.), Computer Vision – ECCV 2000. Part II. Proceedings, 2000. XVIII, 881 pages. 2000.

Vol. 1844: W.B. Frakes (Ed.), Software Reuse: Advances in Software Reusability. Proceedings, 2000. XI, 450 pages. 2000.

Vol. 1845: H.B. Keller, E. Plöderer (Eds.), Reliable Software Technologies Ada-Europe 2000. Proceedings, 2000. XIII, 304 pages. 2000.

Vol. 1846: H. Lu, A. Zhou (Eds.), Web-Age Information Management. Proceedings, 2000. XIII, 462 pages. 2000.

Vol. 1847: R. Dyckhoff (Ed.), Automated Reasoning with Analytic Tableaux and Related Methods. Proceedings, 2000. X, 441 pages. 2000. (Subseries LNAI).

Vol. 1848: R. Giancarlo, D. Sankoff (Eds.), Combinatorial Pattern Matching. Proceedings, 2000. XI, 423 pages. 2000.

Vol. 1849: C. Freksa, W. Brauer, C. Habel, K.F. Wender (Eds.), Spatial Cognition II. XI, 420 pages. 2000. (Subseries LNAI).

Vol. 1850: E. Bertino (Ed.), ECOOP 2000 – Object-Oriented Programming. Proceedings, 2000. XIII, 493 pages. 2000.

Vol. 1851: M.M. Halldórsson (Ed.), Algorithm Theory – SWAT 2000. Proceedings, 2000. XI, 564 pages. 2000.

Vol. 1853: U. Montanari, J.D.P. Rolim, E. Welzl (Eds.), Automata, Languages and Programming. Proceedings, 2000. XVI, 941 pages. 2000.

Vol. 1857: J. Kittler, F. Roli (Eds.), Multiple Classifier Systems. Proceedings, 2000. XII, 404 pages. 2000.

Vol. 1860: M. Klusch, L. Kerschberg (Eds.), Cooperative Information Agents IV. Proceedings, 2000. XI, 285 pages. 2000. (Subseries LNAI).